Create Elegant Spreadsheets

Create Elegant Spreadsheets

Design Principles with Excel ®

Techniques and Applications

Doug Bates

xlegant

Loveland, OH, USA

Doug Bates
Loveland, OH, USA
info@xlegant.com

ISBN: 978-1-7376403-0-1

"With great power comes great responsibility"

-Uncle Ben Parker

Table of Contents

List of Tables

Preface

There is in us an innate curiosity, a desire to *see the forest*, and a tendency to miss it, consumed by the busy work of cataloguing trees, or watching them go by in a green blur from the fast lane. In moments of reflection we must admit that consuming vastly more data has not always led to increased understanding, sometimes even the reverse.

This book is a stop-and-think moment, a chance to unplug from the busy life and remember principles; to be still and look at the trees until the forest emerges. It's a chance that I too often missed, down in the information trenches, where this book was conceived to help the next generation of spreadsheet warriors.

Wait, you're thinking, I thought this was about spreadsheets, not philosophy. Yes it is, and yes, it is. It contains detailed examination of Excel "trees", while respecting their place and role in the information "forest".

What I'm offering to you, and asking of you then, is a candid reflection on the state of our spreadsheets, not for spreadsheets' sake, but as a medium where our mental process is on display. We need to turn off the tool to truly appreciate the advantage it offers. We'll then learn how to use it to see not only the forest, but the pathway through it we can use to guide others.

While there are many expert techniques and tips herein, it is not an introduction nor comprehensive how-to manual. It is selective of what I've found to be the most productive opportunities, to give you what's missing. I have made my best effort to select features and present them accurately. I apologize for any omissions or inaccuracies.

The projects in Part II are available at xlegant.com. Introduction to Part II includes a code for free downloads. It is most fruitful to read the workbooks and the book together, but not necessary. The explanation is carefully written to describe and show how it is accomplished. The purpose is not the workbooks themselves but the possibilities they reveal.

For software I am using Microsoft® Excel® for Microsoft 365 MSO 32-bit, current Version 2107. My intent is to demonstrate the principles and techniques that can be applied in any tool or version, even if the specific features are different or missing.

My hardware configuration is:

Device	HP® ENVY® x360 Convertible
Processor	Intel® Core™ i5-8250U CPU @ 1.60GHz 1.80 GHz
Installed RAM	8.00 GB (7.88 GB usable)
System type	64-bit operating system, x64-based processor

In pushing the envelope on technical design, I sometimes experience a few seconds delay in calculation performance. This is the unfortunate reality of development. The Office VBA Reference has a comprehensive and helpful section on how to improve Excel performance, which I recommend reading. Some of the very features that I love and use the most are flagged as performance hogs. For example, "Defined names are one of the most powerful features in Excel, but they do take additional calculation time."[1]

There are most likely improvements that can be made without degrading elegance too much, but here's why I am sticking with my design:

- My applications are not large and the performance is acceptable.
- Time and effort required to rework the files with little reward.
- I just want Hardware and Software to work out their differences and not bother me with their bickering. (I do realize that there's a certain amount I must live and deal with).

Conventions

> This format is used for formulas and other important notes that are set apart from paragraphs

[1] https://docs.microsoft.com/en-us/office/vba/excel/concepts/excel-performance/excel-tips-for-optimizing-performance-obstructions

```
This format is used for VBA code
```

+ between two keys (e.g. Ctrl+F3) means they must be pressed together

- after Alt and **,** between keys (e.g. Alt-H,L,R) means the keys must be pressed in sequence, with or without holding Alt (i.e. KeyTip navigation)

Proper capitalization (e.g. Name Manager), is used to refer to the actual name of a function or dialog.

Where helpful, **bold** is used in place of quotation marks, to clarify that quotation marks are not to be included in the string.

Part I: Why and How

Chapter 1: What's Missing?

Why?

I didn't set out to write this book, it approached me as a reluctant accomplice. The conversation went something like this:

You have to write me	*No I don't*
It'll be fun!	*No it won't*
You know I'm needed......................	*There's too many of you already*
I'm different. It's important............	*What, spreadsheets?*
You know it's more than that..........	*Really nice spreadsheets?*
Think deeper...................................	*...*
... about principles..........................	*if I have to, I guess...*

I had to admit the book had a point I could not ignore. My years in offices, watching sincere, smart people write terrible spreadsheets, had shown me that something was missing, that this "non-thing" was more common than rare, and that just maybe I could and should make it into something. I've spent most of my career training and helping business users. It's clear that we don't know what we don't know, and we can't even seek it until it's exposed.

On the other hand, I had a point too. Excel has so much ground to cover that there is a large market for training, from beginner to advanced and from general to specialized. There are hundreds of Excel books and videos. Yet, the market is softened by the self-help culture. It is so easy to start using, and to get by with basic skills, that most users are undertrained on what it can do and even on its intended use.

This book will have to be different, not an introduction, and not a comprehensive compendium. There are so many great resources that I must find a niche. The angle I aim to bring is to put why before how; to step back and see the end to which the tool is the means. All work fulfills a need; creative work exposes deeper needs than we have not yet acknowledged. My motivation is to supply what I have found missing, which I must therefore articulate.

Consider the apps we all use every day – applications from simple to complex, for devices from small to large. The plethora of apps available would seem to fill every possible need. We have come to expect an app for everything. There's an app to speak, an app to write and spell, an app to read, an app to play music, an app to do math, an app to tell us where to go and eat and sleep. Apps are so convenient and ubiquitous that we rely on them for everyday tasks. And by golly, they'd better be efficient and spiffy!

The consequence of our reliance on apps is atrophy of the skills that they replace. We see a decline in the quality of language arts, critical thinking, navigation skills. This is not inherently bad but reveals a schism. We might attribute it as a generation gap, one of a series that have grown exponentially. The point is to understand it objectively and take the best step forward. We should not reject nor neglect any old or new thing that can be useful. If I am to offer my dependence to a thing, I wish to do so with respect and trust.

So what is missing, that brought this book to rouse me? A non-thing is inherently difficult to identify.

There are some two million apps available. How can there be so many? They are each designed for a specific, narrow purpose. Smaller and smaller niches are sliced off successful ones. Competition refines design and public reviews make it easy to choose, but we need to know what we're looking for or we'll end up with lots of cool useless stuff.

It's estimated that the average person uses about ten apps a day. Attention is a tough market! To compete, an app must be useful, reliable and easy to use. It should come in a simple package – you open it, you tap or type or swipe, you close it. User interaction is minimal and intuitive.

Ok, so what's the problem? What's not to like about great selection, design and price? Nothing, as long as your need falls into the niche of one of these wonderful apps. Stand-alone apps may well satisfy your personal needs. When it comes to business, there's a need to build our own tools and documents.

Thus we turn to the class of business app suites that allow us to create and customize and automate documents.

There is much buzz about the "democratization" of data management and the rise of citizen developers. Certainly it is a positive sign that more data can be accessed and processed on demand than ever before. The reduction of layers and lead time to achieve visualization is a significant advance. But the human mind must still translate data to information. Easy access accelerates risks as well as rewards. In the hunger for quick conclusions, design is easily overlooked.

In the context of these trends, Excel is but one example of one part of the big data puzzle. It is my focal point, not as an end in itself but as a well known and understood program in which to illustrate principles of design.

The Missing Link

What makes business suite apps different from most other apps? The main point is file creation. You don't just interact with data that resides in the app or online, you create the data yourself. Interaction is therefore much more involved, with thousands of creative options – formats, fonts, colors, graphics, data manipulation and graphical animation. You the user are creating files that are like mini-apps, allowing others to interact with and consume the information you provide. In effect, Office is an "app app", and you are a developer.

In fact, Office includes a development platform called VBA, or Visual Basic for Applications. For anyone who has dabbled in or mastered VBA, the developer-user label is obvious and true. VBA developers are multi-taskers, using the front-end app (mainly Excel) to design the consumer interface and the back-end app (VBA) to control or automate certain features. This coupling of the programming environment with the end-user app has opened up development to the general public. Like Luther's Bible, it has exposed the protected body of knowledge to the citizenry.

For an Office user not using VBA, you are at least an editor, governing the content and appearance of your document. But even if you haven't written macros, if you've written formulas you are a kind of developer, by manipulating data in a way that is hidden from casual view.

Are we getting any closer to defining the non-thing? When you hear the word "developer" you might have a certain image of the kind of person and environment where that happens. Most users don't think of themselves as developers, but neither would they claim to be writers or editors. Yet here we are performing these roles every day without credit!

Office apps have little more governance than spell check and basic error handling. This allows for creativity, but that's not always desirable, like driving with no guardrails. Apps from an app store involve a transaction governed by standards and protections, whereas the files that circulate in a business office have little if any such standards. They also lack the natural governance of competition.

Is this openness a problem? Should we enforce standards? Creative freedom is here to stay, and we should celebrate that. But with freedom comes responsibility. Ah, the non-thing is starting to take form, like a 3D printed object. It is this responsibility that calls each of us individually to respect standards, and to provide protections for ourselves and our consumers. It means adopting a set of core principles for business communication. It is an aspect of how we apply conscience to business life.

Conscience, in business as in personal life, includes standards such as respect, stewardship and integrity. We want to be good and do good. Work life involves interpersonal relations that rely on a common set of values. For most of us most of the time, our conscience is our autopilot. Where it calls us to take control is in the details of the choices we make.

What choices am I talking about? The kind that I make throughout every day. When I click save or send, I feel that I have made adequate effort to convey the information I possess. But have I? Did I present information, or opinion? Did I promote my own conclusion, or even pass on that of my supplier? Did I enable the receiver to trace back to the truth, and draw their own conclusion? How plainly did I show the way? In essence, how truthful was I? The answer is in how well I apply the principles of honest communication.

So there it is, the missing piece. It's about principles. It's an acknowledgement that they matter – that my work matters, my product conveys something about me. I can express it as a manifesto:

> I am an entrepreneur in a niche market. My offering is specific information. It's data with a pedigree, referenced and explained, summarized and packaged aesthetically with respect for your time and mental point of entry. My reward is your comprehension and delight. My goal is to hasten that moment of truth.

This is the attitude I am eager to inspire.

Of course, we have to consider cost. How much effort should we invest to adopt principles? A good start would be training in communication and design principles. A trainer of mine once said, "if you think knowledge is expensive, try ignorance." Training and practice do not make perfect, but make routine what began as strange and awkward. In time you can learn to be equally or more efficient with higher output standards.

In terms of the effort budget on a given project, it is a fine line of diminishing return that I have often crossed and taken home from the office. We need to know when to stop. But the prize is there, in opening the envelope, challenging the limit. Each person has a balance to find between the pursuit of excellence and moving on to the next thing.

To learn, a mind needs three things: desire, ability and capacity. Everyone has learning ability, but it varies in degree just like athletic ability. Some have desire and ability but lack capacity. Some have ability and capacity but no desire. This book is meant to ignite and fuel your desire to learn. How you fulfill it is up to your initiative to make capacity and to apply your ability.

Product and Process

I was the youngest of a well-planned crop of three girls and three boys. My dad looked for ways to incentivize work. We had a lot of dandelions in the yard, so he offered me a penny for each one I dug up by the roots. He thought he'd pay out a quarter or so. I dug up more than 700 dandelions. He never tired of telling that story.

In high school I had a wonderful opportunity to live in France for a year, with a French family. Most of my fellow American students took it as a cultural experience and a time to learn French. I immersed myself so much as a French student that I not only learned French but calculus and physics, and I passed the Baccalaureate exam. When I took it to my American university the next year, they gave me a year of credit.

Yet, I have often caved to mediocrity, the safe and warm. On reflection I have wondered, why? I have health and ambition, why would I not use them to their fullest? The difference in reward between least effort and best effort is much greater than the incremental work. It's not only about the size of the reward, but the kind of reward. There is a great satisfaction in approaching the edge of potential, like standing on the rim of the Grand Canyon. It is to glimpse the true nature and value of the self. But there is a long road to get there, the length of endurance.

The key to avoiding drudgery is vision. When I was a young hiker I spent countless hours plodding through the woods, climbing over rocks and roots, sweating and swatting mosquitoes while carrying my room and board on my back. Most of the time I had to look down at my feet, to find the next safe step. It's a fitting analogy for work, right? I never regretted a single step or minute spent on the trail. Part of the satisfaction was working towards the mountain-top, with the vision of a campfire, a five-star mac and cheese, and a luxurious bedroll. But the best part was in each moment, the inherent surprise of being in untamed nature, the joy of discovery made fresh and personal by ephemerality.

Of course, work must realize some end to be rewarding, even though for many of us that end is beyond the horizon. I might never meet the person who consumes the fruit of my labor. Yet that person is represented at my work station, explicitly or implicitly, by the design and quality and value of the product that connects us. On a trip, the primary purpose is to reach the destination, but the trip also has meaning within itself. The destination and the trip are subject and object, they require each other. A chef produces a delicious meal by immersing himself in the process. An artist calls up the depths of intellect and emotion to create a work. For the creator, the process is the product.

Lessons from Wood

I like to work with wood. I'm an amateur, not highly skilled, but I take great pride in both the product and the process. I love having things around the house that I made myself, from concept to detailed specs, from materials to parts, from rough assembly to finished product. When I behold the product it reminds me of the process and gives me satisfaction. In effect, product and process are one.

Wood is a very responsive medium. It is rigid yet workable; it can be shaped, cut, molded, joined and smoothed. It is mostly muted in color but can be stained and finished to reveal graceful patterns of grain. When done correctly, it perfectly combines utility and beauty, a paragon of elegance.

We have all seen examples of woodworking that were well done and others not so well. If the material has cracks, or is not cut straight or not joined well, it may fail in its intended function and be discarded. If it holds up but is badly finished it might be rejected as unattractive. With each project I learn from mistakes and notch up my standards. I refine my techniques with different tools and different woods, and I've learned that no piece is perfect. The joy is in the pursuit!

The lessons I've taken from woodworking are life lessons. There is purpose to be found in filling any need. Making a table, cooking a meal, writing a program all give satisfaction by being useful to me or to someone else. But the objective need can be filled by purchase just as well. I can buy a table or a meal or an app. What the creative impulse speaks to is a deeper need. It is expression beyond language, a communion. The objective need is subordinated, becoming a vehicle for personal fulfillment. The creator plots to astound and delight, delivering the requirement while achieving self satisfaction. The joy is in the offering!

The happiest people are those who put their whole self into what they do. Even mundane work can be elevated this way. Monetary compensation is a necessity, but what I really want is to know that my work is valued. Therein is the difference between being busy, even successful, and being engaged and fulfilled. The ultimate achievement is to be fully required.

Why Spreadsheets?

I've been around foreigners much of my life. I'm always impressed and grateful how well they have learned to speak English. We anglophones take it for granted that everyone speaks English. Sometimes, with respect, we can enjoy humorous misspeak. The word "spreadsheet" can come out sounding like a colloquial term for a manure spreader. Ironically, this is a fitting analogy for many of the spreadsheet samples I have seen. Like a farmer fertilizing his field, the author is recycling material that has already served a purpose elsewhere, expecting to sprout something new.

Excel has the potential to make us look great or terrible. It is too easy, too kind and forgiving of our good intentions, like blank paper. If you give me a blank sheet and ask me to draw a house, I'll convey the message – here's the door, this is a window – and you'll adopt it right into your circular file.

Is it enough, to convey the message? That's the first purpose, but consider the context. If you ask me how a house differs from a barn, my drawing skills are up to the task. Send, receive, discard. In fact, skip the drawing, I'll just describe it to you. If I'm designing a house to live in however, I need an architect to translate my scribbles with precision.

The spreadsheet is market vernacular. People from all backgrounds and professions can converse and understand enough for daily transactions. Most are satisfied with that and it seldom rises to eloquence. But spreadsheets are like wood. They can be shaped into many things and respond well to attention. Handled with care they can become a creative object that is beautiful and useful.

I have worked with spreadsheets since the 1980's when Lotus 123 reigned. I recall those days fondly, there were some very simple and handy tools. Macros were written on sheets in syntax that in some ways was more intuitive than the modern equivalent. There was a special formatting feature called WYSIWYG – "what you see is what you get". It converted the monochrome display to a light background and enhanced fonts. State of the art!

Later, I worked with mainframe computer data, and built Access databases to create data forms and run queries and reports. Basic principles of data management such as fields and records, data types and joins were inherent and foundational. Data analysis and presentation was a service function. End user interaction was limited and controlled.

With more advanced computers came more power, accessibility, functions and programmability. Along with all that came more risk. Excel became the easiest tool to use, and the easiest tool to abuse. It became the ubiquitous everything, from white board to note pad, from typewriter to calculator to scheduler. It's so easy to use that it's presumed as entry-level skill and little if any training is given on the job. This leaves it vulnerable to huge variation in the level of skill and care that individual users apply.

As people found that you could fill it with anything anywhere, the purpose of Excel as a data analytical tool got lost. Many sheets have only text. If there is a number in a sheet, it might be meaningful or might not. It might be just a number, or text masquerading as a number, or it might be calculated from other numbers in other cells or other sheets. It might have a label or just sit there, naked and dimensionless. What looks like a table might be split by blank columns and rows, and have inconsistent data types, creating non-contiguous areas with unmanageable summary formulas. Often there is no background about how the data were collected, derived or manipulated. Formulas are often cryptic, complex nested structures with no regulation.

There is still a surprising ignorance, or laissez-faire in corporate life about this lack of standards. Most users are innocent, just doing their best with the training they've had, and while they may waste some time they are unlikely to hurt anything but their own effectiveness. They just don't know what they don't know. Most shocking is the extent to which business is managed via Excel, when companies spend enormously on central IT systems. Spreadsheets are local entities, off-grid from integrated enterprise systems. Their value begins to decay almost as soon as they are created, with little thought to data refresh, or reusable modules and templates.

Lost productivity is probably the worst effect, but there can be more severe consequences than wasted time and ineffective presentation. There's an iceberg effect of showing a brief conclusion from large amounts of untraceable and potentially dangerous data. This puts users at risk of drawing wrong and possibly harmful conclusions or missing out on opportunities, giving the tool undue influence.

Working in large corporations, I've seen some great progress towards data tools that offer agility and ease, while respecting the need for control and governance. With demand for more development faster, corporate control must be matched with self control. Individually created spreadsheets will be in use for a long time. The risk of inadvertent, hidden errors and even malicious harm is greater than ever.

What can be done? It's certainly not to change the behavior of millions of busy users who lack the prerequisites to learn, or even the dozen or so in your circle. It's you! If I meet my objective, I'll strike a nerve somewhere, and inspire you to become a change agent. You can be an example, an influencer. You can become a provider, a creator of tools and templates, stemming the proliferation of anarchic spreadsheets. You can be a champion and hero among your colleagues!

It is this idea, the belief in yourself that I am out to convey. My wish is to help you exploit the power you already have, imparting the subtle trajectory that will bring it to fruition. My call is to return to core principles of analysis and communication, to treasure elegance, and to commit to transparency.

Chapter 2: Principles

Purpose

It is self-evident that to have value a thing must have a purpose. All design begins with purpose or quickly devolves into scribbles. The intent of any creative effort is to reverse entropy, to create order, to achieve a purpose. Art and science, a business, a spreadsheet, or a salmon swimming upstream to spawn must have purpose to fight the constant downward flow.

Microsoft and partners have diligently developed many templates for common purposes, which are excellent sources of new ideas for spreadsheet design. Yet templates seem to go largely ignored even when they fit the purpose nicely, or can be easily adapted. As a broader observation, a clear statement of purpose is undervalued and commonly omitted. Many a spreadsheet has had an ignoble birth as a brain dump, storm, fart or whatever graphic noun you choose. Not surprisingly, many of these are stillborn, or if saved end up as numbered orphans; Book1, etc.

Certainly, there is nothing wrong with starting on Sheet1 of Book1 with ideation. In fact, it is good to articulate the purpose, expand the objectives, and give the newborn a good name. Expound the fundamental program elements: input, process and output. But this step does not require Excel and may be more productive on paper or whiteboard. Articulation often exposes hidden needs, and alternate sources and methods. Take some time to let the purpose settle before jumping in.

The first key question of purpose is the customer. Who will consume the product of this labor? You might have a budget or home inventory file that is for you alone, but in business it is almost always for or shared with someone else. Whether it is an actual customer, a project team, your boss or the CEO, you need to define purpose from their perspective. Start with a good name, then connect the design, features and documentation to the purpose as simply as possible. Simplicity leaves the comforting impression of exposing purpose.

The second key question is use. How will the product be used? Is it stand-alone or linked to other data sources? Is it ongoing or temporary? Will users input data or only read and output the data? Is the data sensitive? What is the shelf life of the data, and how will it be renewed? Is VBA a must-have, nice-to-have, or not applicable?

Once the use case is clear, the next important step is to assess the market competition. Is there a standard solution already available? Can one be modified? Is there a template that can be adapted? Is there a ready-made solution available for purchase? If there is nothing available for the specific need, then it's time for reality check. Is there enough value to justify the cost? This is hard to answer objectively, maybe impossible, so common sense applies. In the absence of a formal solution, users will proliferate informal ones. The tipping point to justify development might be the need to regain control, over any quantifiable payback. Coupled with the use case of any shared tool is the purpose to entice willing adoption.

Having a clear purpose enables efficient design and test, and leads directly into training and adoption. A good project, like any good presentation, begins with objectives and ties everything back to them.

Integrity

Integrity pertains to the character of the author and of the product. Personal integrity means honesty and uprightness. Consider advertising or journalism standards, paraphrased: never misinform, present factual evidence, cite references. Internal advertising appears in many forms, filling the inbox daily – dashboards, reports, presentations, and of course "see spreadsheet for details", if not all-in-one. The reader has the right to draw their own conclusions. A good provider respects and encourages that.

Structural integrity means reliability. "Built to last" is a mantra of manufacturing and is the deserving goal of any project worth undertaking. Taking pride in the integrity of your work is not a requirement – it's compensation. It begins with a long-term vision leading to obsolescence-resistant design, fault-proof engineering, skilled construction and rigorous quality testing. There will be defects, the goal is to catch them all in build-test iterations. Testing goes beyond intended features to anticipate unintended use, ensuring that it will work every time for diverse users.

Think about a product you use daily that you expect to work every time – your car. Every one of the thousands of parts in a car has a purpose, most of them you never see. When you buy a car, you take a test drive to see how it feels – performance per design is presumed. But way before that point, the maker checked that every part and subassembly performed its function and did not break under stress. Entire cars were destroyed in crash tests in order to design and test safety features that you expect never to use but would not buy without.

The quality and integrity of public products involves trust. Especially for something like a car, which can cause death, you rely on trust, backed by the legal and insurance systems and decades-long reputation. You don't have that foundation when you are building a spreadsheet. Adoption is based on trust, and trust comes from a subjective threshold of experience. If a defect or design gap appears early, the user may never reach their threshold, but once they do, they will come to you for help rather than abandon your product. Your objective is to help them cross their threshold by removing all obstacles.

Trust grows organically, but needs some selling to germinate. This can be provided by video, demo, or built into the sheet, with sample data and help text to expose the more subtle features. Help should be unobtrusive, concise and easy to access. Most help is needed once, maybe more if the app is infrequently used. The ideal help is never needed, because the design is simple and intuitive. Elegance sells itself.

When you invest yourself in a project, you might even wish for help requests, because you love explaining and demonstrating your creative work. Be careful what you wish for. Plan from the start to make yourself dispensable. You do not want to be under the gun for embarrassing and expensive repair work once it's in use. The goal is to make it as fault-proof and self-explanatory as possible.

This is a core principle of product development and change management: test, and test some more, and test again before you release it, and validate after release. This is your chance to get the consumer's perspective, by being one. Use it, over and over again. Not only will you find and fix bugs but make improvements as well. Consider a production pilot to limit the risk until proven. Don't rush to market. First impression is key.

Transparency

Transparency in communication means using plain language to say only what must be said – the whole truth, and nothing but the truth. It means no secrets, even unintentional ones. As you become more fluent in Excel and VBA, remember that your users are not as fluent as you are.

Minimalism is a foundation of transparency. The fewer objects that are in my field of view, the further I can see. Articulate the process from input to output in small steps, and get rid of anything that obscures the logic. Give the user what they need to know about how to navigate and interpret the information you give them, no more or less. Design features to be self-evident, minimizing the need for instructions.

Consider a user encountering a cell with a number in it. How many different ways can it be interpreted? It could be a user input cell, a non-editable lookup cell, a cell filled by a macro, or the result of a formula. When the user is not given clear clues about the source and usage of the data, confusion and errors are inevitable.

When subtle shades are applied to the sheet background and read-only cells, and only the user input cells are not shaded, the user intuits that white means editable, and knows where to enter data without searching or being told. Elegant use of formatting and space similarly helps focus attention.

Complex formulas are of special concern for two reasons. First, they are vulnerable to errors in both logic and range selection. Second, they are intimidating to read. Every nested level makes them more opaque. They can get to a point of no return, where even the author is hard pressed to retrace the logic.

Name Manager can be used to make formulas readable, by giving ranges logical names. It can also define intermediate formulas to help break down complexity, with comments to explain. It is thus like a dictionary of words that are used to build formulas like sentences that anyone can read. Using tables to structure the data similarly provides named referencing and some added transparency.

Most users won't know or won't bother with Name Manager, and many will not even try to read formulas. Name Manager can be pointed to or downloaded to a sheet for reference. The principle of transparency is that those who do read beneath the surface can readily grasp the meaning and appreciate the lucidity.

You may have a secondary audience of support personnel, or colleagues who want to reapply your model. They may need more detail than an end user. You can leave subtle breadcrumbs, but the more you can make it easy for the end user to understand, the less you need to think about anyone else. The difference may be that the consumer will ignore the breadcrumbs that a developer will eagerly follow. You should be able to hand it off with minimal explanation. Any VBA procedure should be commented thoroughly to explain the logic.

Think about owner's manuals for your home appliances. They explain how to use it, for the consumer, and how to troubleshoot and maintain it, for the handyman. Some people never read manuals, and of course controls are made as self-evident as possible. I always read manuals and keep them in a binder. If a manual is well written and informative, it gives me greater confidence in the machine.

Know your customer and provide an appropriate level of detail. If you use protection in the file, then be clear about when and how to contact you for support.

Elegance

Definitions of elegance note two aspects of the word, appearance and structure. One is refined beauty, the other a refined solution. Together they encapsulate the primary design objective of practical works.

"Elegance is beauty that shows unusual effectiveness and simplicity. It is frequently used as a standard of tastefulness, particularly in the areas of visual design, decoration, science, and the aesthetics of mathematics. Elegant things often exhibit refined grace and suggest maturity, and in the case of mathematical problem solving, a deep understanding into the subject matter." (https://en.wikipedia.org/wiki/Elegance)

As freedom of expression has exploded in both forms and outlets, the aesthetic spectrum has expanded. There are many new fascinating and wonderful works to enjoy, and many that bore, disturb and even disgust. With ubiquitous instant access to publish and consume content, it's as if a race was kicked off with a booming "anything goes!"

If we unplug for a moment though and think about it, there is common purpose in human expression. Centuries of art and science prove that universal principles do exist. There is truth and beauty that lasts. And there are many, many things that don't go at all, evidenced by a short life.

Elegance is a principle that is universally valued, and universally accessible to everyone, in any profession. Any undertaking has an object, the physical output which is sold to a customer or to an employer as the fruit of labor. But the result is more than that.

An artist's objective is not just to complete and sell a work, it's to express his unique inner self and give beauty to others. An engineer is not only building a machine, but one that performs a useful function reliably. The desired end result is not the product itself but a delighted consumer. It is this refinement of purpose, to be beautiful, useful and simple that is captured in the word elegance.

A formula or macro can be elegant by accomplishing its assigned task concisely and intuitively. Since they are mostly invisible, there is no aesthetic aspect to their elegance. This internal elegance is about how the data are structured and manipulated to produce a robust and transparent result in the simplest way. Those who know what to look for can see the skill and care applied. For those who can't see or appreciate the internal elegance, it just works.

External elegance is the aesthetic aspect of the visual and interactive design. It is the art that sells the science, the moment of truth that captures and engages the user's precious attention. Failure here negates internal elegance, if the user cannot follow enough to engage. A spreadsheet as a whole assembles the internal components, adding visual elements and qualities to achieve an elegant end product.

Transparency is inherent in elegance. A structure that is easy to read and understand must also be simple and effective. In addition, elegance addresses aesthetics with a clean visual presentation and intuitive user interface. Complementing minimalism is tasteful use of layout, fonts, colors and locking.

Many users do not appreciate the role of elegance in the office. Too often we succumb to time constraints and throw together spreadsheets that are both quick and dirty. Also too often, this results in miscommunication and rework, or worse. Careful investment in elegance takes more time, but can avoid these pitfalls. Which approach is really more productive?

Even for quick, one-use reports, keeping principles in mind will add value, and with regular use you will learn to apply them efficiently. As with social media, with office documents you never know who is going to end up reading your report. Do a good job, respect your customer and they will want more of what you offer.

The two sides of elegant design are complementary and interdependent, like strength and beauty. To embrace them together as a singular objective is a profound experience of nature itself and a path to personal fulfillment.

Chapter 3: Excel Techniques

Thoreau said, "If you have built castles in the air, your work need not be lost; that is where they should be. Now put the foundations under them." (Henry David Thoreau, Walden). Having put forth a rationale and some lofty principles, I must now bring them within reach. As warned, this is not a comprehensive how-to guide. As promised, these tools will help bring principles to life.

These techniques are collected from areas that I have found to be easy gains towards design and use of Excel with elegance, methods that are not hard to learn but are often overlooked, or poorly used. The techniques and their application in the projects are interlinked, so you can navigate between Chapters 3 and 4 for the best learning experience.

Basics

I have presented the case for internal structural elegance, and external aesthetic elegance. A third type of elegance to master is that of motion, or what could be called navigational fluency. If you work in an office you undoubtedly expose your screen performance skills frequently. Whether you face individuals, small teams or large groups, this is part of the package you present.

As with design principles, the best impression you can give is not to wow the crowd with tricks, but to get yourself out of the way. Hone your skills to be more productive, and let the result speak for itself. If you struggle to navigate or edit the sheet in a public setting, you draw negative attention to yourself, detracting from your message. By contrast, when a well-designed sheet is presented and interacted with natural ease, focus remains on topic.

By avoiding distraction, your fluency contributes to your impression as a good communicator.

To develop skill requires study and practice. As noted earlier, there is a huge volume of training material to study. Here it is important to prioritize and focus on the basics. Even if you think you know Excel well enough and have written formulas and macros, take time to renew and improve basic skills. Study and practice.

A good place to begin is to review keyboard shortcuts. Most people use only a few clipboard shortcuts, unaware of the hidden treasure in the keys. Mastering shortcuts makes you more productive by leveraging muscle memory and reducing mouse-to-keyboard transitions. This helps you in both private and public settings. The Keyboard Trainer project explains more and provides an easy learning tool.

First, review the purpose and use of the modifier keys, Shift, Ctrl, Alt:

- Shift capitalizes letters or types the “upper” character of a key
- Ctrl with most keys invokes whatever hot-key function is assigned
- Alt with a few keys invokes a hot-key function (e.g. =,↓, some F-keys)
- Alt begins a key sequence to invoke a ribbon function

Navigation Shortcuts

Walk before you run by getting fully comfortable moving around in the sheet and selecting data. Of course you know how the four arrow keys move cell to cell, and how PgUp, PgDn and Home keys work. The End key is more subtle. It toggles End Mode, as seen in the bottom left status bar, and must precede each key press.

End-navigation is easier with the Ctrl key. For example, say I’m in the top left corner of a filled rectangular range, and I want to go to the other three corners and back. I can go End →, End ↓, End ←, End ↑, or instead, I can hold down Ctrl as I hit →, ↓, ←, ↑.

Now, experiment. Add and hold down each modifier key – Shift, Ctrl, Alt – first one by one, then in pairs, as you move around with the four arrows. Practice this with different kinds of sheets – contiguous data region, non-contiguous regions, table, filter. Next, repeat the exercise with PgUp and PgDn keys, with multiple sheets, and finally, with Home and End. You will notice the following:

- Shift+ any navigation key extends the selection
- Ctrl+ arrows goes to the end of the contiguous range
- Ctrl+Home goes to cell A1
- Ctrl+End goes to the bottom right cell (as of the last save)
- Ctrl+PgDn goes to next sheet, Ctrl+PgUp goes to previous sheet
- Ctrl+Shift+ arrows, Home or End extends selection to the jump-to cell
- Alt+↓ opens a pick list, or creates a dynamic one in a text column
- Shift+Alt+→ groups, Shift+Alt+← ungroups
- Shift+Alt+↓ within a table column opens the filter

Not every combination is assigned a function, but this is how you discover what's available. Some functions depend on the context, so study is still the way to understand the intended use. Practicing basic navigation skills is like the Karate Kid's wax-on, wax-off exercise. You will see the value later, as you apply them in edit mode, in the ribbon and in dialogs as well as the sheet. In some contexts you'll add the Tab key, and Space or Enter to select an option. In any case, you can always try any combination. See what happens!

Another key to add to your navigation vocabulary is F6. It cycles between panes, including the sheet, panes within the sheet if split, the sheet tabs, the status and zoom bar, and the ribbon. In each pane, try your moves and watch where the focus goes. With modifiers F6 cycles open workbooks.

The greatest agility is gained when you're able to efficiently combine all input methods. Practice modifier keys with mouse actions to learn techniques such as:

- Shift+ left click extends the selection
- Ctrl+ left click adds to the selection
- Alt+ left click opens the research pane (looks up first word in a text cell)
- Ctrl+ scroll zooms in and out (scroll on the zoom bar does a finer zoom)
- Shift+ scroll opens and closes groups
- Ctrl+Shift+ scroll scrolls horizontally

Compete with yourself to find the best methods for you.

Function Shortcuts

The next level of shortcuts perform functions. Almost every key on the board has one or more hotkey functions assigned to it, and the F1 to F12 keys have stand-alone functions as well. It would be difficult and unnecessary to memorize them all, but they should all be assessed so that you can select and memorize those that give you the most benefit.

Of course, to know what hotkeys to use you must be familiar with the functions they perform. As an example, I was once in a meeting where the presenter had learned to copy and paste by Ctrl+C, Ctrl+V, but had not learned how to paste values only. When the target cell format was changed, the person reformatted the cell, causing an awkward distraction. Had they studied, they would know first that there is an option to paste values only, and second that while there is no direct hotkey, there are at least three easy keyboard methods:

- Ctrl+Alt+V, V, Enter
- Alt-H, V, V
- Ctrl+V, Ctrl, V

Most hotkeys are assigned mnemonically or spatially to be easy to remember. Appreciation of that will be to your advantage as you recall or even guess your way to productive use. They are also spelled out on the related ribbon icon tooltip, as you hover the mouse over it.

The Ribbon and Toolbar

The ribbon menu is rich with features, each with nice graphical representation. It is worth some quality time to get familiar with each tab, section and function, to know what's available and where to look when you need it. Hover the mouse over each function to see a description, and whether a hotkey exists.

The entire ribbon is accessible via key sequence. Press Alt or F10 to start ribbon mode navigation. This reveals small black boxes with one or two characters called KeyTips, which are the shortcuts to each tab and function. You must always start with the KeyTip for the tab, then add the KeyTip for the function. For example, if you remember that the Name Manager is in the Formulas tab, you press Alt to see the letters on each tab, then M for the Formulas tab, then find the Name Manager icon and hit N to open it. Alt-M,N.

Now, you may already know that Ctrl+F3 also opens Name Manager, so now you have options and can choose which way you like.

Generally, the most frequently used functions are those that have predefined hotkey shortcuts. If you get good enough at using the hotkeys, then use the KeyTips method for anything else. Or use hotkeys for navigation, and KeyTips for ribbon tools. It's all about your personal productivity. KeyTips are less important to memorize because it is easy to open and follow the signs on the fly, easier if you can at least remember which tab to start with.

Another way to use the ribbon with keys is simple navigation. Start with Alt or F10 as with KeyTip navigation, then use → and ← to move between tabs. ↓ goes down into the tab, ↑ goes back up to tab navigation. Within a tab, Ctrl+→ or Ctrl+← to move between sections, → or ← or Tab to move between functions. To open a drop-down menu, Alt+↓, then ↓ or ↑ within the menu, Space or Enter to select an item, or Esc to close the menu.

Once you have a mental list of your personal favorite functions, keep them within easy reach in the Quick Access Toolbar (QAT). These are your choicest functions. They can be functions that don't have a hotkey, or a redundant method for those that do. They can be tools you use everyday, or ones you rarely use but don't want to hunt for again, and can recognize by icon. They can be standard tools, contextual tools or even personal macros that you keep in your startup file.

Customize the QAT by the drop-down at its right end. I like my QAT below the ribbon because it is quicker to access, and the buttons are in color, like they are in the ribbon. The downside of putting it below the ribbon is that it takes up about two rows of screen space.

To add a function from the ribbon to the Quick Access Toolbar, right-click it and select "Add to Quick Access Toolbar". Not everything is in the ribbon, and not everything in the ribbon can be added this way. Sometimes you can only add the gallery when what you want is one item within the gallery. You really owe it to yourself to spend some quality time in the QAT customizer, Alt-F,T,Q, or via the QAT menu, "More Commands..." Here you can add specific items from any menu or gallery, explore available features, reorder items and add separators. Give special attention to the first nine items, as these will have KeyTip shortcuts Alt-1 through Alt-9.

In the QAT customizer "Choose commands from:" drop-down menu you can select from commands not in the ribbon, from macros, or from any standard or contextual tab. You can also customize the ribbon itself, Alt-F,T,C, by adding a tab, or group within a tab, then adding items to it. I have a tab I call "Mine" where I dump anything that looks interesting, allowing me to experiment without messing up my QAT. You can also remove groups you don't need, and don't worry, you can reset the tab or the whole ribbon to standard.

Formatting (Ctrl+1)

Formatting is like fashion, it's how you make yourself look good. We say a person has good fashion sense when their appearance is enhanced by their attire. Type, color, pattern, accessories and grooming are all coordinated well with an aesthetically pleasing effect.

Even for people who have decent personal fashion, aesthetic sensibility does not always translate to good spreadsheet formatting. Let's face it, it is not easy to make Excel both function well and look good. But don't underestimate the impact of formatting on your first and lasting impression! Here we'll see some built-in help and some simple techniques.

Coordination

Office tries to help us groom and dress up our documents by packaging elements that look good together. It gives us freedom to choose while protecting us from too many choices. This gentle guidance comes in two voices, themes and templates. I'll deal with templates in a later section.

A theme provides a consistent appearance throughout a document. This plays out as a combination of complementary colors, fonts and object effects. Think of each theme as a department store mannequin dressed in an ensemble that clicks. You can simply point and say, "I want to look like that." Excel, Word and PowerPoint all have the same 34 themes, and allow you to create your own.

For fonts, Alt-H,F,F, there are two Theme Fonts at the top of the list, labelled with (Headings) and (Body). Some themes are the same font for both, some are different. Some themes have fonts that are larger and can cause the loss of five or more rows of screen space.

For colors, Alt-H,H, Theme Colors provide an ample palette of 60 colors; 10 base colors in the top row defined as 2 Background, 2 Text and 6 Accent colors, plus 5 shade variations, 3 lighter and 2 darker of each base color.

The Themed Cell Styles gallery, Alt-H,J gives 24 of the 60 Theme Colors, based on the 6 theme accent colors with the 3 lighter shades of each. Be aware that the Themed Cell Styles are named with the percent shade value that is opposite the one on the Theme Colors dialog tooltip. For example, the lightest shade is "20%" in Styles, and "80% lighter" in Colors. This matters if you are programming the shade property in VBA, which uses the value from the Theme Colors tooltip.

The main benefit of using Cell Styles is the ability to define custom styles (Alt-H,J,N) that can be merged (Alt-H,J,M) across open files. Thus, you can fine-tune the coordination of formats for specific purposes, like input cells, formula cells, background, etc. If you define styles in your startup file they'll be accessible to import to any other file. Still, be conscious of whether you are using themed formats or non-themed formats in your styles.

You might be satisfied with the default theme and never use the other 33, but you should at least check them out. The gallery gives you a miniature encapsulation of each, and you can easily scroll the themes with the arrow keys to see the effect on your sheet. Chapter 4 Startup Themes Sheet provides an overview.

If you do decide to change theme, be aware of their behavior. As you apply formatting to your sheet, if you stay within the theme fonts, colors and styles, then they will change when you apply a different theme. If you stray outside of these theme-controlled elements then you must manage each style element individually, or create your own theme. If you never change theme, then it doesn't matter. If you share the file, others might choose a different theme, but it's unlikely and not a good reason to avoid themed elements.

The lesson for me on themes is to respect the default. I'm not an artist, and I appreciate the helpful suggestions the theme gives me. It has plenty of nice coordination, and I seldom feel the need to explore outside of it. Then I can focus my attention on applying its nuances to enhance and balance the total picture that the sheet presents in both static and Conditional Formatting. That said, themes don't have a monopoly on aesthetic coordination, and it is fair game to use any other features, particularly if you have artistic talent.

Not to be confused, there is another type of theme called Office Theme. Office Theme is much less interesting and is only for you. It sets how your screen looks as you are using Office, with four options. This can be set in File – Options – General in each app, or File – Account once for all apps.

Alignment

More than most formatting, alignment has a way of exposing the common spreadsheet malpractice of "too many words." Long text is meant to flow freely across the page, as in a book. When it's crammed into a cell, juxtaposed with columns of short text and numbers, it strains against its bounds, demanding unwanted attention.

A common case is a sheet used to track project tasks, or meeting notes. You would think to use Excel – why not? It starts off with some generic columns – task, priority, etc. – until the one with all the notes begins to take over. Soon you find that by wrapping long text, the row height grows, exposing alignment inconsistencies in other columns.

There are better ways to manage notes without excessive text in any cell. The most obvious is to use fewer words. Then, if you designate columns for things you might want to filter for, such as dates and names, you start the journey back to Excel's strength. Still, a small amount of wrapped text can look ok and help manage space. If you use any wrapping, be intentional about alignment.

Consider the appearance of the table below. The left shows Word table alignment, showing the normal wrapped, top-left alignment for any data type. The right shows Excel wrapped alignment, with the default bottom-left-text, bottom-right-number alignment.

Table 1: Cell Alignment

Word Alignment			Excel Alignment		
A	1	Num	A	1	Num
In Word, cells align top left	Numbers align the same as text	345	In Excel, text spills across columns or aligns bottom left when wrapped	Numbers align bottom right	345

The point is that Word and Excel are cousins with very different talents. Word treats letters and numbers the same for best readability, wrapping paragraphs and table cells alike with consistent left-alignment, easy on the eyes. Excel, on the other hand, clearly distinguishes numbers from letters, because they may be subject to transformation and validation. A number in a cell is likely to be accompanied by other numbers in the same column. Naturally then, numbers are right-aligned, as we learned in school, to clearly show their significance.

Excel always defaults text to the left and numbers to the right, and everything to the bottom. When you have text headers for numeric columns, the headings are left and the data are right. The wider the column and taller the row, the worse it looks. A quick answer is to align headings of numeric columns to the right, but the best answer depends on the case.

If numbers in a column are all the same number of digits, like percentages, then alignment is not an issue and might be right, left or center. A column with various orders of magnitude should be aligned right. Similarly, a column with variable-length text should be aligned left. Sometimes an indent looks good, to pad the cell edge a bit.

Variable decimal places can be made to line up on the decimal point by custom number format with a "?" placeholder per decimal place. For example, 0.???? will line up the decimal point for 0 to 4 decimal places. However, it may be a better choice to format a constant number of decimal places, such as 0.00.

While I can logically understand the rationale for right and left alignment differences, I can't say the same for the default bottom alignment. Tall rows are ugly enough to start with. With wrapped text in one column determining the height, and a single word or number at the bottom of another, it looks just awful.

I try to minimize row height and keep it uniform if possible. Again, if you're writing paragraph-length cells then stop and think about what you're trying to do. You might do better using Word, or splitting out the text into smaller cells. If I need to wrap at all, I select the whole sheet and top-align.

Clean Screen

An Excel sheet has more than 17 billion cells. One screenful has less than 1000 cells (on most screens), and even that can tax a user's grasp if not designed well. I design for one screenful whenever possible, but the key objective is to "un-busy" the screen. There should be enough space and format variety to naturally draw attention to the point. If the screen is filled with data then there is no room for information.

An introduction or summary sheet can help provide the stepping stones to the detail. A few clean sheets with good names is better than one that looks crammed or requires scrolling. If one screenful is not possible, try for one screen width, so that only vertical scrolling is required. Think about how it will look on different computers with different screen sizes. You can't please everyone, but you can try to please most.

View Options

Various parts of the screen can be hidden, to gain space or just to look clean. Hiding headings and gridlines are sheet-level settings, and transfer to other users. They are thus design options for a dashboard, instructions, or other sheet in which the user has no use for columns and rows. Both can be hidden per sheet from the View tab, Alt-W,V,H to hide/unhide headings, and Alt-W,V,G to hide/unhide gridlines.

I leave both on during design and build, then decide in refinement whether to hide or not. I sometimes hide headings, and I normally either hide gridlines or cover them with full-sheet background color. Formula bar can also be hidden, Alt-W,V,F, but this is an application-level setting so it is not a good design option.

You can also leave tips for users on how to enhance sheet visibility with user-level settings. There are various ways to manage the space on the screen to give a comfortable, uncluttered appearance without the need to zoom out. This table lists several ways to increase screen space, with the number of rows gained, beginning with the placement of the QAT.

Table 2: Options to Gain Screen

Option	Path	Rows gained
QAT Below Ribbon	(reference)	0
QAT Above Ribbon	Customize QAT menu, S	+2
Show Tabs only	Ctrl+F1 (toggle)	+5
Auto-hide Ribbon	Ctrl+Shift+F1 (toggle)	+10
Full Screen	Add "Toggle Full Screen" to QAT	+12

All of these options retain headings, and all except Full Screen retain the formula bar. Auto-hide keeps the ribbon accessible, by Alt key or by click at top; Full Screen does not, and is canceled by Esc key.

Grouping

Groups are applied to complete rows or columns to enable summarizing and convenient hiding and unhiding of the subordinate rows and columns. When you group a range of rows, you get a group bracket outside the row header, and a button at the bottom to expand or collapse the group.

If the grouped rows contain numbers, you can use =SUBTOTAL() in the summary row, the one with the button, to subtotal the group. Then, all groups can again be grouped to a grand total row, where =SUBTOTAL() ignores the subordinate subtotals within the range, to give an accurate grand total. The groups can then be collapsed to show just the total or subtotals, and the same can be done with columns.

This is a neat effect, especially with the automatic Subtotal function in the Data ribbon, Alt-A,B. Once you have a proper data table, that is, where the first row has headings and every record has every field filled, the Subtotal function groups by the primary sort column, inserting subtotal rows at each change in that column. For example, if you have economic data by country, sorted by region, it could give you subtotals by region, with your choice of statistical function.

As cool as that sounds, it is dated and has limited value. You cannot use it If you have formatted the data as a table, versus a range that's structured like a table, and you must ensure that the data are sorted by the summary field. And oh yeah, there's this thing called pivot table that does all that and a lot more. I would go ahead and format as table, and spend the time to learn how to work with pivots.

The reason for this background is to explain how grouping is still useful as a screen management tool. However, because it is based on the subtotaling model, the summary row is by default below the group, and the summary column to the right. This is awkward for outlining, in which the more significant rows are followed by the less significant.

I sometimes use row groups to create a text outline, and column groups to hide configuration data columns. In either case, I uncheck both summary checkboxes in Outline Settings, Alt-A,L, to reverse the summary position – i.e., summary row above the group, summary column to left of the group.

To create a group, select the range of subordinate rows or columns, then Shift+Alt+→, or Alt-A,G,G. To ungroup, Shift+Alt+←, or Alt-A,U,U. If you forget to select, it will prompt you to select either columns or rows.

Group buttons consume space and add clutter when not needed. You can regain that space by hiding them with Ctrl+8. Grouped rows will usually contain a heading, and grouped columns can use a single character or symbol in a small header column, with a cell note or Data Validation message as a reminder that there is a group and how to expand and collapse it.

If the project will contain VBA code, it is simpler and more versatile to hide sheet sections with code. This is used in Startup Colors Sheet, Project Tracker and Fun and Games. The benefit of learning to use grouping is when you want to avoid VBA.

Camera Tool

One of clunkiest limitations of Excel is the way that column width and row height affect the entire sheet. It's a common need to have multiple areas on one sheet that you would like to format independently, yet keep close together. You have to choose between formatting and positioning, right? Not necessarily. You can use the camera tool to get a remote view of another area or another sheet.

For example, you have one table that wraps text and has variable-height rows, and you want to put another one next to it that has standard-height rows. Or maybe you have a flow chart on a sheet that has a tight grid like graph paper, and you want to combine it with a freely-sized column area. With camera you can copy an area and paste it as a live view – not as a static picture, but as a true remote image. When the copied area changes, the image dynamically reflects the change.

The camera tool works well when one area is user-interactive, and the other is responsive to the first, or for setting up the screen for PDF or print. Navigation between areas may be acceptable for a developer, but a hindrance for a user. If both areas are interactive then you might need to provide navigational aids, or a different solution.

The camera tool is not in the ribbon. To try it, copy some data and paste somewhere as linked picture, as shown below. Then change the source data and see the copy change. The copy can be formatted like any picture, enlarged, reduced, etc. If you like it, add the tool to the QAT via Alt-F,T,Q, select "Commands Not in the Ribbon", and scroll to find Camera.

Table 3: Camera Tool

Method	Copy	Paste
Clipboard	Ctrl+C	Alt-H,V,I (Paste Linked Picture)
Camera	Click the Camera button	Click the target

Examples of linked images are in Team Calendar and Fun and Games Poker.

Custom Number Format

Custom number formats are convenient and powerful ways to enhance the display, both as static and conditional formats. They're like a miniature set of conditional formats for four conditions: >0; <0; =0; text. Each of the four conditions can be formatted differently, combined with text, or hidden, and additional criteria can be entered as well. Here are a few simple examples:

Table 4: Custom Number Formats

To do this	Try this
Include unit with a number	0" KG"
Set a custom date format	mmmmm-yy
Hide zeroes	0;-0;
Hide text	0;-0;0;
Hide everything	;;;

Furthermore, custom conditions can be entered into the formatting string. The conditions are entered in brackets and are applied in the order entered, and are limited to two conditions. For example, this string formats millions with "M", thousands with "K", and anything smaller as entered.

[>=1000000]0.0,,"M";[>=1000]0.0,"K";0

The number format string can set conditional font color as well, also in brackets, such as [Red]. More details can be learned by reading the custom codes that are included in Excel, and from online or other sources. The value of using number format alone versus Conditional Formatting depends on how many conditions and formatting options are required.

Hiding data is a common need for control parameters or for whatever the user doesn't need to see. Column or row groups and hidden sheets can be used to store data out of sight, and format can simply hide the data from view. An example is to hide column data with ";;;" when it's the same as the cell above, such as year and month in a calendar table.

Formatting Navigation

Most of the Home tab is all about formatting. It's a rich set of options, with multiple ways to use them. First, the ribbon has them neatly laid out, with 17 buttons and 10 drop-downs just in the Font, Alignment and Number groups. The right-click context menu includes a small palette chock full of the most common format options, 11 buttons and 6 drop-downs. There are at least 13 direct shortcut keys to common number formats, font styles and borders. Finally, the Format Cells dialog has every possible option, too many to number.

The most important tool to master is the Format Cells dialog, Ctrl+1. It gives you all formatting types and options in one place, some that you might easily miss with other methods. For example, the ribbon Fill Color palette, Alt-H,H, has all colors available, but the Format Cells dialog adds gradient and pattern fill effects. If you only use the ribbon palette you might never realize these options exist. The ribbon Font group has most font settings, but the Format Cells dialog adds effects like subscript and superscript, as well as a one-click reset to normal font.

Spend time practicing navigation within the Format Cells dialog. Use → and ← between tabs, or hit the first letter of the tab name; use Tab key into the tab and between options; use any underlined character to jump to options, or with Alt key to jump from a text box to the option; use ↓ and ↑ within picklists. Practice setting options with Space or Enter, across multiple tabs, before hitting OK.

Here's an example key sequence to hide cell contents: **Ctrl+1, N, Tab, ↓** (hold it down until it reaches the last item, "Custom"), **Tab, ;;;, Enter**. The whole thing takes maybe three seconds. The other tabs take a little more practice, or mouse clicks, to use efficiently.

All font formats – font, size, style, effect, and color – can be set on selected text within a text cell as well as on the whole cell. This can be useful for emphasis or if symbols are used.

Conditional Formatting (Alt-H,L)

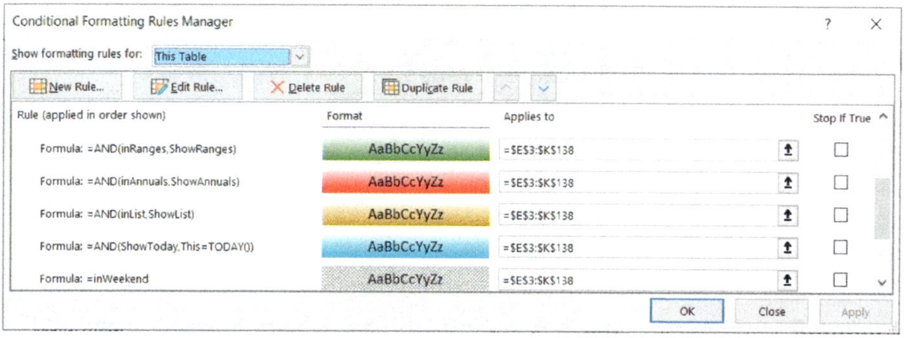

As much as formatting does for image, Conditional Formatting enhances the effect with dynamic relevance. It automates outlier highlighting; it offers special formats, like traffic lights and icons; it makes a sheet interactive, responding to input or control values.

Conditions are input criteria that produce special formatting. See the section on Logical Formulas for more detail on Boolean conditions. In Conditional Formatting there are numerous preset conditions and condition builders, as well as a formula option, that are all worth exploring. I most often create custom formula rules, but occasionally use presets for convenience.

Select any data range and open the Conditional Formatting menu, Alt-H,L. The menu has five types of preset rules in two sections, which I'll call highlighting rules and visualization rules. The third section of the menu has tools to create and manage rules.

Highlighting Rules

Highlighting rules highlight the data based on how they compare to a reference value. There are two groups of highlighting rules called Highlight

Cells Rules and Top/Bottom Rules. Most of these rules have a default reference value which can be changed, and a default format with a short picklist and access to custom formatting with a slightly reduced set of the Format Cells dialog.

Highlight Cells Rules

These rules highlight cells by comparison to a static value, a cell or a formula. Within this group there are four numeric rules and three other rules.

Table 5: Highlight Cells Rules

Rule	Default criterion
Greater Than...	middle of range
Less Than...	middle of range
Between...	25% and 75% of range
Equal To...	middle of range
Text that Contains...	active cell
A Date Occurring...	Yesterday
Duplicate Values...	Duplicate

The four numeric rules start you off with a calculated default value. When the rule is invoked with a numeric cell range selected, the selection is analyzed to default the middle value of the range, or the middle half of the range in the case of Between, as the rule reference. As a starting point this gives a quick and reasonable view of the data.

The default value can be overwritten with any value, or with a cell reference or a formula. If the data won't change, a constant reference value can be used. To make it dynamic, change the value to a cell reference or a formula such as =AVERAGE(*range*).

The Text rule defaults the active cell value, if it is text, and can be overwritten with any text or cell reference. For example, this could be used with an input cell labeled "enter search text:" to highlight any cell containing the input string.

The Date rule has a picklist of ten periods relative to today; Yesterday, Today, Tomorrow, In the last 7 days, Last week, This week, Next week, Last month, This month, Next month. To customize further, use a "Between" rule. For example, to highlight the past year enter between =TODAY()-365 and =TODAY().

The Duplicate rule is a picklist with two options, duplicate values or unique values. These can be replicated or customized as a formula condition. For example, =COUNTIF(*absolute range, relative active cell*) returns how many of the active cell value are within the range. This count can then be made Boolean by =1 (unique cells), >1 (duplicates), etc.

The New Formatting Rule builder, Alt-H,L,N, adds more options to most rules. For example, in addition to duplicate or unique cells, by using the Rule builder or Rules Manager you can highlight blank or error cells.

Top/Bottom Rules

These rules are based on statistics of the data range selected. Even though the four Top/Bottom rules say "10", that's just the default and can be overwritten.

Table 6: Top/Bottom Rules

Rule	Criterion range
Top 10 Items...	spin or type, 1-1000
Top 10 %...	spin or type, 0-100
Bottom 10 Items...	spin or type, 1-1000
Bottom 10 %...	spin or type, 0-100
Above Average...	no option
Below Average...	no option

Above/Below Average rules have no input, but the New Formatting Rule builder, and Rules Manager, add the option of 1, 2 or 3 standard deviations in each direction.

Visualization Rules

We've seen how highlighting rules use conditions to select the cells to apply a format. With visualization rules, conditions select the format to apply to the cells. With highlighting rules, the formats available are a subset of standard cell formats. With visualization rules, a whole new set of formatting choices is introduced.

Color Scales use standard fill color with gradual shading between two or three colors; Data Bars and Icon Sets are unique to Conditional Formatting. The objective of visualization is to see the numbers without reading them; to give a stratified, visual summary, or "heat-map" of the data.

On the Alt-H,L Conditional Formatting menu, with the highlighting rules, you could get a preview of the rule before saving it, but you could not go back to the menu from each rule. In the visualization rules section, since there are no inputs, you can browse around all of the presets without ever closing the menu. Thus you can window-shop to settle on the look you want.

Select the data, open the menu, and mouse-hover over Data Bars to open the gallery. Hover over the gallery, watching the sheet change, then back to the menu, and do the same with Color Scales and Icon Sets. To use the keyboard, arrow down the menu, then right to and around each gallery; hit Esc to return to the menu.

Visualization presets use default thresholds to assign values to formats. For example, each traffic light color gets a third of the range. These thresholds and other options can be customized in the New Formatting Rule builder, or in the Rules Manager. Bars and Icons can be set to hide the cell value; Bar direction and negative axis can be changed; Icon order can be reversed, and each Icon can be customized.

In this section I have most often used Data Bars, sometimes Icon Sets. Over-use of visualization can look busy and detract from elegance, but tasteful use adds sizzle.

Custom Rules

I've noted above how the New Formatting Rule dialog builds on the preset rules with more customizing options. There are six options; the first contains all the visualization rules, the next four correspond to the highlighting rules. It is worth some time to browse each to see what it can do. Now I'll describe the last option, the formula.

Formula conditions are not intuitive at first, but it's what I use most often. With a formula, you can base the condition on a cell outside the format range, use hybrid range referencing, and more.

Boolean Conditions

As I've previously noted, conditions are Boolean, having only true or false state. When you select the formula option, the formula bar says "Format values where this formula is true:". The word "true" is the clue that the formula must be Boolean. If you think about it, each of the preset conditions discussed can be expressed as true or false; the cell value is greater than the average, or not. Some combine several conditions; “if bottom third then red, else if mid third then yellow, else green.” Each “if” is true or false.

Boolean formulas are discussed further in the Logical Formulas section. For now, note that the formula itself does not need to return true or false in order to be evaluated as true or false. An equation that compares two values, such as =A=B, or =A>B, or =A<B can only be true or false. Math functions return numbers, but also evaluate as true or false when used as a condition; any non-zero number is true, zero is false. True/False can be converted to 1/0 by multiplying by 1. Either type of formula is a valid Boolean condition.

To practice condition formulas, start by replicating a preset. Say you have a sheet, A1:A20 is filled with numbers 1 to 20. Copy the range to C1, then format A1:A20 with the preset “Greater Than...”, which gives you the default threshold 10.5. Then format C1:C20 with the formula =C1>10.5, and select any highlighting format. Note that C1 is relative, and is the active cell when the formula is entered. You should see the same rows, 11 to 20 highlighted in both columns. Try others as needed to gain confidence, like “Above Average...” and =C1>AVERAGE($C$1:$C$20). Change some numbers in both ranges to verify that the conditions match.

Some common math functions used as Booleans are =COUNTIF (*range, value*) = “value exists in range”; =SUM(*ref1, ref2*) = “ref1 or ref2 (or both) are non-zero (presuming they are not negative of each other)”; =PRODUCT(*ref1, ref2*) = “ref1 and ref2 are both non-zero”.

Reference Type

Preset conditions apply to each cell in the selected range. This makes them mostly applicable to a single column. Even though they can be applied to multiple columns, this would only be appropriate if all the columns have similar ranges. For example, if you have several columns of indicators or percentages, you might want to highlight the same values in each column. Don’t be fooled by relative conditions like “Top 10%”, which applies to the whole range of selected data, not column by column.

Consider what kind of hybrid reference to use in the rule. For example, if you select a single column it makes sense that the reference is relative, so that any cell that meets the condition is formatted. For this you can use any preset condition or create your own. If you use a formula condition, enter the active cell in the formula, as a relative reference (no "$"). To check which is the active cell, it's the one in the Name Box.

In a table, each row is a record of related data that should be treated as a unit, not column by column. But you can't just select all columns and set a relative condition, it will evaluate each column based on all columns' values, and you'll have a mess. You want all columns, whether text or number, to be formatted based on a condition applied to a single column. You can do this with hybrid referencing to draw attention to the full record, resulting in a more elegant look.

Table 7: Formatting Multiple Columns By One Column

Condition	Result		
	Note	Name	Due
= TODAY()-D5>7	due date extended 2 weeks to account for delays	Jose C.	08/04/2021
	Grace expects evaluation to begin by 7/23	Grace Y.	07/28/2021
	no update; Mary's team will meet next week	Mary M.	07/28/2021
	added deliverable to confirm transport access	Jose C.	07/28/2021
	Note	Name	Due
= TODAY()-$D5>7	due date extended 2 weeks to account for delays	Jose C.	08/04/2021
	Grace expects evaluation to begin by 7/23	Grace Y.	07/28/2021
	no update; Mary's team will meet next week	Mary M.	07/28/2021
	added deliverable to confirm transport access	Jose C.	07/28/2021

The way to do this is to select the whole table and use a formula condition. In the formula, enter the cell with the evaluated column as absolute, and the active row as relative.

For example, say you have a ten-column table of demographic data, headers in row 1 and income in column G, and you want to highlight the rows where income meets certain criteria. Select all ten columns, with the active cell in row 2, then use a formula to compare $G2 to a calculated or constant value, such as = $G2 > 100000, or = $G2 > PERCENTILE($G$2:$G$101,0.9). The result is that each row in which income meets the criterion is highlighted all the way across.

When writing formula conditions there are a few disadvantages. Table references and references to names scoped to other sheets are not accepted. To get around this, use Name Manager to create an alias name for the reference as a Boolean formula, then use the new name as the formatting condition.

In the example above using a table, I could create the name: InTop10Pct =Data[@Income]>= PERCENTILE (Data[Income],0.9). Then in Conditional Formatting I would select the whole table and enter the condition formula =InTop10Pct, with an appropriate fill or font effect. It is implicit that the name InTop10Pct is only relevant and valid within the Data table context.

If you have a sheet background format and several areas on it with different formats, changing the background can be cumbersome. You would need to select all ranges avoiding the foreground areas, or format the whole sheet, and reformat the foreground areas. Another way is to set the foreground formats in Conditional Formatting, with the condition =TRUE, that is, always on. Then you can format the whole sheet and the foreground formats will remain undisturbed.

With formula conditions, always be aware of the formula range reference in relation to the applies-to range. If the formula reference is relative, it should match the first cell in the applies-to range.

Rules Manager

Conditional Formatting rules are managed in the Conditional Formatting Rules Manager, Alt-H,L,R, an important tool to master. It gives you access to all the rules in the workbook, one sheet at a time, or only those in the current selection or table. Here you can maintain the conditions, the formats, and the ranges of individual rules, and the order and dominance between the rules.

When you first open the Rules Manager, check the "Show formatting rules for:", and select or accept the default scope of the rules. The first rule is gray-selected. This means you can Alt+E to edit the rule, or Ctrl+↓ to change its priority.

To select any other rule, Tab or → to the toolbar, then use → or ↓ to move across the toolbar, and continue to the first rule and down the list of rules. Now the rule is blue-selected. This means you can Tab to the "Applies to" bar, and navigate the sheet to change the range, and Tab again to the "Stop If True" box, Space to set or unset. The next Tab will land on the OK button, or Shift+Tab to backup and select another rule.

Audit becomes important as the number of rules mounts. Rules Manager gives the main points, including a preview of the format. With a long list of rules it is worth maximizing the window, but this window exhibits some odd behavior. The double-click-the-header trick to maximize the window doesn't work, like it does in Name Manager. Double-click on the top or bottom edge maximizes the height, and the sides or corners can be dragged to manually resize. I have also written a macro ListFormatConditions which collects formula conditions from all sheets and tabulates them, with some of the most commonly used formats listed and displayed. There are too many properties to list them all, but this helps if you are mainly using formula conditions.

Conditional Formatting becomes a powerful tool when combined with user interaction, making the interface dynamic and interesting. For example, when you click a button an area lights up, or when you complete a record it changes color, or when you click a checkbox select data are hidden. It can also provide some governance, with or without Data Validation, to help the user to recognize errors and missing inputs.

Templates (Alt-F,N)

Templates included with Office are professionally-designed Excel files that you can adopt and adapt for your own purpose. The benefit of using a template is that it already works well and looks good. This can save a lot of time and give a better result than starting from scratch. Even if you build your own, experimenting with templates is a great way to get ideas to reapply. Try out what you have for free, and to know your base competition.

Use a Template

To use a template, go to File-New and browse the thumbnails. Here in the "back office", you'll see select templates at top, and at bottom, tabs for Office-provided templates and Personal templates. A template is a special file type, extension .xltx, that once opened becomes a standard .xlsx file. Thus you are not opening the template, you are applying it to a new workbook.

You can also open a template while in a workbook, without creating a new one. Right-click on the sheet tab and select Insert... to select from templates. Whatever sheets are in the selected template will be inserted into the current file. Interestingly, this method does not allow folder navigation, and includes personal templates in the startup folder but not in the personal templates folder.

As you experiment with various types of templates, you'll probably see some interesting techniques that you want to adopt yourself. Explore for hidden treasures. Use the Find & Select menu, Alt-H,F,D, to select parts of the sheet with certain features, to check for learning and reapplication opportunities. This can also apply to auditing your own or a shared file.

Select Formulas, Alt-H,F,D,U: while selected, read the formula, then hit Enter to go to the next, and so on. Learn how they're constructed, and if there are any named references in them.

Select Conditional Formatting, Alt-H,F,D,C: while selected, open the Conditional Formatting Rules Manager, Alt-H,L,R, and scroll through the rules to understand how they are constructed, by value or by formula, and the output formats and ranges.

Select Data Validation, Alt-H,F,D,V: while selected, open Data Validation, Alt-A,V,V, but beware the warning you'll receive if there are more than one rule in your selection; the only options are to erase all rules or cancel. If this happens, cancel. Select an individual cell, open Alt-A,V,V, and check the box to "Apply these changes to all other cells with the same settings" to select the rule's range. Review the three tabs to see the rule, the input message and the error message, then cancel. Repeat with other ranges until you understand the Data Validation model.

Name Manager, Ctrl+F3: see what kind of convention is used, scope, fixing type, and if there are any named formulas to be learned.

Templates are a good source of learning, because you can easily enter some data and see the effects. In addition to internal inspection, look at it aesthetically. How do you like it? These are vetted, so they should be fairly attractive. What might you do differently? Keep a healthy sense of confidence that you can do better, and plagiarize at will. If a template is close to what you need, resist the urge to reinvent, or tweak it only as much as needed.

Create a Template

If you find yourself frequently repeating the same steps to set up a sheet, consider creating your own template. Before you start, check your default template folder. Go to File-Options-Save, Alt-F,T,S, and look for "Default personal templates location". The standard is ...\Documents\Office\Templates.

To create your own template, start from an existing template or from scratch, and create the workbook template-to-be. Spend extra time on formatting, and add just enough data to demonstrate the functions and formats. Once you are satisfied with it, F12 to save. Open the "Save as type:" drop-down menu, and select "Excel Template (.xltx)". This automatically selects your template folder. You can also save templates from the File tab, but you will need to navigate to the template folder.

Once you have saved it, close the file and take it for a test drive. Go to File – New, open the Personal folder, Alt-F,N,Y,3, and select the template. See that the file name has a 1 appended to it, and F12 defaults to Excel Workbook.

Two standard templates require special attention. They are normal templates, but have prescribed names and are stored in the startup folder instead of the templates folder. They are completely optional and can be used separately or together.

- XLSTART\Book.xltx becomes the default for new workbooks e.g. via Ctrl+N. The new workbook is numbered with the next available number, like Book1.xlsx, as with any template.
- XLSTART\Sheet.xltx becomes the default for new worksheets e.g. via Shift+F11. The new worksheet is numbered with the next available number, like Sheet2, etc.

These are personal defaults and like your startup file, are to be shared cautiously. A user should know that they are adopting their own preference, and understand how to revert to Excel defaults by deleting or renaming files in XLSTART.

For your own use, devise a strategy that gives you the most convenience and flexibility. Set up your favorite sheet as the default "XLSTART\Sheet.xltx", and save other templates in your startup folder as well. This makes them available via right-click on the sheet tab → Insert.

If you want to share a template for repeated use, provide instructions to save it to the user's default template folder, or share it as a normal workbook, with instructions to convert it to a template by F12 as explained above.

Note the behavior, if you open a template file from recent files, it will reopen as a template file, and default save-as a template file. If you select the template via File-New, or open it via Windows Explorer, the name will have a number appended to it, and save-as will default to Excel Workbook. Be conscious of this when instructing users.

If your template includes macros, then save as "Excel Macro-Enabled Template (.xltm)". This will subject it to the same macro security as a macro-enabled workbook (.xlsm). Make sure your users are ok with that. Treat your template like an app, and test it thoroughly with enough data to ensure it will perform reliably. Use it yourself many times before you share it.

To edit a template, either open it from recent or pinned files, or open it as a new workbook, make the changes, and use F12 to save it again, overwriting the same template name.

Table 8: Template Locations and Use

Folder	Filename	Use
XLSTART	Book.xltx (or .xltm)	Ctrl+N
	Sheet.xltx (or .xltm)	Shift+F11 *
	Other names (.xltx or .xltm)	Right-click sheet tab → Insert *
Templates	Office templates	Alt-F,N,Y,2
	Personal templates	Alt-F,N,Y,3
	Blank workbook	Alt-F,N,L

* Note that inserting template sheets includes VBA code that resides in the sheet, but not in other modules. Plan ahead to store code in the sheet if you want to use it as an Insert-Sheet template.

Functions (Shift+F3) and Formulas

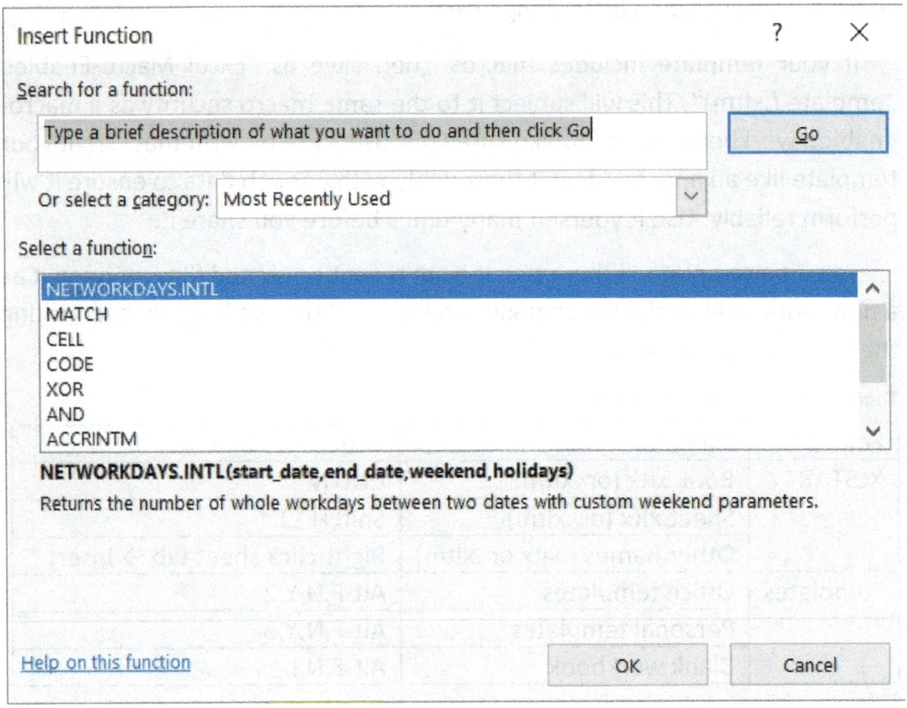

Approach

A function refers to a standard built-in operation such as SUM, AVERAGE, etc., and a formula is your creation, as you apply and combine functions with references and values. Formulas are a strong dialect using the function vocabulary. The syntax is more familiar than VBA code, but still far from natural fluency for novices.

A formula can be as simple as =A1 or as long as 8,192 characters. They can be nested and combined in unlimited ways that as you have probably seen, can quickly become unintelligible. Actually it is not quite unlimited, according to an Office tip, "Nest no more than 64 functions", to which I reply, "are you kidding me?!". The risk is more than an affront to fluent users. Complex formulas can become unsustainable to the point where you can't explain their logic even to yourself. The risk of "I don't understand the process" quickly leads to "I don't trust the result."

You do not want to perform surgery to try to "cure" poorly constructed formulas, so prevention is important. Before you get tongue-tied in formula-speak, think about basic communications. We converse effectively in short sentences with subjects, verbs and objects. Apply this principle to formulas and they won't get out of hand. Let's look at techniques:

Function Choice

Get to know functions well enough so that you don't get stuck trying to make do with the obvious few that you first learn. With each new application, research the list and look for the best one or combination for your purpose.

Pick any empty cell and type "=a" to see a list of functions beginning with a. Backspace and type b, then c, and so on. Arrow down through each list to see function descriptions. Tab on one to select it and open the list of arguments. This method gets you familiar with the function names and also how to enter them efficiently, directly in the cell.

Next, browse functions by category, by clicking *fx* in the formula bar or via Shift+F3. This gives you explanation of the arguments, and a link to a help page to complete your understanding.

There are over 100 functions ranging from the common SUM to esoteric financial and engineering operations. You can quickly scroll through many you'll never use, and frequently revisit those that look interesting. Think through your purpose and strategy before you start.

One of the most common needs is look ups, for example, to link two tables. There are several ways, and many articles written on their virtues; VLOOKUP, HLOOKUP, the newer XLOOKUP, DGET, or a combination of INDEX and MATCH. This is an example where you need to evaluate and make your own choice, then master it.

A common novice attempt to manage complexity is the nested IF. It only takes a few levels to get lost in the logic. This can be avoided with CHOOSE, or by INDEX of a range or array constant. As a rough guide, if you need more than two IFs, try CHOOSE, and if you need more than four or five, use INDEX with a lookup table.

Consider the following, where two array constants are defined for input and output, and we need to return the correct output for each input.

```
InputList ={"a";"b";"c"}
OutputList ={"alpha";"bravo";"charlie"}
```

The cell named Selection is where the user enters one of the three input values. There are at least three ways to get the desired output from the selected input:

```
1 =IF(Selection="a","alpha",IF(Selection="b","bravo","charlie"))
2 =CHOOSE(MATCH(Selection,InputList,0),"alpha","bravo","charlie")
3 =INDEX(OutputList,MATCH(Selection,InputList,0))
```

The best choice will depend strongly on the complexity of the input and output lists, and the possible need to expand and maintain them. If you hard-code the choices into IF or CHOOSE, you must find and edit all such formulas if the list changes. Further, if you don't limit inputs with Data Validation, you must have an "or else" clause for unexpected values. A lookup table makes the process transparent and change-ready, and with a range name such as InputList = Table[Input], can double as Data Validation.

Modular Formulas

Long formulas can be broken down into stages to make them more readable and more portable. This is particularly helpful if the intermediates are used in multiple output formulas, so that you can edit and audit the part once for many. It also helps just for comprehension, like learning to read in syllables. If you get to the point where you are counting parentheses in your formula, think about splitting it into stages.

Intermediate formulas can be written on the sheet, if it aids transparency, or hidden in Name Manager. Beware of getting too granular with components, this can lead to frustration as the logic becomes a treasure hunt.

Two projects in particular illustrate the benefit of modularizing. Startup uses step-by-step formulas in Name Manager to break apart the complex calculation of Holidays. The MRP Demo uses a table of intermediate calculations to illustrate MRP logic, as explained in the Formulas section.

Named Arguments

Operations within a table record, that is, in the same row, automatically use structured reference. If you refer to another row, such as one up or one down, it reverts to the default cell address reference. You can maintain structured reference by using OFFSET, or use a relative range name. See the example below.

Outside of a table, create fixed or relative range names for ranges that you perform operations on. See the section on Name Manager for more information. Names go a long way to improve transparency.

Self-Documentation

The formula bar allows for spaces and line breaks and even comments to improve transparency. The function N() converts any text to the number 0. This means you can add it anywhere in a numeric formula to explain the step by step process without affecting the calculation. Consider the following example:

```
= OFFSET([@Inventory],-1,0) + N("previous inventory...")
+[@Demand]+[@Supply] + N("...plus net change = ending inventory")
```

The formula is written on two lines for legibility, using Alt+Enter to create the line break, and each line ends with + N("explanatory text") for that stage of the formula. Formulas with several lines may be more readable with appropriate indentation on each line. To help users read multi-line formulas, you can start the first line with N("F2 or Ctrl+Shift+U to read the formula").

Logical Formulas

Boolean or binary logic is the DNA of computer hardware and software, yet we seldom see it in its raw form. Ever since CDs replaced audio tape we've known that what we hear is made up of zeroes and ones, but it's hard to grasp how that's possible. We would need a super-microscope to see the individual bits of the digital content we consume. Boolean logic is nonetheless an important element of spreadsheet design.

A variable refers to something whose value can vary, as opposed to a constant which has only one value. Variables that can only ever have true or false values are called Boolean. The value itself might be referred to as a state or a condition. Functions that return or use Boolean values are called logical functions.

An easy way to think about logical conditions is to compare a variable with many values to a constant. Age can have over a hundred values, but age > 40 can only be true or false. Some logical functions take Boolean input and return variable output. For example, IF (Age > 40, *Then, Else*) has two output values based on the Boolean input condition.

Boolean conditions are essential elements for building powerful formulas. They are also the basis for two important features, Conditional Formatting and Data Validation. These features allow you to construct the Boolean logic in various ways, or to use a formula that returns a Boolean value, then set the effect of that value.

In Conditional Formatting, you define the effect you want based on a TRUE condition. The condition identifies records that you want to format specially, to bring attention to them. In Data Validation, you define the effect you want based on a FALSE condition. The condition defines what values are valid, for which you want no effect. When the condition is FALSE the value is invalid, and you define whether to reject it or allow it, and what message to give.

To learn to use logical functions, set up two cells, A1 and A2, with values 0 and 1. If you evaluate them with logic, =IF(A1,TRUE) returns FALSE and =IF(A2,TRUE) returns TRUE. In fact, zero is always FALSE and any non-zero number evaluates as TRUE.

If I want to know if both cells are TRUE, logically I can use =AND(A1,A2), or mathematically I can multiply them, =PRODUCT(A1,A2), or =A1*A2. If either cell is 0 (FALSE), AND() and PRODUCT() are FALSE. Only if both operands are TRUE can the result be TRUE. I can also count zeroes in the range and flip the result – if there are any zeroes then the result should be FALSE, as in =NOT(COUNTIF(A1:A2,0)).

Similarly, to find if either cell is TRUE, I can use =OR(A1,A2), or by math =SUM(A1,A2), or =A1+A2. In this case, only if both operands are FALSE can the result be FALSE. To use count to find if there are any non-zeroes I use =COUNTIF (A1:A2,"<>0"). Note that COUNTIF() is used here to determine existence rather than actual count. To summarize the logical equivalencies:

PRODUCT (*refs*) = AND (*refs*) = NOT (COUNTIF (*refs*,0)) =	"all TRUE"
SUM (*refs*) = OR (*refs*) = COUNTIF (*refs*,"<>0") =	"any TRUE"

Note that if the data include negative numbers, SUM does not always equal OR, unless ABS is added. ABS accepts only a single argument, which can be a range.

=SUM (-1,1) = 0 = FALSE, whereas OR (-1,1) = TRUE.
=SUM (ABS(*range*)) = 2 = TRUE, where *range* contains -1 and 1

The Information function category has several Boolean functions with names beginning with "IS", indicating the binary result, "it is or it isn't". They report the type of data in the reference cell, including error trapping functions. N() and LEN() are ways to convert text to number or logical, but do not handle errors. Shaded cells in the table below evaluate FALSE.

Table 9: Logic Functions

Formula/Value	12	0	Blank	Abc	Space	N/A	1/0
N()	12	0	0	0	0	#N/A	#DIV/0!
LEN()	2	1	0	3	1	#N/A	#DIV/0!
IF(ref,TRUE,FALSE)	TRUE	FALSE	FALSE	#VALUE!	#VALUE!	#N/A	#DIV/0!
ISNUMBER()	TRUE	TRUE	FALSE	FALSE	FALSE	FALSE	FALSE
ISBLANK()	FALSE	FALSE	TRUE	FALSE	FALSE	FALSE	FALSE
ISTEXT()	FALSE	FALSE	FALSE	TRUE	TRUE	FALSE	FALSE
ISNONTEXT()	TRUE	TRUE	TRUE	FALSE	FALSE	TRUE	TRUE
ISNA()	FALSE	FALSE	FALSE	FALSE	FALSE	TRUE	FALSE
ISERR()	FALSE	FALSE	FALSE	FALSE	FALSE	FALSE	TRUE
ISERROR()	FALSE	FALSE	FALSE	FALSE	FALSE	TRUE	TRUE

Notice the relationships: ISTEXT() is the opposite of ISNONTEXT(); besides errors, LEN() is the opposite of ISBLANK(); ISERROR() is the equivalent of OR(ISNA(), ISERR()), and can be used as an outer wrap on a formula to catch any error.

For convenient error handling, ISNA() and ISERROR() each have special versions of IF(). This avoids the duplication of the output formula required for standard IF().

A common example of IFNA is used with MATCH. When the lookup value is not found in the lookup array, MATCH returns #N/A. To show this condition as a blank or as "not found", enter it as the IFNA result: =IFNA(MATCH(*lookup, range*,0),"not found").

Table 10: Special IFs

Special IF	Equivalent IF
=IFNA(*value,value if na*)	=IF(ISNA(*value*),*value if na,value*)
=IFERROR(*value,value if error*)	=IF(ISERROR(*value*),*value if error,value*)

Tables (Alt-H,T) and Pivots

Purpose

An essential foundation of data management is the two-dimensional table structure of fields and records. It is an elegant and simple way to store and retrieve data. Intuitively, it mirrors how we remember and communicate information.

Think of all the people you know, or scroll through your phone contacts. Based on fields that describe significant attributes of a person – name, address, birthday, etc. – each contact is stored, in your phone's memory or your own, as a record. Because they all possess similar attributes – with different attribute values, you can store hundreds of them and easily find the unique one when you need it.

Columns and rows are the DNA of Excel, yet despite this implicit invitation to adopt fields-and-records structures, the opportunity is too often lost. Users jump to visuals, treating the sheet like a white board. Blocks of disconnected data are separated by blank or colored columns and rows. With no logical framework, formulas are cell-by-cell with anonymous and cryptic references.

According to Excel's big brother Access, the data table is to be protected, to ensure the security and integrity of the source data. To input data, you create a form; to output data, you create queries and reports. You don't mess with the tables. Access clearly separates the duties of data management.

Excel is less strict about the rules and more popular than his brother, and has had some discipline problems. He's matured a lot and become more responsible about data management. To draw out this better nature we can use tables.

When you define a range of data as a table you are taking a step towards principled design. The table gently guides you back to the two-dimensional data model with these standard features:

- A single row of unique text column headings = field names
- A contiguous region of data rows below the headings = records
- Boundaries that adjust automatically as data are added or deleted
- An intuitive reference model

Tables are more than a convenience and will become your favorite tool to manage data, from complex datasets to short, single-column lists. To convert a range to a table, Ctrl+T to apply the default table format, or Alt-H,T to browse styles.

Table Referencing

The table reference model begins with the header row to define unique field names. If you try to reuse a name, the table will automatically append a number to make it unique. To avoid this, define the fields and make the names unique from the start.

Within the table, a field is referenced with square brackets as [Field]. This refers to the entire data field, all table rows excluding the header row. This gives the data set a meaningful name, making table formulas transparent and easy to read, such as =AVERAGE(Data[Income]).

For the rows there is a special reference for the current row. To refer to another field in the same record, use [@Field]. @ means intersection of the current row and the [Field] column. You might see @ automatically appear in other contexts outside of tables if there's an implicit intersection, but it won't affect calculation. Within the table it is intentional and explicit.

There are special notations for each part of the table. Review the list below, and practice with a sample table, navigating all around the table to see what kind of reference you get in each area. Note that OFFSET allows reference to the current cell, which would otherwise be a circular reference error.

Table 11: Table References

Reference to	From	Format
A table cell	Inside table, same row	=[@Field]
A table cell	Outside table, same row	=Table[@Field]
A table cell	A different row (default)	=C3 (e.g., from C4)
A table cell	A different row (alt)	=OFFSET([@Field],-1,0)
A table row	Outside table, same row	=Table[@]
A range of table cells	Same row	=[@[Field1]:[Field2]]
A table data column	Inside table	=[Field]
A table data column	Outside table	=Table[Field]
A column with header	Inside or outside	=Table[[#All],[Field]]
Table header row	Inside or outside	=Table[#Headers]
All table data rows	Inside or outside	=Table
All data and headers	Inside or outside	=Table[#All]
Table totals row	Inside or outside	=Table[#Totals]

To become fluent with Table referencing, practice navigation using the square bracket notation. When you type "=[", a picklist of all the Table's field names opens for convenient selection. At the top of the list is the "@ - This Row" option. Tab to select it, and only field names remain. Arrow down to the field you want, and Tab to enter it.

The fields are listed in the order entered, not alphabetically. This is helpful because primary key fields are most likely the first columns, and likely to be target references. The list is also filtered as you begin to type.

To step through an example, imagine you have a table, or create one, in which the first two columns are Name and DOB (date of birth), and you want to calculate Age. You begin typing your formula, and when you're ready for the DOB, hit five keys: **[Tab ↓ Tab]** ; **[** opens the field list; **Tab** enters @; **↓** selects DOB; **Tab** enters it; **]** closes the reference. With practice, this becomes an efficient sequence for formula entry.

For your interest, to be perfectly precise requires a longer formula for Age, but this one is simple and very accurate: =ROUNDDOWN((TODAY()-[@DOB]) /365.25,0).

Table Behavior

The table likes to stick together. Think of the table edge as a rubber band that expands and contracts as columns and rows are inserted or deleted.

Practice using it to select table contents. There's a fine line between selecting a data column, a table column and a spreadsheet column. Place a table with the header in row 1 to practice the following selection methods.

Hover over a table column heading. Slowly move the mouse up until it first becomes a down arrow. Click to select the table data column. This is a good trick for selecting the field as a function argument. Click again to add the header cell to the selection. Now you can drag the column to rearrange the order, or Ctrl+ to insert a column. Continue moving up until it becomes a down arrow the second time, when it's above the sheet column heading. Click to select the entire sheet column.

Likewise with rows, practice selecting records from the left table edge. Once a record is selected you can drag it up or down to manually sort. When doing so, notice the subtly different drag behavior in the table versus an open range.

When you drag a range on the open sheet and drop it onto a filled range, the default behavior is to move the data, that is, to cut and paste, overwriting (with your permission) any data in the target range. By holding down Ctrl as you drop, you can change cut to copy, and by holding down Shift you can change overwrite to insert, pushing the existing content down or right.

In the table, the default is cut and insert, like rearranging the pieces of a picture puzzle. You can still change the default with Shift and Ctrl. Table drag and drop only works with complete columns and rows. You cannot drag a single cell or group of cells that does not extend to the table edges.

Finally, hover over the top left corner of the table, until the cursor becomes a diagonal arrow, then click to select the data area, and again to select the entire table with headers.

With the active cell within the table, hit Ctrl+ to insert a table row or Ctrl- to delete a row. This is a nice shortcut, bypassing the dialog you would get on the open sheet. Particularly if you have multiple tables or table and non-table data next to each other, it inserts or deletes the row in the table only without affecting the rest of the sheet. In effect, the table is like a sheet within a sheet. Watch out for data below the table, which can be affected. As you will see in the Projects, tables can be stacked if the lower table has the same number or fewer columns as the upper table.

When you enter a formula anywhere in a data column, make sure the column is empty. The table will graciously copy the formula to the entire column, even to new rows inserted or added at the bottom. It will not prevent you from later typing in a number or a different formula in any row. Error checking will warn you of the inconsistency, and you will learn discipline.

Adopting tables gets you into the mindset of robust structural design. While less formal than a relational database table, the Excel table offers integrity, elegance and transparency. The expectation is that you are intentionally structuring your data to exploit these advantages and will respect their humble requirements.

Treat each table row as a record. Keep each column a consistent data type. Use a table format from the gallery or create your own. If using Conditional Formatting, apply it to the whole table or whole columns, never format individual rows. To manually highlight rows, insert a small flag column, such as a single digit or letter, and base the format on it. Apply formulas to whole columns, never to individual rows. Don't insert blank columns or rows or otherwise insult the table, and it will treat you well.

Pivot Tables

Pivots are powerful tools for analyzing significant amounts of data. They are a great payoff for the effort to structure your data. If you have tabular data you can use a pivot to cross-reference any two or more fields.

In a table, columns are fields and rows are records, period. With a pivot, you discover relationships between fields. You can put one field in rows like the table, another in columns, and summarize a third at each column-row intersection with statistical functions. Thus you pivot your view of the data.

Take an example from an Order detail table, with columns for Customer, Item, Quantity and Price. If you pivot Customer rows and Item columns, and sum Revenue = Quantity * Price in the middle, you then have a statistical summary view to customers, items, and to who orders what.

As another example, think about monthly records. It's common to see accounts in rows and months in columns. This is a quick and easy entry method, but "Dec 2020" is not a field, it's a value. Good data management reserves columns for fields, which can then be pivoted. You can't pivot data that's already pivoted.

With month as a column, data entry takes amount, account and month. The pivot can then select the date range with months as columns, if desired. This entails more table rows, but so what? With pivot power for data display, you specialize the table for data storage. Rows are cheap.

Choose pivot column fields carefully. You don't want so many columns that you have to scroll left and right a lot. In the Order table example, you might have product category that would fit better in the columns range. The power of the pivot is in summarization, to expose patterns and trends. If you get too granular, you may as well just read the table.

The Keyboard Trainer is an interesting example of a pivot used for selection rather than output. The Team Calendar Analysis Sheet has output pivot tables and charts.

Data Joins

Integrated data models are split into multiple tables. If you are entering sales orders, you don't want to type in the customer information and product information as you enter each order. You want these data to be stored in other tables, so that you can look them up and retrieve their details, saving effort and errors as well as data storage space.

Database structure requires that every table has a key that makes each record unique. When you use a value from a table field to look up other fields for the same record, you first need to know that the lookup value is unique within the lookup field. This is an essential principle of data management.

A key can be a single field or a combination of fields. For example, a customer table has a unique account number; a product table has a unique product code; an order table puts customers and products together, and has a unique order number; an inventory table may have material and location numbers, which are not unique in themselves, but are unique when combined.

Table joins come in different types, the most common is many-to-one. The order table can have many records with the same customer, all joined to a single record in the customer table. This enables efficient and secure data management. The first step to creating a coherent data model is to learn these principles, take stock of table and field names and keys, and draw a diagram of table/field joins.

Table links can be set up in the Data Model via the Relationship Manager, Alt-A,A. Use the "Create Relationship" dialog (no, that does not refer to pickup lines) to connect tables by linking a "table / foreign key" (the "many" side) to a "related table / primary key" (the "one" side). Each table must have its own unique primary key, which can also be called the lookup column. The Data Model can then be used to generate pivot tables with all fields from both tables.

In the Order table, Order[Number] is the primary key. In the Customer table, Customer[Account] is the primary key. Order[Account] is a foreign key because it resides in the Order table, but its values come from the Customer table.

Tables can also be joined by lookup functions. There are various ways to look up data. The first one learned is usually VLOOKUP. I prefer INDEX-MATCH because it describes precisely what I'm doing, and because the input ranges are more direct and flexible. I can MATCH on one column and INDEX on another without concern for their relative positions. MATCH type 0 finds the exact ordinal (nth) record number of the unique value within the lookup field, passes it to INDEX, and INDEX uses that to retrieve the value of any other field in the same record. For example, if Account is a named input cell and Name is an output cell,

```
Name = INDEX(Customer[Name],MATCH(Account,Customer[Account],0))
"Lookup this Customer's Account and give me their Name."
```

You can choose to join the tables via the Data Model, or just retrieve a few columns from the reference table to add to the analysis table. Think about your purpose and which table you're most interested in. In either case, joining tables requires a single key field. If you have a multi-field key used in multiple tables, concatenation is a simple way to turn it into a single field for easy lookup.

For example, you have city-level data, geographic characteristics in table Geo and demographic data in table Demo. The key to both tables would be state and city together, since neither is unique by itself, but the combination is unique. To link them, add a column to each table, "CityST", then use CityST as the key for MATCH and INDEX. If you're interested in the demographic data and you want to add city area to it, you can now add column Area to table Demo.

```
Geo[CityST] = Geo[@City]& ", " &Geo[@ST]
Demo[CityST] = Demo[@City]& ", " &Demo[@ST]
Demo[Area] = INDEX(Geo[Area],MATCH(Demo[@CityST],Geo[CityST],0))
```

Note the ", " in the middle of CityST is optional, but makes it easier to read and potentially useful as output. If you're not sure if every record has a match in the remote table, protect the formula with something like =IFNA(formula, "no data").

Slicers

Table and pivot filters are really great tools, with filter by value, by range, by text, even by cell color. But if users commonly need to filter, consider all the clicks required. Click the filter button, uncheck all values, scroll to find the desired value, check the value, click OK to activate. Do you really want to presume that they are inclined to do that, and will do it efficiently and effectively?

A slicer gives you a button for each value in a field, offering one-click access to filter the data. It makes it obvious that the filter is set, and makes it easy to unset it.

Slicers are applied to fields that represent data drivers or categories, fields that you would normally think of filtering or pivoting. The idea of using slicers is to replace and turn off the default filters, so they should be selected and arranged with care.

Pay attention to Slicer sorting. In Excel options you can define custom lists with custom sort. Find this option by Alt-F,T,A, then repeat Alt+O four times and hit Enter. These enable you to flash-fill and retain the custom sorting. You can add your own lists, for example, company divisions, markets or product categories. Slicers can use these custom lists to sort the button values, however this does not transfer the sort to other computers. What looks good to you may not look good to others. To convey custom lists to others requires an export-import of the registry entry, or a macro to recreate the lists. That's probably more trouble than value.

As an alternative, create a column for the purpose of customizing and sorting slicer buttons, with concatenated or prefixed values. It can be hidden from view. For example, if you have a column of course numbers and another with course titles, create a hidden column concatenating the number with a shortened title to feed the slicer buttons. With any column you can add a one or two digit prefix to sort buttons without detracting much from the look.

The downside of slicers is the real estate they require. One way to manage it is to put slicers across the top or on the left side of the screen, and freeze panes. Slicers default as a single column of buttons but you can set the size and number of columns to make them horizontal or rectangular.

Slicer examples are found in the Keyboard Trainer and the Startup Outline Sheet.

Data Entry

Tables are great for storing and accessing data, and for calculating columns from other columns. They're also not bad for data entry. Using the Tab key you can move across the columns, and once you reach the last column Tab takes you back to the first column and down a row, just like a typewriter "carriage return". This works well when you have a reasonable number of columns, so Tab key might be all the data entry help you need.

If a given column's entry must be one of a defined list, use Data Validation, List option. For example, a survey might have an affiliation field. With the list range defined and set as the only valid entries, you get a drop-down list in each cell. This reduces keystrokes and errors, and makes the table more like a form. Another option to simulate a data form is the Form tool.

The Form tool is a nice partner for a table, giving an alternate view and entry point for the data. The special service it provides is to put a single record on the stage, where you can see all or most fields at once. Field names are displayed in a column that adjusts to fit the longest name, with a column of uniform value boxes next to it that hold about 10 characters before it begins to scroll. This makes it hard to use with longer entries.

To use the Form tool, install the button on your Quick Access Toolbar or custom ribbon group. Alt-F,T,Q, Alt+C to look in "All commands", type F and scroll to Form. Then with the active cell in a table, click the Form button. Form can display up to 32 fields, with calculated columns grayed out. Due to the limited size of the entry box, it is best suited for numeric or other short entries.

Name Manager (Ctrl+F3)

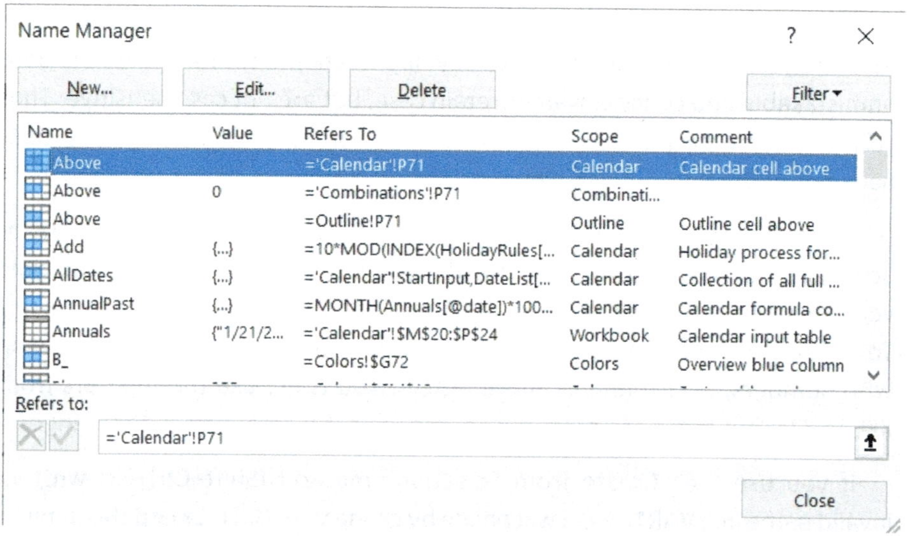

Using names to refer to cells and ranges improves transparency. Good choice of names is a way of self-documenting your project. Name Manager also has a comments field to elaborate the genealogy of each name. Names can also define custom formulas.

Rules

There are few rules for names. The most obvious is that a name cannot be a cell address. Everything from A1 to XFD1048576 refers to a cell and cannot also be a name. An attempt to define such a name will be rejected with a message that is not entirely helpful. It lists three things to verify: the name starts with a letter or underscore, doesn't have a space or disallowed character, and doesn't conflict with an existing name. If it's the first name in the workbook, that might make you wonder; it just means that you've entered a cell address.

The message is also not entirely accurate, the name can also start with a backslash. And how is "don't use a character that isn't allowed" help, if you don't tell me what's allowed? Below is a summary of what is allowed.

Table 12: Allowable Characters in Names

Place in name	Allowed characters
First character	A-z, _, \
Rest of name	A-z, 0-9, _, \, .

A name can be as long as 256 characters! That's crazy – a name is meant to be a shorthand reference. Try to develop a scheme for names that is both unmistakable and concise. Names retain case, but are not case-sensitive. Thus you can create easy-to-read names like AvgScore or NetSales, but you can't have both NetSales and netsales.

You might think of short clever names that use 3-letter abbreviations or acronyms, such as APR or VAR or GDP. That's fine, but if you have multiple versions and try to number them like VAR1 or GDP2017, you'll get the error. To get around it you can add underscore or backslash or period, avoid ending with numbers, or use four or more letters. You could use three letters from XFE to ZZZ, but there are probably not many useful acronyms in that range.

If you use the "Create from Selection" method (Shift+Ctrl+F3) with an invalid name like VAR1, Excel will oblige by giving you VAR1_. Keep this in mind whenever you need to number similar names. Try to keep names concise, but use whole words if you think it will enhance clarity.

When you begin or continue typing a formula and enter a few letters, the look-ahead picklist includes functions and names. After the first few characters, use down arrow to highlight and tab to select. This is a reason to design names well to be easy for you to remember and select this way. Avoid using the name of a function to prevent confusion.

Scope

Name scope can be either workbook (global) or worksheet (local). The default is global, which is good for most cases. Global names are easy to use in formulas anywhere, and do not require sheet reference since they are unique within the workbook. However, locally-scoped names can play a role in elegant design, especially the more sheets and names that you have.

Table 13: Name Scope

Image	Description
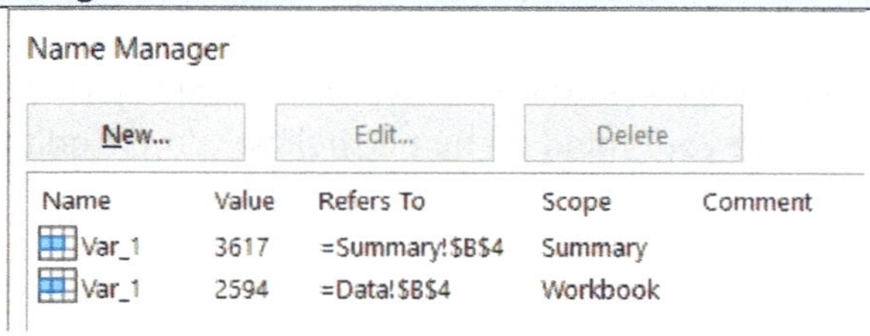	The same name has Workbook and Summary sheet scope
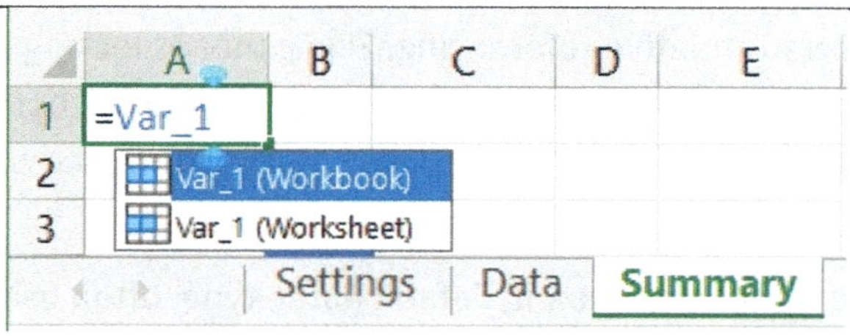	On Summary sheet, both names are visible
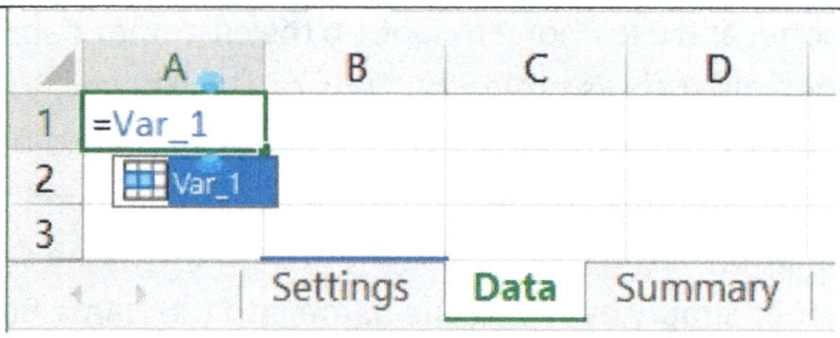	On other sheets, only Workbook-scoped name is visible
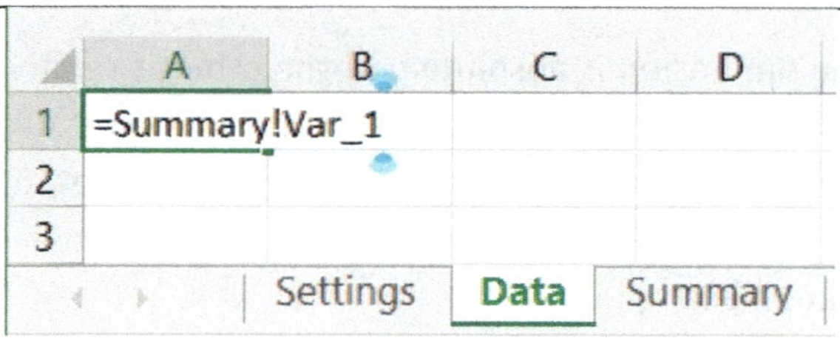	The locally-scoped name can be explicitly called with sheet!name notation

Global names are unique and visible from all sheets. Local names can duplicate names that are either global or local to other sheets, and are only visible from their own sheet. They can be seen in Name Manager, but not in any other sheet. Even though not seen, local names from other sheets can still be used by explicit reference including the sheet name, as shown in the table above.

The lesson for names is to think about the design ahead of time. It will surely evolve as the project develops. If you're prepared and keeping up with changes as you go, you'll avoid rework. If you create names after writing formulas, there are ways to apply names, to replace common cell references in existing formulas. If you change your mind on name spelling, simply edit in Name Manager and all formulas where the name is used will be updated. If the name is referenced in VBA, however, it must be manually edited.

Fixing type

Fixing type is absolute versus relative referencing. Fixing means locking in position, with absolute reference to the column, the row, or neither, or both. All four fixing types can be useful. By building them into names, formulas will be clean and intuitive.

An absolute range name is the simplest and default name type, often used with a single input cell. For example, you might have a cell labeled "enter phone number", name it Phone, and use Phone to look up the customer name, account, etc. If you have controls such as option buttons or checkboxes, you would want to pass the control's value to formulas by a name with absolute reference to the linked cell. You might also use a multi-cell absolute name to store a pick list for Data Validation or a List Box control. An absolute name can be defined in Name Manager or simply by typing the name into the Name Box at the left end of the Formula Bar.

Hybrid fixing is when one dimension is absolute and the other is relative. Most often the column is absolute because you have columns of input data and columns of output formulas. With relative row reference, every output formula within a column is identical. This is a common and powerful use of hybrid names, so let's look at an example.

Let's say you have two columns, C with inventory and D with unit cost, and you want to calculate the inventory value per item. If the data begin in row 2, you start in E2, enter =D2*C2. If you use arrow keys to enter the formula, the sequence would be: = ← * ← ← **Enter**; and you would get the default relative fixing type. Then you copy it down the column, and get E3 = D3*C3, etc. and all is good.

Now, with the cursor in E2, create the name "Quantity" to refer to $C2, absolute column, relative row. To enter the Name, follow these steps:

1. Ctrl+F3 to open Name Manager
2. Alt+N to open the New Name dialog
3. Enter "Quantity" in the Name box
4. Tab three times to the Refers to box
5. Hit ← twice to select column C
6. Hit F4 twice to fix the column and unfix the row
7. Hit Enter to save the Name
8. Hit Esc to exit Name Manager

Repeat the steps to create the name "Cost" to refer to $D2. Then in E2, enter the formula =Cost*Quantity, and copy it down. You get the same result, but now your formulas are not only readable, but are the same in every row.

If you are using the input column (Cost) in only one output column (Value), technically it doesn't matter whether the column in the name is absolute or relative. Cost = D2 gives the same result as Cost = $D2. However, by naming it Cost, you are committing to the meaning of the name, which is only valid in column D. As a principle, fix what should be fixed to ensure it cannot be misinterpreted. If you ever need to add another column using Cost, it's ready.

Column fixing is common and relates directly to table reference style. If the example above is a table, the names come from the column headings, and the Value formula will be =[@Cost]*[@Quantity].

Row fixing is handy for matrix calculations. For example, a multiplication table can be created by entering operands down column A and across row 1, and writing a formula in B2 =$A2 * B$1. Copy B2 to the inside region of the matrix, and as you select different matrix cells notice how the formula changes. To use hybrid names, again with B2 as the active cell, create names Operand1 =$A2 and Operand2 =B$1. The matrix formula is then =Operand1 * Operand2, the same for every cell. Another option is to define a formula name Product =$A2 * B$1, and enter =Product in the matrix cells. Formula names are discussed in the next section. The Startup file Functions sheet has an example calculation matrix.

Finally, there's a use for names with both column and row relative. For example, I often need to refer to the cell above in formulas or Conditional Formats. If the active cell is D9, create the name Above = D8. Don't use it in row 1, and beware of the scope. Even though you can refer to a global name from any sheet, the reference is to the sheet on which the name was created.

If you create global name Above on Sheet1 and use it on Sheet2, you think you're getting the cell above, but you are actually getting the cell above on Sheet1. If you want to use a relative name like Above on multiple sheets, create it in each sheet, scoped to the sheet.

When writing hybrid or relative reference names, pay attention to the cursor position. You must be aware of the active cell address to ensure proper reference. Remember what cell you have selected, or with Name Manager open, check the name box on the sheet behind it. If the active cell has an absolute name, the name box displays it, otherwise it displays the cell address.

Named Formulas

A less known but powerful use of names is the formula name. By working in the Name Manager you can create logical names for formulas. You can use any standard or custom function, table references, and other named formulas. Use the comments field to document the purpose and logic of each name.

One way to use this is to build component formulas that are easy to understand and document, then snap them together for the actual output function. You can thus have numerous intermediate formulas that don't take up any sheet space but are quietly working behind the scenes.

For example, the Team Calendar project has date tables that need the date type – is it a workday, weekend or holiday. This requires multiple lookups that would make the table formulas unnecessarily complex. By using Name Manager to define a DateType formula, the lookups are done invisibly and passed to the table as an index.

This can help you from a documentation and maintenance perspective, and for troubleshooting. To see all calculation steps, select a cell with the output formula and go to Formulas → Evaluate Formula, Alt-M,V, then use the Evaluate and Step In buttons and watch as it unfolds. If needed, insert some temporary columns to fill with the internal formulas so you can see what each one returns.

The caveat for building formulas in Name Manager is that they can only be used where they are relevant. In the Team Calendar example, there are three date tables that each have their own version of the DateType named formula. If they were table formulas that would be obvious, but by setting them apart in Name Manager it takes a conscious awareness and careful naming. Use name and description purposefully to keep it clear, and avoid getting carried away with complex name chains. If you have several sheets, organize names by scoping them to the sheet where they are used.

If the formula uses a table reference it must include the table name. When you reference another column from within the table you just get [@Field]. Name Manager won't accept that. You either need to type the table name in front of the field, or create the formula outside the table. Select a cell two columns away from the table on any row, and use the mouse or keyboard to select the target table column in the same row. This way you'll get the Table[@Field] reference format. While still in cell edit mode, copy the formula for paste into Name Manager.

This in effect creates an alias name to reference the table. Table referencing is not accepted in Conditional Formatting or Data Validation. The options then are to discard the structured reference, or to create an alias in Name Manager. Using aliases this way requires the diligence to apply them only where they are valid (i.e. within the table). The benefits are to make formulas easier to read, and the aliases keep structured references.

Behavior

There are aspects of the Name Manager and other formula bars that behave a little differently than you'd expect. They are subtle enough to miss, and pesky enough to cause frustration. It's worthy to call them out so you can adjust to the context and work like a pro.

First let's review how the worksheet formula bar works. When you type = to start a formula, and use an arrow key to reference another cell, the initial reference is relative column and row, A1 style. Depending on the context, you accept the default, or to change it, hit F4 one or more times to cycle through the fixing style options, A1 → $A$1 → A$1 → $A1 and → back to A1. This F4 cycle works the same way in all formula bars, but some start the cycle at a different point.

Also, within the sheet, if you click in the formula bar, or double-click the cell, or hit F2, you are in Edit mode. In Edit mode you can navigate within the cell contents by the keys – Home, End, ←, →, Ctrl to jump, Shift to extend, etc. Then if you're at a point in the formula to insert a reference, you can hit F2 again and select the cell or range on the sheet. This is called Point mode.

The other formula bars toggle between Edit mode and Point mode as well, but start in the opposite mode. You want to step into the formula with arrow keys, but instead you get cell references you don't want. This can be aggravating if you don't know about the F2 toggle, so it's a good point to practice.

To practice all cases, create a sample sheet with one of each: formula cell, named cell, named formula, Conditional Format formula, Data Validation formula. In each case, open the respective formula bar and hit ←, while watching the bottom left mode indicator. Only in the formula cell does "edit" start you off in Edit mode, and does ← move the cursor one character into the formula.

In Name Manager, Conditional Formatting Rules Manager and Data Validation, "edit" starts in Enter or Point mode, and becomes Point mode as soon as you hit an arrow key. Try it again, hitting F2 before ←, and note the difference. Make a mental note that to edit a reference in Name Manager, F2 (or Tab) to select the formula bar, F2 again to switch to Edit mode. Practice until it becomes natural.

Three of the four formula bars are expandable. Data Validation is not, and only holds about 48 characters before it starts to scroll and become difficult to manage. This is one reason to create a formula name in Name Manager. Another is simply to manage complexity in one place.

The table below summarizes the behavior in these four formula entry bars. Once these behaviors and the means to tame them are understood you will easily master them all.

Table 14: Formula Bar Behavior

Formula bar location	Initial mode	Initial fixing style	Expand entry bar
Worksheet	Edit mode	A1	Vertical
Name Manager	Point mode	$A$1	Horizontal
Conditional Format	Point mode	$A$1	Horizontal
Data Validation	Point mode	A1	None
To change	F2 to toggle	F4 to cycle styles	Drag edge

When you copy sheets within the file, names on the sheet are copied as local names on the new sheet. When you copy sheets between files, names can be created with link to the source file. This can cause the file to prompt you to update links the next time you open it. You might wonder where the links came from, and wonder why you can't find them anywhere on the sheet. Check Name Manager, and see if any references include a file path. Edit or delete these names as needed.

Name Manager as a strategy centralizes complexity where it can be modularized and enhanced with comments. For long calculation chains it is indispensable. It's also good for creating logical references, shortening entries elsewhere and improving transparency.

Navigation

Name Manager does not have a maximize button, but can be maximized by double-click on the header. Columns are sortable and column widths are changeable. The filter button has six options, two each for scope (workbook, worksheet), errors (with, without) and type (defined, table). Note, the worksheet scope filter is not for the current sheet, it applies for any name scoped at the sheet level.

To change a name that refers to a cell range, click Edit to change the name itself or the comment, or F2 or Tab into the reference bar to change the reference. Since you start in Point mode, navigate to the new selection, or hit F2 again to type it in. To change a named formula, be sure to hit F2 for Edit mode.

Tables have a different icon than defined names, and the reference box is grayed out when selected. Table size can only be changed on the sheet. However, in Name Manager, table name and comment can be changed. If you use a lot of tables, use the filter to show and manage them all.

As you learn to use Name Manager regularly, you will find the methods that make it routine. For example, if you have several sheets and many names, you might sort by Scope, or Refers to. You can use Comments to sort as well as to document names.

Listing Names

If you get into using a lot of names, you might need to list them to audit and document the project. There is an easy way to list all names and what they refer to in a sheet, but watch out – it asks neither permission nor forgiveness for overwriting data! To be safe, insert a sheet. It will consume two columns, and as many rows as you have names. To paste the names list, Alt-M,S,P, Alt+L.

Remember that relative names will refer to a cell relative to the cell where the name is pasted.

Another way to list names is with VBA. If you have invested in writing Name Manager comments, you'd want the list to include them, and If you've scoped names to sheets, you'd want that too, and in that case you can't use the Paste List method unless you do it sheet by sheet. The Startup project includes the ListNames macro to create a table of all names with scope and comment, and allows comments to be uploaded from the sheet to Name Manager.

Controls (Alt-L,I)

As part of an elegant design, controls add professional look and feel to your Excel project. They make selections intuitive, giving users a friendly interface. Think of an online survey or quiz, and the usefulness of controls is evident. Purpose comes first, and the simplest solution is best. Like macros, controls are advanced tools in your kit to be used when there is no simpler answer.

Consider for example the case of data entry. A typical data entry form has many controls, so it's natural to think of adding controls for entering data in a sheet. But where do the data go once they're entered? Controls have a "linked cell" property to catch the entry, but then what? You would have to process that cell to commit the record to a table. The simple solution is to enter data directly in the table or via the Form tool, as described in the Data Entry section. If you really need a business form and you're struggling to make it in Excel, stop and think about purchasing the right tool for the purpose.

The most common control I see people use is a button to run a macro. If you've written a macro for the user to run, you wouldn't expect them to find it the long way. A button control is a natural way to say "run something", but there's nothing special about a button; any shape, picture or icon can also do the job, which gives you a lot more visual options. Simply right-click the object and select Assign Macro. Make it clear that the object is interactive and what it does, either by appearance or by label.

I like to use controls to enhance the user interface even without VBA; a checkbox to switch a condition on and off; a spin button or scroll bar to slide from low to high value. These are intuitive invitations to interact safely with the sheet.

Another type of control is used to select data from a list, such as a combo box. Such controls add the value of exposing not only what was selected, but from what options. For this purpose controls can be used with or without VBA coding. Their input and output are linked to sheet ranges. Competing options here include table filters, pivot tables, Data Validation and slicers.

Control Families

Controls like VBA are on the Developer tab, which if you have not yet enabled you must select in options; Alt-F,T,C, then check Developer on the right. Once you decide to use controls, the first question is, Form or ActiveX? They have mostly the same controls, so what's the difference? Initially, not to worry, either one will do. Form controls are easier to set up and learn, and are adequate for most uses. As you encounter limitations, you can start to learn and incorporate ActiveX into your toolkit.

Table 15: Form vs. ActiveX Controls

Family	Properties	Programming	Use on	Gallery
Form	Basic (e.g. Combo Box has 4)	Assign Macro	Sheet	
ActiveX	Enhanced (e.g. Combo Box has 49)	Sheet – Object – Event (14 events)	Sheet, VBA UserForms, web pages	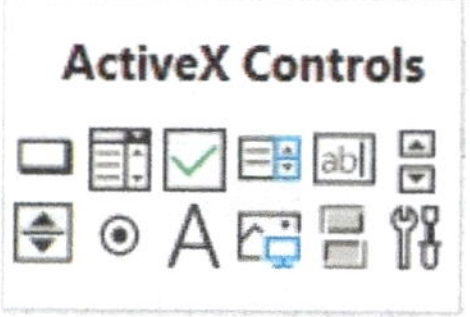

Once you understand Form vs. ActiveX, learn their navigational differences. To set Form control properties, right-click and select Format Control. To set ActiveX control properties, first set Design Mode on the Developer tab, Alt-L,D,M, then select the control, then Properties, Alt-L,L. To program a Form control, write the macro, then right-click the control and select Assign Macro. To program an ActiveX control, in Design Mode double-click the control to open the default event in VBA, or, in VBA double-click the sheet, in the first drop-down list select the control, and in the second drop-down list select the event.

Control Types

Here are some points to consider when selecting controls. I've included some non-control options I call "faux controls" that look and feel like controls, for comparison. In the descriptions following, I'll refer to ActiveX properties in the format [Property], and Form control properties, if they exist, as {Property}.

Table 16: Control Types

Control type	Control	Selection	Validation
Text selection	Combo Box	Single	Choice
	List Box	Choice	List range
	Check Box group	Multiple	Implicit
	Option group	Single	Group
Number selection	Spin Button	Single	Min/max
	Scroll Bar	Single	Min/max
Toggle	Toggle Button	Boolean	Implicit
	Check Box	Boolean	Implicit
(faux)	Data Validation list	Single	Choice
	Slicer	Multiple	Field values

Combo Box combines features of List Box, presenting a list of pre-defined values, and Text Box, allowing new entries. The [Style] property gives you the option to either limit entries to the list (List style) or allow non-list entries (Combo style). The Form Combo Box does not have the new entry option and thus is not a true combo box. A Combo Box does not reveal its value list until the drop-down is clicked.

List Box can be sized to show its entire list, eliminating scroll bars. It does not have an option to accept non-list entries, but it does have the option to select more than one entry from the list with the [MultiSelect] {Selection type} property. Combining [MultiSelect] with [ListStyle], an ActiveX List Box can be made to look and behave like an Option group or a Check Box group.

Table 17: ActiveX List Box Options

Option	ListStyle	
MultiSelect	0 – Plain	1 – Option
0 – Single	Click to select one item	Looks like Option group
1 – Multi	Click to add items	Looks like Check Box group
2 – Extended	Ctrl+click to add items	Looks like Check Box group

This is a convenient alternative to set up a single control instead of several. Note, a multi-select List Box negates the simple output cell link, and VBA is required to retrieve the selections. Stick with single-select to keep it simple, or a checkbox group to retrieve each selection without VBA.

A Check Box group is like a multi-select List Box, but since each control has its own linked cell, there is no need for VBA. Check Boxes can be used individually as a toggle (see below), or in a group for independent options. Here the group is a convenience only, each option is retrieved and evaluated on its own. On a form this might be labelled “check all that apply”.

An Option Button group is a collection of dependent options. An individual Option Button has no purpose by itself, it can only exist in a group with at least one other Option Button, like a single-select List Box. Each button must be identified with a group, because only one option within the group can be selected. With Form Option Buttons, the {Cell link} property defines the group; all Option Buttons linked to the same cell are logically grouped, and the cell displays the index number of the selected button. With ActiveX, the [GroupName] property defines the group, and each button has its own LinkedCell that contains its Boolean state.

Spin Button and Scroll Bar are both ways to select a number between the defined [Min] {Minimum value} and [Max] {Maximum value} by a defined [SmallChange] {Incremental change} increment when the arrow buttons are clicked or an arrow key is hit. Scroll Bar adds a [LargeChange] {Page change} increment when the bar between buttons is clicked or a page button is hit. As an example guideline, I think of Spin Button for a range of 1 to 10 and Scroll Bar for 1 to 100. These are useful for any numeric field with reasonable range, or to navigate a set of pre-defined numbered scenarios.

Toggles are Boolean controls, Toggle Button (ActiveX only) and Check Box. These are great for output controls with clear yes/no, on/off options, like “show chart”, or “include holidays”. They can be used for any two-answer question, but are best reserved for true Booleans. For example, “domestic or global” appears to only have two values, but might later evolve into a list. ActiveX toggle controls also have a [TripleState] property. If [TripleState] is true it adds #N/A to the standard true and false cycle with a grayed-out appearance. The Form Check Box displays gray if the linked cell contains #N/A, but it cannot set the #N/A state.

The Startup file Controls sheet gives examples of these controls and features. Various controls are used in MRP Demo, and the Startup Calendar and Startup Colors.

The first faux-control, Data Validation is like a Combo Box that can be set up once for a range, and the drop-down list is enabled when each cell is selected. The choice to allow new entries or not is made in the Error Alert tab; if Style = Stop, no new entries are allowed, like Combo Box "List" style, otherwise new entries are allowed, like Combo Box "Combo" style. This method is used in several projects for configuration settings. An input example is in Team Calendar.

The second faux-control, Slicer is similar to an "extended" multi-select List Box; multiple options can be selected while holding Ctrl. A Slicer is an output selector linked to the data itself, so as new values are added to the sliced field, new buttons are added to the slicer. Examples of Slicers are noted in the Slicers section.

There is another faux-control option using symbols that look like controls. This requires VBA to control interaction and set the appearance. This method is used in Project Tracker.

Sheet Design

The choices of Form or ActiveX and which control to use in each case are numerous. Adding visual criteria helps narrow the choice. How do you want the sheet to look? How many controls do you need, and how much space do you have? It is important to have a deliberate design strategy, including logical and visual flow, labelling, spacing and alignment. Think about your car dashboard to get the idea.

A Combo Box consumes little space. It can be but does not need to be sized and aligned to a cell, although font size might need adjustment to avoid cropping. The drop-down exposes a good chunk of the list. The default is eight items and it can be increased to avoid a scroll bar. A Data Validation drop-down list is of course by nature a part of the cell, so how good it looks depends on the size and position of the cell. It also shows eight items, which cannot be increased.

A List Box looks better as an expanded list, requiring more space. Sized well it will have no scroll bars. The color palette is limited, but enough to blend nicely into the sheet. As noted above this is a nice alternative to an Option Button group.

Get familiar with the Align tools, Alt-P,A,A. Start with Snap to Grid, then nudge to balance. If controls are poorly balanced with other elements of the sheet, they will detract from the appearance rather than enhance it. If not aligned to the grid, then at least align and space them nicely as a group. For example, for a vertical option group, select all the option buttons and Align Left, and Distribute Vertically. A Group Box control is not technically required, but is a good way to set groups of controls apart.

Control size is visible for all except check boxes and option buttons, which have an invisible border. Only when you select the control – right-click for Form, Design Mode-click for ActiveX – do you see the border. Make grouped controls the same size with Shape Format, Alt-J,D, H and W, and such that once arranged, their borders do not overlap. A click anywhere within the border sets the control, and if they overlap this can cause clumsy behavior and unexpected results.

Meanwhile behind the scenes, each control needs to be configured. For Combo Box and List Box, input range is best stored and named, hidden or on a separate config sheet. Output cells can also be stored and named on the same config sheet. Use naming convention to logically connect the control with its input list and output cell. For example, if an input list of brands is named *BrandList*, name the control like *BrandBox*, and the output cell like *BrandSelected*.

Some pick lists never change. Others may seldom change, but are best designed to accommodate change, such as a product line or customer group. In these cases it's worthwhile to create a table and a name to make it easy to update. The format for the name is Name=Table[Field]. You don't need to use a table for pick lists, you can simply name the range, but if you ever add items to the list, be sure to update the range name. If you insert a cell within the list, the named range will be naturally extended. If you add an item at the bottom of the list, you must manually update the list name to include the new item. The table does this bottom-extension automatically.

The linked output cell may or may not require processing to achieve the desired effect. Form selection boxes output the index of the selection within the list, while the ActiveX counterparts output the selected item itself. To retrieve the item from a Form selection, use =INDEX(*InputList,OutputCell*). On the other hand, if you need the index from an ActiveX control selection, use =MATCH(*OutputCell,InputList*,0). Unless used directly, OutputCell can be hidden.

Navigation

All true controls, as well as Data Validation dropdowns and Slicers, are objects on the sheet, like shapes or pictures. They can be viewed, selected, renamed, sorted and hidden in the Selection Pane, Alt+F10. They are mass-hidden and un-hidden by Ctrl+6, but this does not change the individual object's hidden setting. If you can't find a control or drop-down, try Ctrl+6 and Alt+F10 to see if it's hidden.

User interaction with Form controls is by mouse. There is no need to select the control except to configure it. As developer, you can use Ctrl+Alt+5 to select the first object on the sheet, which is at the bottom of the Selection Pane, and Tab to move up the list from there. Objects can be sorted to change Tab order.

The user can interact with ActiveX controls by key once they have the focus, that is, when they appear selected – but without the resizing handles. For example, if you click an ActiveX Check Box, it puts a dotted outline around the name. You can then use the Spacebar to set or unset it. Esc releases the focus back to the sheet. ActiveX controls can only be actually selected in Design Mode, and will interrupt the Tab cycle if Design Mode is turned off.

Users can navigate Data Validation dropdowns by key, first to select the cell, then Alt+↑ or Alt+↓ to open the list, ↑ or ↓ to scroll it, and Enter to select.

Slicers can be user-navigated and selected by Ctrl+Alt+5 followed by Tab, arrows, Shift+arrows, Space, Ctrl+Space, Enter, Ctrl+Enter. With a little practice this can be very productive. Multiple Slicer banks should be sorted in the Selection Pane to support object Tab navigation.

Allow users to use but not select controls. To disable selection of Form controls, or ActiveX controls in Design Mode, protect the sheet with Edit objects unchecked. Linked cells must be unlocked when the sheet is protected, if on the same sheet.

If the sheet has Slicers, Edit objects must be checked, as well as Use AutoFilter if table slicers, and Use PivotTable if pivot slicers. Since you can't disable slicer selection with sheet protection, a good alternative is to set Size and Properties → Position and Layout → Disable resizing and moving. This removes resizing handles and prevents inadvertent nudging.

To create a form with Tab navigation between controls, use a custom VBA form. This is seldom justified and is out of the scope of this book.

Governance

Data Validation (Alt-A,V,V)

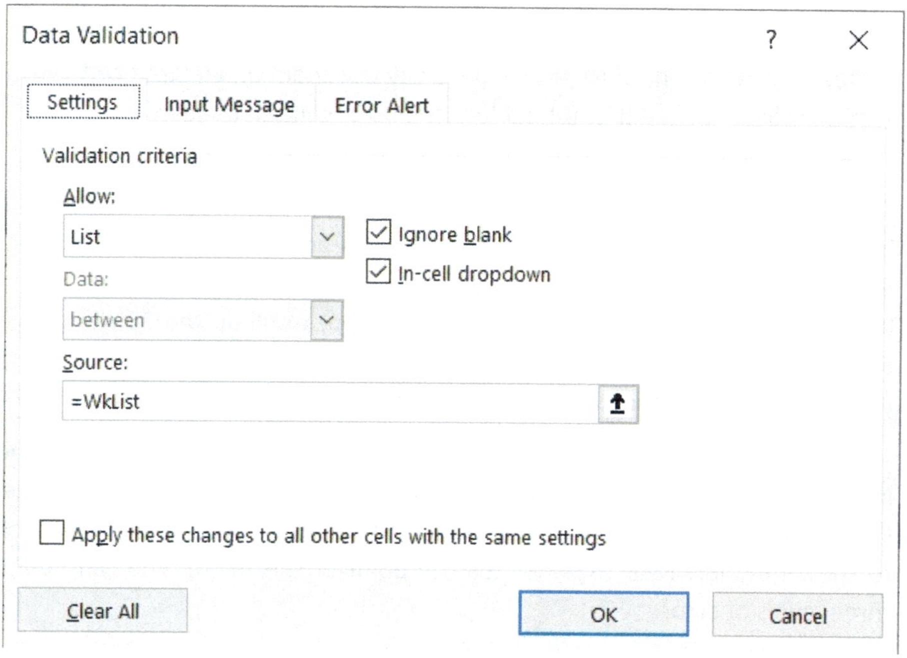

Data Validation serves two purposes; one, it enforces rules on what can be entered in a cell, and two, it is a convenient way to deliver feedback to the user. Several types of conditions can be applied, such as a number or date range, text length, or list. With list you can reference a range on a sheet for allowed values, or type them in, separated by commas. The rule can then offer an in-cell drop-down list of the valid selections to pick from.

User Messages

Two kinds of feedback can be given. Input Message can be used with or without a validation rule to raise a small popup of instructional text upon selecting the cell. It is similar to a cell note or comment, but does not put a corner flag in the cell, and is opened by selecting the cell rather than by hovering over it. It's a matter of choice which kind of message to use. I like Input Messages because they don't flag the cell, they support keyboard navigation, and they can include rules.

Because they don't flag the cell, I use Input Messages in obvious places like column headers, or a cell marked with a symbol or made to look like a button. They're limited to 256 characters, so they need to be concise. I've also put them on entire columns. This might be a bit intrusive for some users, but it makes instructions hard to miss. I generally use them on all input cells, help-symbol cells, and on either full table columns or column headers.

The message box has a bold header and a normal font body, with no formatting options. The header is a single line, up to 32 characters, and the body can have multiple lines, total 256 characters. If text wraps in an undesirable way, you can stretch the width a bit by adding spaces to the header, with a character at the end like a colon, to fill up the 32 characters allowed. You can use the body with no header for a non-bold message. To use the header with no body for a bold message, enter a single space in the body.

The second type of feedback is Error Alert. It requires a validation rule and raises an error popup when an invalid value is entered. Once you've set a rule, the user will get a message if they don't follow it, unless you uncheck the box to show the alert (and then, what's the point of the rule?). You can define three levels of error.

Table 18: Data Validation Error Alert Styles

Style	Icon	Behavior
Stop (default)		The user can only retry or cancel the entry
Warning		The user is informed of the violation and asked if they want to continue or not
Information		The user is informed of the violation
None		No message ("Show" checkbox unchecked)

If you leave on the Show setting and don't give them a message, Excel will give them a generic one, and the default is Stop style. When setting rules it is good practice to give messages that tell what valid entries are, rather than simply reject invalid ones with a "guess again!" taunt. For example, I'll give the title "Oops!" and the message "Please pick or type a member of the drop-down list", or "Please enter a number between 1 and 4".

Validation Criteria

When the validation criterion is Any value, it means that error checking is turned off. Otherwise, criteria are set to define what types and ranges of data are allowed. There are seven data types: Whole number, Decimal, List, Date, Time, Text length, and Custom.

Numeric Criteria

All except List and Custom are numeric criteria that use the same settings; the data type, the inequality expression, and the boundaries. The inequalities are: between, not between, equal to, not equal to, greater than, less than, greater than or equal to, less than or equal to. The boundaries are an upper and lower limit for between or not between, or a single limit for the other inequalities.

The limits can be typed in, or can refer to a cell, or can be calculated. For example, you could allow a date between =TODAY()-365 and =TODAY(), with an error message, "enter a date within the past year". To allow 0% to 100%, you would select decimal between 0 and 1.

List Criteria

Selecting the List data type disables the inequality selector, prompts for the list Source, and enables In-cell dropdown as a checkbox option. Source can be a comma-separated list, numeric or text with no quotation marks, or a cell range or name.

The section on function choice presents a case where a Data Validation picklist is used to select from a list of inputs, which selection is then used to derive one from a list of outputs. Attempting to set up the pick list and the conditional formulas reveals a dual maintenance risk.

Whether you use nested IFs, comparing the selection with each input value as a condition, or CHOOSE with MATCH of the selection against a list, the list of possible values in the formula need to match the values in the Data Validation list source.

In the formula you can use either an array constant or a table column reference, but Data Validation does not accept either of these as the list source, so you would need to enter the same list there as well. The best way to avoid dual maintenance then is to use a sheet range to hold the list, which can be referenced in both formulas and Data Validation.

The list range must be one-dimensional and can be vertical or horizontal, normally vertical. It doesn't require a table or a range name, but I recommend both. By using a table column as the input source, you can add output and other columns as reference or for use in formulas. All you need for the Data Validation source is to create a name for the input column, such as List=Table[Field], then enter =List as the Source.

For a short list that's not likely to change, dual maintenance is a reasonable option. Type the list in the Data Validation list source. For formulas, type the list, or create an array constant name if helpful.

Custom Criteria

The Custom validation type takes a formula entry. An example of this is to validate email address format, =NOT(ISERROR(SEARCH("*@*.*",C10))). Another example is in the Startup File Calendar sheet, where the Work Week string is validated by this formula that refers to the same cell it is validating: =AND(LEN(WkCustom)=7, NOT(ISERR(BIN2DEC(WkCustom)))).

By using Data Validation together with tables and Name Manager you create a transparent and sustainable configuration and governance model for the user interface.

Protect Sheet (Alt-H,O,P)

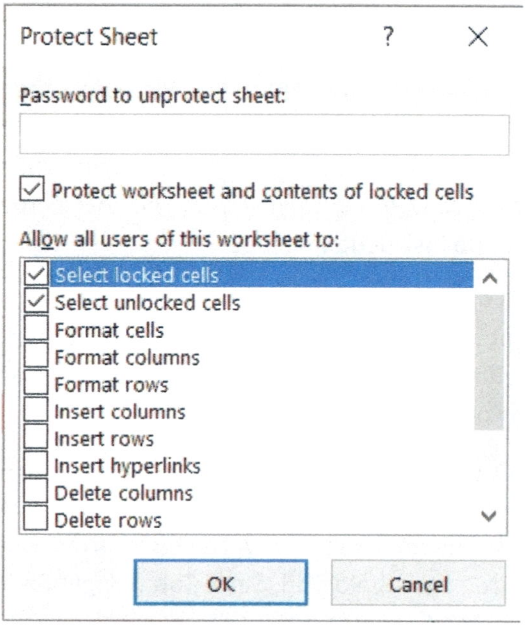

While Data Validation controls what can be entered in cells, Protect Sheet controls what cells can be entered, and other sheet-level actions. It has fifteen options of what can be allowed once protection is turned on, with an optional password. This gives it quite a range of control, from mild to strict.

As with Data Validation dropdowns, Protect Sheet offers more than its name implies. It is a navigational aid that can make a sheet behave like a data form. When only input cells are unlocked and protection is turned on, the user can hit Tab or Enter to navigate from one input field to the next.

The first step is to set cell protection. The default is protected, and any cell that the user inputs, or that any control links to, must be unlocked. Use fill color so that only the unlocked interactive cells are white. Store control-linked cells on another sheet so that the user can tab through input fields without landing on a control's cell.

To make the sheet act like a form, use Protect Sheet, Alt-H,O,P or Alt-R,P,S, without a password. Omitting a password makes it possible for anyone to unprotect the sheet, but it avoids problems and is really meant to protect the user from inadvertent errors, as well as to aid navigation. Most of the permissions can be left off. Always allow "Select unlocked cells", and decide whether to allow "Select locked cells" or not for the desired behavior, as described next.

With locked cells allowed, Tab cycles through all unlocked cells, across then down, and all other navigation keys behave normally. With locked cells disallowed, Tab and → cycle through unlocked cells, across then down, while Enter and ↓ cycle through unlocked cells, down then across. This makes the sheet nearly foolproof with little or no instruction needed.

If the sheet has Slicers, allow Edit objects. If they are Table Slicers, allow Use AutoFilter, and if they are Pivot Slicers, allow Use PivotTable & PivotChart. Always check every intended function and control on the sheet to be sure the user will not encounter frustrating obstacles.

If there is a data entry table that requires inserting and deleting rows, Protect Sheet is not a good solution. Even with all actions allowed, insert and delete of table rows does not work. The entire sheet row can be inserted, but cannot be deleted unless the entire row is unlocked. Since Tab navigation is already active in tables, the Protect Sheet navigational advantage really applies to non-table ranges, or to tables with a static structure.

There may be cases that you want to password-protect, for example, if you store sensitive data or quiz answers in a sheet. Protect Sheet cannot disallow hide/unhide of the sheet, but you can either hide the columns or rows on the sheet before protecting it, or you can Protect Workbook, Alt-R,P,W.

Error Checking (Alt-M,K,K)

Standard error checking rules automatically trap common errors. It's important to understand why Excel looks down on these conditions, and not to ignore them. Error checking rules are like a seat belt. The intent of safe driving is never to need the seat belt, but always to fasten it just in case. It is far better to start with all error checks on while learning than to hide mistakes for others to find.

The rules are not just there to flag cells, though. They enable comprehensive audit of the sheet using the Error Checking tool, Alt-M,K,K. This tool is like a spell check. It brings up each offense and suggests a remedy, letting you fix it on the spot or review other options. This only works for errors that are set to be checked in options. The bigger the used range on the sheet, the more important this feature becomes.

The "auto-correct" feature is like a formula tutor. It exposes the specific cause and offers suggested ways to correct it, or to put you in edit mode and make you think about it. For example, if you have a number stored as text, it offers a button to convert it to a number; if you have a text date with a 2-digit year, it gives you two buttons, to convert XX either to 19XX or to 20XX. It is a worthy exercise to build a test sheet, try to create all or some of the errors, and see what the tutor suggests.

Table 19: Error Checking Rules

#	Error Checking Rule
1	Cells containing formulas that result in an error
2	Inconsistent calculated column formula in tables
3	Cells containing years represented as 2 digits
4	Numbers formatted as text or preceded by an apostrophe
5	Formulas inconsistent with other formulas in the region
6	Cells containing data types that couldn't refresh
7	Formulas which omit cells in a region
8	Unlocked cells containing formulas
9	Formulas referring to empty cells
10	Data entered in a table is invalid
11	Misleading number formats

With experience you'll get accustomed to robust design principles that prevent errors, like defensive driving. You might wish to disable a rule, for example, if you have a dashboard range with inconsistent formulas, or you use text-formatted numerals as indicators. Rather than disabling alerts, resolve the root cause, or ignore the error instance and own the fact that you have an inconsistent design. Because error checks are set in user options, other users can get alerts that you don't get, unless you eliminate them in design.

Formula Auditing

Use the Error Checking tool as described above to test your work. Catch errors early to avoid rework. If you turned off any checking options, turn them all on again before running the check. The tool gives you access to change the rules during the check, but not to save them. To save rule settings, return to options, Alt-F,T,F, or go with the temporary settings, and resume checking.

Besides Error Checking, other tools in the Formula Auditing section of the ribbon enable tracing, watching and dissecting formulas. In addition to auditing your own projects, these tools are helpful to analyze someone else's sheet or template. It's worth the time to learn what they offer. They will help you understand the logic and potential risk of how the sheet is built. You might learn something you can reapply or avoid in your own work, or simply validate your own skills.

The Formula Auditing tools include Trace Precedents (Alt-M,P) and Trace Dependents (Alt-M,D), which link interdependent cells with arrows; Show Formulas (Ctrl+`) to toggle display from formula to result; Watch Window (Alt-M,W) to monitor select cells in a popup as you move and change other cells; and Evaluate Formula (Alt-M,V).

Evaluate Formula opens a dialog with the selected cell's formula, and allows you to see the result step by step. To illustrate, in this example I have an input cell $P$3 named Diameter, and a formula Name Radius = Diameter/2. The output cell in $P$4 calculates the area of the circle with the formula, =PI()*Radius^2. The evaluator steps into the formula following operation precedence rules, underlining the portion being evaluated at each step, and opening a second pane for named ranges and formulas.

Table 20: Step-Wise Formula Auditing

Step	Evaluation	Click
0	$P$4 =PI()*Radius^2	Evaluate
1	$P$4 =3.14*Radius^2	Step In
2	Radius =Diameter/2	Step In
3	Diameter =$P$3	Step Out
4	Radius =4/2	Evaluate
5	Radius =2	Step Out
6	$P$4 =3.14*2^2	Evaluate
7	$P$4 =3.14*4	Evaluate
8	$P$4 =12.56	Close

This can be a lifesaver when troubleshooting complex nested formulas, and a good practice for validation of any complex formula logic that you have so carefully constructed.

Visual Basic for Applications (Alt+F11)

The Developer tab is disabled by default. This is a hint that you should at least think about what you are getting into before enabling it. If you don't see it, customize the ribbon, Alt-F,T,C, and set the checkbox next to Developer on the right. This tab has a Code section with VBA tools as well as Controls to add buttons and other interactive tools to your project.

To Code or Not To Code?

VBA is a powerful tool and a must if you are serious about being an Excel developer, but it is not for the novice. It is another language. Like any language, you can easily pick up casual phrases, but sustaining a meaningful conversation requires significant investment. Avoiding offense and articulating nuance is a full-immersion commitment. Using it in public without full command risks your reputation.

When your workbook includes VBA code you cross the border from ".xlsx" to ".xlsm" file type. This alerts anyone who opens it, unless they've disabled macro security, to beware and be sure that they trust the source. This is like going through customs, warning of an inherent risk in distributing code.

Opening a macro-enabled file from an untrusted source can have serious consequences. Hackers can write malicious code that runs automatically. Digital certificates provide assurance on public files, and allow you to trust other files from the same publisher. Go to the macro security page, Alt-L,A,S. I would not recommend making any changes in the Trust Center, but it is a good first step to learn how security works.

With colleagues and acquaintances who share macro-enabled files with you, you know and trust the author, but you might not know their level of programming skill. Initially this may leave you feeling uncomfortably dependent. This feeling will pass, but don't forget how others might perceive your files. VBA is very opaque to non-developers.

The most obvious and strongest lesson on macros is justification. When you have a compelling need, use it with care. The more significant the user value, the more successful your macros will be. But many macros provide only marginal value over standard Excel and can be seen as frivolous. To avoid this, consider VBA as part of a mature and elegant design.

I don't mean to discourage you but to help your reputation. Don't let your method dominate your message. VBA will not make your tool cool. Elegance makes it cool. Applied appropriately, VBA can make it elegant. First, compress your work to its essence. Don't automate work you can eliminate or simplify.

Exploit all native Excel tools before creating your own. For example, let's say you have groups on a sheet and you want to toggle the outline button display. You search and find the DisplayOutline property of the window, and write a clever macro. Then someone tells you, "oh, I just use Ctrl+8". Hmm, yeah, it's cooler to use your first language well before showing off your second. Some macro buttons do nothing but select another sheet. If VBA is justified for other reasons, small tasks can be included, but are usually not justifiable by themselves.

Ok, but what if the user doesn't know there's a shortcut, and I want to make the function accessible to them? Accessibility is a valid reason to code, but think it through. To make my macro accessible I'll need to put a button somewhere, or assign a hotkey and inform the user. Instead of a button, I can put a "Help" cell that looks like a button, which when selected displays a Data Validation message to inform them of a shortcut tip. It is barely any more effort for them, less for me, avoids code and helps the user become more fluent.

That said, macro scope need not be complex to be worthy. Think about your project scope, dumbed-down. Not to look down on your users, but don't expect them to either know how or care enough to perform tasks that don't add value for them. Most macros simply protect the user from the need to learn and execute actions the long way.

For example, if you have defined data scenarios, it adds value for a user to be able to see and compare them. What doesn't add value is the process to go find Scenario Manager and select a different one. Your audience might not be familiar with scenarios, or have the time to make the connection between scenario description and data. Instead, a macro can cycle scenarios with a spinner button, and can display a scenario number and description on the sheet. This saves user effort and missed opportunity.

More complex cases like data manipulation call for a more involved strategy. Useful information comes from well-analyzed and well-presented data, which Excel itself does so nicely, but getting the raw data in the first place is often the challenge and justification for macros. It is also where an inexperienced coder can do damage. If the data are not already Excel-friendly, or are stored in multiple tables, retrieval is a daunting task of formatting and joining tables and defining which fields and records from each table to output.

In the corporate environment, it is important to work with the IT department to develop solutions that are secure, scalable and supportable. The strategy is to minimize the distance and delay from data source to destination, but data integrity is the implicit governor. Macros can serve to prototype or mock up the business requirements for more permanent solutions, but because they are so open they usually cannot be supported.

For a small business, you might be the IT department, and Excel your only solution. In that case it's up to you to make sustainable design a deliberate strategy.

Let discretion guide you to code or not to code. Do it for the sake of the user, not your resume. What will they take away from the experience you give them? You might elevate their skill a little, but the primary objective is to shortcut the result. When they reach that without even realizing how they got there, you have closed the sale.

VBA Tips

VBA training is available in many forms. Microsoft has an excellent introductory page, look for "getting started with VBA in office", which includes a section on when and why to use VBA. There are many great tutorials and examples on the web. Below are a few tips from my experience, with more elaboration in the projects.

Basics

Start with navigation, learn your way around. Alt-L,R to record a macro; Alt+F8 to run one; Alt+F11 to open VBA. In VBA, look through the menus, try them out, review each screen section. Open the Object Browser, F2, and spend time browsing it.

To simplify, Objects are nouns, Methods are verbs, Properties are adjectives. Like some human languages, order is not like English, and some verbs are implied. To "select B2" is Range("B2").Select; to "make it red" is Selection.Interior.Color = 255; the verb is implied by the equals sign. Once the essential syntax is learned, work on building your vocabulary with Object Browser. Use the help and study Concepts and Object model in the Excel VBA reference: https://docs.microsoft.com/en-us/office/vba/api/overview/excel.

Recording vs. Typing

Object Browser and the Excel VBA reference library are essential references, but cannot teach you how to speak the language. To begin learning on your own, recording and reading macros is like listening to a language tape, and repeating the words. Once you begin to understand VBA syntax, start typing, adding your own variations – "I like to eat chicken... I like to eat rice...".

Not all Excel actions are recorded, and often, many more things are recorded than you actually do. For example, if you record while setting fill color, in addition to the .Color property, VBA will list several other format properties that you didn't set, like .Pattern, .TintAndShade, etc. In this way it packages related properties to recreate the exact effect. If you run the macro on a cell that has a pattern fill, it will overwrite the pattern in addition to setting the fill color you recorded. You can remove that effect by removing or commenting out the respective lines from the macro.

You can record with Use Relative References in order to apply the action anywhere, but you'll also need to learn range referencing within VBA. The Excel VBA reference has a section in Concepts all about cells and ranges.

Before reapplying a macro on other sheets, think what can happen. Is there a chance your macro will overwrite data, or mess up the formatting? You can edit the macro to check the affected range before taking action, but you can't record that kind of governance.

There are many VBA techniques that are not based on Excel actions, such as branching, looping, input box and message box. To truly leverage its power and avoid its dangers, you'll need to learn concepts and methods of programming. You will get a lot more from such training once you have mastered the basics.

Even when you learn to type complete macros, recording is useful to capture the relevant object and properties that you want to control, and the enumeration of property values. For example, to set fill color you need to know the color number or RGB values, or you can record while setting the color. In this sense recorder is like a translator app that saves time from reading the dictionary.

Error Handling

Early success can make you cocky until you encounter an embarrassing run-time error. The lesson is to be humble, expect errors, and learn how to find and handle them. Test repeatedly with various inputs and conditions, and build in error handling. First you need to learn the different kind of errors.

Syntax errors appear as you type, within the offending line. This is like grammar check at the sentence level, for example, telling you that you have not provided required arguments for a function, or you've written an If statement without Then, etc.

Compile errors are raised at runtime. These are like grammar checks at the paragraph level, such as "Block If without End If" or "Expected End With". Sometimes these are a little inaccurate, for example I might get "End With without With" when in fact the error is "For without Next".

Runtime errors are like fact-check flags. If you call an object which does not exist, for example, the code cannot run even if it is grammatically correct.

Finally, you can trap and resolve all the above errors, and still have incorrect results. A key task of the programmer is to validate and document the logic of the program.

Don't use "On Error Resume Next" too easily, until you understand potential errors. It does bypass nuisance errors, but also hides serious errors that you need to manage. Set traps at key points in the code to see what's happening.

Of course, if we knew what errors would occur, we would prevent them, right? Limiting values, using If...Then statements, and other techniques reduce risk, and rigorous testing exposes it. Learn to find subtle errors by getting familiar with the Debug menu. Cause intentional errors to practice.

The bottom line is that the user should never be dragged into VBA debug mode because of a runtime error. If there's any chance of one, they should rather be given a helpful message within Excel. This is like the Data Validation of VBA, where it's important to customize the default message.

Modular Code

VBA chapters are called modules, but modular construction refers to the "Lego" concept of packaging reusable code segments for efficient assembly. As a principle, code should be as compact as possible, and never repeat itself. That may not be entirely possible, but it's a guideline. For example, if you have several buttons or target cells that will perform similar actions, put all the common code into a subroutine that each action calls by name.

In VBA, a workbook is a VBAProject. In the Project Explorer, Ctrl+R, the project has a folder called ThisWorkbook in which you can select and code all the workbook-level events. To see what events are, double-click ThisWorkbook, and on the right you'll see two drop-downs, with (General) and (Declarations). In the first, select Workbook. This creates Private Sub Workbook_Open(), which is the default event. To see other events, open the second drop-down list.

Project Explorer also has a folder for each sheet, which has its given number and the name on the tab. Within each sheet's folder you can select and code the worksheet-level events, as well as any controls on the sheet. Repeat the steps to select the Worksheet and view the events, noting how they differ from Workbook events.

The folder icon in the Project Explorer toolbar toggles a folder level that separates Microsoft Excel Objects from Modules. Modules are still part of the file's VBAProject, but apart from the workbook structure. If you record a macro, it creates a new Module, or you can manually insert one.

Your file can thus have many places to store code, and you need a strategy.

A Worksheet must contain the code linked to its own events and objects, which are private in scope, meaning they can only be run from that sheet. But, they can call other, manually created routines in the same sheet, or public routines in a module. When routines get complex, look for ways to split out segments as separate subs and functions, and plan organization.

Consider a workbook in which configuration data are stored on a special sheet, in cells named with workbook scope so they can be referred to from any sheet. This is analogous to a module of public routines that can be called from anywhere in the file. In VBA you're not hiding anything, it's about organization and accessibility.

A public module is a good idea for routines that are reusable, for example, it does some general function that can be applied to any sheet. A routine can be more broadly usable by feeding it arguments instead of hard-coding with fixed inputs.

Portability

If the code is specific to the sheet and could never be used elsewhere, keep it within the sheet. A benefit of this approach is portability. If you ever want to copy the sheet to a stand-alone workbook, the code that resides on the sheet is copied with it. Code called from the sheet in any other module would need to be manually copied, or you will have runtime errors.

Copying a sheet to a new file doesn't always work perfectly. One unavoidable issue to deal with is shape controls. If you have macros on the sheet, chances are you have some shape objects to run them. When the sheet is copied, the macros assigned to the shapes still point to the origin file. The best way to manage this is by a special macro to update the .OnAction property of all the shapes on the sheet.

VBA Options

Editor options (Tools → Options...) include various features such as syntax check and quick info that are normally all on. I have turned off Auto Syntax Check. If a make a mistake it still shows in red font, but it no longer pops up and tells me. A popup is an annoyance if you occasionally leave commands to be completed later. Some people turn off Require Variable Declaration, which allows variables to be self-defined on the fly. I prefer to explicitly define variables by Dim statement at the top of the procedure or even the module, so I keep this on to enforce it.

The editor has limited text formatting features. There is no way to format selected text, but you can set the format for different text types such as normal text, keywords and comments, in Editor Format options. The default differentiates these three by font color only, which may be hard to see for some people or on some screens. You can set font, size, foreground and background color by text type. I like to give comments a background color to make them stand out. Be sure that you are not duplicating any other text type format so that you can always distinguish the types from each other.

Part II: Application

Introduction to Part II

If principles are the soul of design, techniques are the bones, and projects are the flesh and blood that bring it to life. These works are vehicles to convey the principles in practical terms, to catalyze learning and adoption. They each have a specific use, but are intended primarily as demonstrations of what can be done, for you to plagiarize and improve.

The projects in Part II are files available at xlegant.com. Use coupon BOOK50 for $50 worth of free downloads. It is most fruitful to read the workbooks and the book together, but not necessary. What follows is a full description of each file, so that even without them you can learn how they are designed and to create your own.

If you want to build your own but you want to reapply the VBA code, or just want to see how it's written, all code modules are available for free download in the xlegant store. A few notes:

- .bas and .cls files can be read with Notepad to copy, or imported
- In the VBA Editor window, Ctrl+M to Import File
- Modules export as .bas files and .bas files import as Modules
- Sheets export as .cls files and .cls files import as Class Modules; the code should be cut/pasted to the sheet, or use Notepad to copy
- All references in [square brackets] must exist in Name Manager

The projects are as categorized and summarized here. Those marked * contain VBA code.

Table 21: List of Projects

Category	Projects	Ch.	Purpose
Business	Gantt Chart	6	Project scheduling
	Team Calendar	7	Team vacation and coverage
	Project Tracker *	8	Project notes and status tracking
General	Startup File *	4	Personal reference and macro library
	Keyboard Trainer	5	Keyboard productivity
	MRP Demo *	9	Inventory management training
	Fun & Games *	10	Collection of games

Chapter 4: Startup

Purpose

It is fitting to start up with Startup. This was not done before the others began, but grew as a collection throughout their development. The Calendar was reapplied in whole or in part in other projects. The Controls and Symbols sheets have been frequently used as a reference. These and other sheets were made to shine a light into places where I could not see well.

A well-designed personal startup file is like a home-made multi-function tool. It has all your favorite tools and stays within reach in your pocket. When you need it, you take it out and open the tool for the job. When you're done, you fold it up and put it back in your pocket. Even if you seldom use it, you are comforted knowing it is there when you need it.

Any file in your startup folder opens automatically when you start Excel, that much is given. How to take advantage of that is up to you. First, you need to find the startup folder. Search the local drive for XLSTART. This path should also be in your trusted locations, see Trust Manager. There is also an alternate startup folder that you can set in Options: Alt-F,T,A, then keep hitting Alt+L until you find it.

Putting a file in the startup folder is like clipping it to your belt. It's there for you, but you might not want it to be so visible. To stow the file in your pocket, hide the window, Alt-W,H. It will no longer be visible in thumbnails, Alt+Tab, or anywhere. The only clue to where it's hiding is the unhide button, Alt-W,U.

To make it open hidden, hide it, then when you shut down Excel, click Save when prompted. Restart Excel, and Alt-W,U to confirm it's there. You can continue to build it as you learn and develop tools, avoiding multiple files to keep track of. Unhide, maintain, hide, and save on exit. You can also manually save it in the VBA window, it is always visible there, even if it has no VBA code.

Macros in the file remain accessible while it's hidden. In fact, if you're starting with macros, Excel provides PERSONAL.xlsb for this purpose. When you record a macro, Alt-L,R, look in the Store macro in: box, you'll see Personal Macro Workbook. This file is hidden by default, but you will see it in the VBA window (Alt+F11) or in the unhide window (Alt-W,U). When you exit Excel, it will offer to save the file, with a little sales pitch on the benefit.

If you don't have a startup file yet, you can use this option as a convenience, since it is automatically named, hidden, and saved to your startup folder. Just record a simple macro in it, and save it. The .xlsb extension is a binary file that bypasses macro security warnings, since this particular file is for you only. It has other advantages and disadvantages over .xlsx and .xlsm, but there's nothing special about it. You can manually name and store your own startup file, or you can use PERSONAL.xlsb as your startup file. Just unhide it to store stuff in sheets.

My own preference and usage of the startup file is more as a reference than as a macro library. Most macros I write are specific to a project, I have just a few in my startup. Many people who write macros are not aware of the Personal Macro Workbook option, nor of how to make code reusable.

I've included several sheets that serve as tools or references. The intent is to collect the kind of help that's hard to find, with examples and reminders. Start your file with whatever you like. Consolidate every such thing into one file, naming sheets sensibly. If it gets large, think about a dashboard, and consider .xlsb format to make it save and open faster.

This is just for you, it doesn't have to be pretty, but you'll want to keep it reasonably organized like a proper toolbox. You'll also find it's a convenient notepad with temporary sheets for anything from trip itineraries to shopping comparisons. Don't forget to clean it out once in a while.

If you use your personal file to store and run macros or define functions, you can use those macros and functions in other workbooks you have open at the same time. If you share those other workbooks, other people will not be able to execute the same code. Be stingy with your own tools to prevent breaking shared files, or copy selected code to the shared file as appropriate.

Macros are only as good as their marketing. It's easy to forget the cool stuff you've done when it's not visible. When you design a workbook with macros you can put a button on the sheet. If you write general macros that you want to be file-independent, you need a way to see and run them.

For your own use, you can add macros to the Ribbon, Alt-F,T,C, or to the Quick Access Toolbar (QAT), Alt-F,T,Q. Select the macro in Choose commands from, then Add > >. Optionally, select Modify... to change the button. If you elect to Customize Ribbon, create a new tab to organize your macros without changing the standard ribbon. The QAT is all custom and you can use <Separator> to create a macro group.

Calendar Sheet

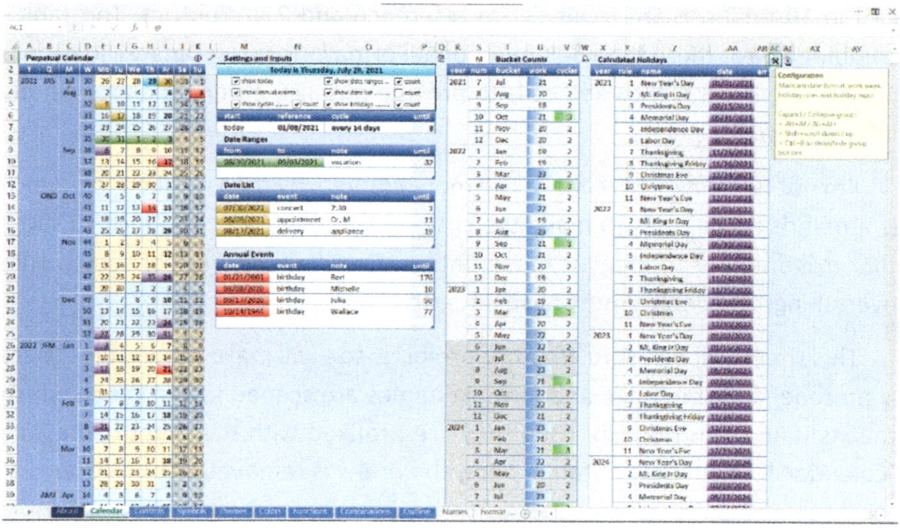

Purpose

There are some nice Excel templates to create, annotate and print monthly or annual calendars in Excel. Check them out before you start creating your own. If you're like me you don't print much, and if you want a perpetual calendar you have many options of course, including Outlook, Google, Apple and others. These full-featured calendar apps allow you to manage your detailed schedule, highlight events, or as you may be chagrined to admit, control your life.

So why build a calendar in Excel when there are so many great ones available? Clearly I like to customize things, but what's missing?

I want small day cells, yet see clearly what's happening and coming up. With an input table next to the calendar, I can enter dates and descriptions, then highlight the calendar with those dates. As this concept gestates, I think of other types of inputs, like date ranges, and annual events like birthdays. I think I can calculate holidays with configured rules. Finally, I want another output table to count workdays and custom cycles per week or month bucket. These are all opportunities to demonstrate various features and techniques working with dates.

From humble birth this sheet grew and matured into a showcase, with 6 column groups, 9 controls, 10 tables, 19 range names and 37 formula names. Of the 10 tables, 5 are input, 3 are reference and 2 are output. The tables combined have more than 30 Conditional Formatting rules. Data Validation is used on multiple ranges and cells to provide pick list, enforcement or simply information.

I'm not boasting. This sounds like more complexity than is called for, which is a real risk. My job is to make the case for the complexity, in fact, to show that it is integral to elegant presentation. One flaw in one part could ruin everything. The details must have integrity.

This sheet will be useful in other projects, so I will make it portable. There is no code, and the range and formula names are scoped to the sheet, which means that when they are used they are prefixed with the sheet name, like **'Calendar'!**. To simplify notation here, the prefix is removed from references.

Calendar Table

The main output table is Calendar, in the form of a continuous perpetual calendar, with eleven columns; year, quarter, month, week, and the seven days of the week. I use the international standard of weeks starting on Monday, putting the most common weekend at the end of the row (as in weekend). Weekends will be configurable, but not the Monday start. If desired, the table and formulas can be modified to start on a different day.

In preparation for writing formulas and conditions, I create two relative names in Name Manager, This = the current cell and Above = the cell above it, hitting F4 three times to make both column and row relative. Thus, with active cell A2, This = A2 and Above = A1. I accept the implicit disclaimer that Above cannot be used in row 1.

To begin the table, I type in short headings, create the table, name it Calendar, and turn off the filter buttons. I start with a width of 3 for all columns.

Formulas

I'll calculate the Monday column and use it to derive all the other columns. The Monday formula must combine two things:

1. For the first row, retrieve start date, calculate Monday of that week
2. For every other row, increment the previous row by 7

For start date I can use =TODAY() most of the time, but I want to be able to set it as well, so I define an input cell named StartInput, and a formula named Start. If there is a date in StartInput, it is used, if not, the current date is used.

```
Start =IF(N(StartInput),StartInput,TODAY())
```

Next, I need to derive the Monday of the week of Start. This calls for WEEKDAY, which returns an ordinal day-of-week number with several options. I usually use type 2, here I use type 3, Monday=0 through Sunday=6, to simplify the formula. For example, if I enter 1/1/2022 in Start, then =WEEKDAY(Start,3) returns 5, that is, Saturday. To get to Monday of that week, I subtract the weekday: Saturday – 5 = Monday.

```
Monday = Start-WEEKDAY(Start,3)
```

Finally there is the point of distinguishing the first data row from the others. All the data are numeric and only the header is text, so I can use that to differentiate the top row from others. I can use ISTEXT(Above), TRUE only in the top row, or ISNUMBER(Above), FALSE only in the top row. N(Above) converts text to zero, so if I know the numbers are never zero, this is also FALSE only in the top row. I wouldn't use N() if the column data are not guaranteed never to have 0 value, but here they are. Whenever N(Above) is TRUE, I add 7 to it, for "next Monday". When it's FALSE, "first Monday" applies.

```
Monday = IF(N(Above),Above+7,Start-WEEKDAY(Start,3))
```

This formula could be entered on the sheet versus Name Manager, but I'll be able to use this again elsewhere, so having a name adds value. In column [Mo] I enter =Monday, then every other column is derived from it. Each other day is an offset; Tu=[@Mo]+1, We=[@Mo]+2, etc. Once the seven days are established, I select all seven data columns and use custom number format "d" to show only day numbers, 1 to 31.

For week number, I use =ISOWEEKNUM([@Mo]) and leave it as format General. ISO is the International Standards Organization, which defines the first week of the year as the one containing the first Thursday of the year, which is also the first 4-day week of the year, counting from Monday.

The seven day columns plus week number column will all have values that change by row. Month, quarter and year will each have repeat values that I'll want to hide. Considering this, I need to choose between calculation and formatting.

For example, I can use custom number format "m" or "mm" to format a date as month number, or "mmm" as abbreviated month name. To do so I would simply copy Monday, M =[@Mo]. The display would be constant for the weeks of each month, but the underlying value would change in each row. Thus, I would not be able to hide repeating values.

To create constant values per month, quarter and year, I calculate:

```
Month M =MONTH([@Mo]); result is 1 to 12
Quarter Q =ROUNDUP([@M]/3,0); result is 1 to 4
Year Y =YEAR([@Mo]); or, for 2-digit year, use MOD(YEAR([@Mo]),100)
```

Later, I decided that I preferred to use text names for month and quarter. To do this while keeping constant values, I created two text arrays:

```
Mons ={"Jan","Feb","Mar","Apr",... etc.}
Qtrs ={"JFM","AMJ","JAS","OND"}
```

The final formulas:

```
Month M =INDEX(Mons,MONTH([@Mo]))
Quarter Q =INDEX(Qtrs,ROUNDUP(MONTH([@Mo])/3,0))
```

Basic Formatting

I set initial base and Conditional Formats:

Table 22: Calendar Basic Formatting

Range	Condition	Fill
Sheet	Base	Blue, Accent 1, Lighter 80%
Headers	Base	Blue, Accent 1, Gradient from Lighter 40% to Darker 50%
[Y] to [M]	Base	Blue, Accent 5, Lighter 40%
	=This=Above	hide values (;;;) and clear top border
[Mo] to [Su]	Base	Blue, Accent 5, Lighter 80%
	=ISODD(MONTH(This))	Gold, Accent 4, Lighter 80%

Border color is also set for contrast. The point here is not to overstate the details, but to impress on you that they are very receptive to attention.

I try entering some start dates in the input cell, and drag the table bottom edge down to expand. How far down to copy? I'll mostly be looking at the first screenful, about six months, but extending it for a couple of years doesn't hurt. Just for fun, I try some outrageous dates. With 12/1/9999 start, I confirm that the computer is not Y10K compliant, and that the "end of time" 12/31/9999 will be a Friday. Y10K is one error I will not bother protecting against.

User Inputs

Now that I have the main output table, I want to design a user interface that will take different types of inputs and reflect each type differently in the Calendar. Collecting my earlier design notes, I'll have a list of discrete dates, a list of date ranges, and a list of year-independent dates. I previously mentioned the start date input cell, and I'll add two more input cells to define a cycle; reference date, and cycle length.

As I start to plan how to arrange all these inputs neatly, the advantage of tables becomes clear. When tables are stacked on the sheet and have the same number of columns, insertion and deletion of rows in the upper table move the lower table down and up without disturbing any other columns.

The three individual input cells, StartInput, First and Cycle, can be in one row, with three input tables below it in the same columns. DateRanges table needs two columns for from and to dates, the third will be free text. DateList and Annuals tables will each have one date column and two free text columns.

With the tables set up, I practice navigation. Ctrl+ inserts a row and moves lower tables down, Ctrl- deletes a row and moves lower tables up. Tab in the bottom right corner of any table adds a row to the bottom of the table and moves lower tables down. Unfortunately, this does not guarantee correct formatting. Tab in the bottom row of the bottom table adds a row, but adopts the blue sheet fill instead of the white table fill. This can be avoided by using Ctrl+, or corrected by copy down from the row above.

Since these date entries will be full dates, date format is a concern and will be handled via configuration. They will also share the same Conditional Format that they cause in the Calendar, as a visual link.

Holidays will be configured and calculated. A holiday input table is also included, for holidays that don't fit the rules defined, or for other non-work days that are not regular holidays. This table resides with configuration rather than inputs.

Configuration

Configuration settings are inputs that are a step removed from the output purpose, and therefore likely to be set once or very rarely. They can be hidden most of the time. In some projects I put them on a separate hidden sheet. Since this sheet is designed to be self-contained, I place them in a column group.

The configuration area contains tables and individual input cells. It's important to consider how to make them easily maintainable. When tables and non-table data are stacked vertically, the tables should be below, or occupy the same columns as the non-table data, to allow for table row insert/delete. A static lookup table can have fewer columns, since it will not be maintained.

Configuration comprises four input cells, the Weeks reference table, the HolidayRules input table, and the HolidayInput table. Holiday logic will be explained in the next section.

The first three input cells are selections from a validation list. The fourth, WkCustom, is a custom weekend string, following the format as defined in WORKDAY.INTL and NETWORKDAY.INTL functions.

Date Format

The format in which dates are entered is controlled by the computer's regional settings, but Excel does not automatically display them in the same way. To display them in the selected regional format requires one of only two date formats that begin with an asterisk (*), or to make the format user-selectable.

For control and convenience, I make them selectable via two choices; DateOrder and DateSeparator, each with three choices. DateOrder is one of **dmy,mdy,ymd** and DateSeparator is one of **.,/,-**. These two cells define nine total format options. All ranges with full dates are set in Conditional Formatting with nine rules based on these two selections, following the example:

```
Condition:    =AND(DateOrder="dmy",DateSeparator="."), etc.
Format:       dd.mm.yy, etc.
```

Work Week

Weekends are of course an important feature of any calendar, but do they need to be customized? From my cursory internet research, approximately 90% of the world's population work Monday to Friday and have Saturday and Sunday off. Most of the remaining 10%, which are mostly Muslim countries, work Sunday to Thursday, or some close variant. Some countries or companies might work six days, or other pattern. I try to be as inclusive as possible. It is not much trouble to offer work week selection and even unique pattern definition.

Here I use the seven-digit binary string format to define the week, as per the functions WORKDAY.INTL and NETWORKDAYS.INTL. There are simpler ways to select standard, two-consecutive-days weekends, but there is no simpler way to define a custom pattern. The seven-digit string gives me a consistent method of identifying weekends, whether standard or custom.

Holiday calculation references the work week in order to move the holiday from a weekend to the next or previous workday. This is not practically feasible to set up for all weekend possibilities, but it works for any of the seven patterns with two consecutive weekend days.

Work week is selected from a table that lists these seven options; "Mon-Fri", "Tue-Sat", etc., and an eighth option for "custom". The second column in the table lists the WEEKDAY return type, using 11 through 17 for the standard cases, ensuring the weekend is always on days 6 and 7 for the holiday logic. The third column is the binary string, e.g. 0000011 for Saturday-Sunday weekend.

One cell in this table, the custom string cell, is a formula to retrieve the string entered by the user. Here I reluctantly violate a table rule by mixing text and formula in a table column, but it is all read-only. Meanwhile, the name WkList =Weeks[Work] passes the pick list to Data Validation on the selection cell, WkSelect.

Custom week string input cell, WkCustom, has a gray font to make it look inaccessible. When the user selects the custom option in the WkSelect cell, the gray-font cell WkCustom reverts to automatic font color, indicating it is now relevant and ready for input. Data Validation is defined for the input cell, with appropriate instructions, and the following condition:

```
Allow: Custom
Formula: =AND(LEN(WkCustom)=7,NOT(ISERR(BIN2DEC(WkCustom))))
Error message: must be 7 digits of 0's and 1's
```

Name Manager formulas WkString and WdType retrieve the week string and weekday type based on a match of WkSelect against WkList.

WkString is used in the workday count formulas, and also provides access to a Boolean "is weekend" condition by dissection of the string. The formula segment below picks the character from WkString corresponding to the weekday of the reference date. Since the seven characters of the string always represent Monday to Sunday, it is based on weekday type 2.

```
(is weekend) = ... MID(WkString,WEEKDAY(Date,2),1) ...
```

Can the start day of the week be customized? It's possible if I don't use a table (then I could use a formula header), or if I use VBA, but that's a cost I'm not willing to pay. Monday start is a common international standard, letting most people see their weekend at the week's end.

Table 23: Calendar Configuration

Range	Type	Name	Data Validation
Cell	Format	DateOrder	List: dmy,mdy,ymd
		DateSeparator	List: .,/,-
	Work Week	WkSelect	List: =WkList (=Weeks[Work])
		WkCustom	Custom: =AND(LEN(WkCustom)=7,NOT(ISERR(BIN2DEC(WkCustom))))
Table		Weeks	
	Holidays	HolidayRules	Numeric range per column
		HolidayInput	

Holidays

Holiday calculation itself is a worthy of an app or add-in, and there are no doubt some available. Here it's an opportunity to illustrate a process.

Holidays are defined at various levels – country, state, local – and employers choose which ones to give employees as days off. Some are standard, but there are a lot of choices, and some are made up. Some factories shut down for the first day of hunting season. It's not hard to input a list of dates once a year, but holidays do follow rules, and if I can discover the rules then I can use them to calculate the dates for any year. This presents an intriguing challenge.

I chose a list of eleven US holidays that are representative of various rules – first Monday of the month, last Monday of the month, fixed date unless weekend, and some "Eve/Day" pairs that require special rules for weekends. There's even a day after the last Thursday of the month. Other religious and national holidays may have more complex rules which may need other logic or manual entry.

When I looked at all the US rules, I realized that they fall into two general types, or forms:

1. The "not weekend" form: fixed date unless on a weekend
2. The "nth weekday" form: a certain weekday of the month

The goal here is to come up with a single formula that covers both forms with all their variants. The formula must work for any given input year and rule. To enable this, each holiday is defined as a rule in a table with four parameters, and several stages of calculation. But before I could define the parameters and formulas, I had to work out the logic.

Not Weekend

For now assume that the weekend is Saturday and Sunday. This form has three cases. The first is a stand-alone holiday, which moves to the nearest business day. If the date falls on a Saturday it is moved to Friday, and if it falls on Sunday it is moved to Monday. The second and third cases are for two consecutive holidays, "Eve" and "Day", which need special rules, depending on which date or if both dates fall on the weekend.

Each of these cases has a nice simple formula, derived empirically by laying out Friday to Monday with the offset that occurs whenever the holiday is on a weekend. For example, move type 1 moves from Saturday to Friday, offset -1, and from Sunday to Monday, offset +1. For move type 2 and 3, if the Eve/Day pair is Friday/Saturday, Eve doesn't move, Day moves +2 to Monday. The table below summarizes the observed logic, the shaded area showing three possible scenarios for Eve/Day.

Table 24: Not Weekend Holiday Logic

<table>
<tr><th></th><th>Wd=</th><th>5</th><th>6</th><th>7</th><th>1</th><th></th></tr>
<tr><th>Move</th><th>Holiday type</th><th>Fri</th><th>Sat</th><th>Sun</th><th>Mon</th><th>Offset if Wd > 5</th></tr>
<tr><td>1</td><td>Single</td><td>0</td><td>-1</td><td>+1</td><td>0</td><td>=ODD(Wd-7)</td></tr>
<tr><td rowspan="3">2 and 3</td><td>Pair (Fr-Sa)</td><td>0</td><td>+2</td><td>→</td><td>→</td><td rowspan="3">(for illustration)</td></tr>
<tr><td>Pair (Sa-Su)</td><td>←</td><td>-1</td><td>+1</td><td>→</td></tr>
<tr><td>Pair (Su-Mo)</td><td>←</td><td>←</td><td>-2</td><td>0</td></tr>
<tr><td>2</td><td>1st of pair</td><td>0</td><td>-1</td><td>-2</td><td>0</td><td>=5-Wd</td></tr>
<tr><td>3</td><td>2nd of pair</td><td>0</td><td>+2</td><td>+1</td><td>0</td><td>=8-Wd</td></tr>
</table>

Here are the form 1 calculation stages in descending order. The bottom three names retrieve the rule parameters, and two others transform them to date and weekday.

Table 25: Not Weekend Calculation

Name	Formula
NotWe	=Date+IF(DWd>5, CHOOSE(Move,ODD(DWd-7),5-DWd,8-DWd),0)
DWd	=WEEKDAY(Date,WdType)
Date	=DATE(HolidaysCalc[@year],Month,Day)
Move	=INDEX(HolidayRules[par2],HolidaysCalc[@rule])
Day	=INDEX(HolidayRules[par1],HolidaysCalc[@rule])
Month	=INDEX(HolidayRules[month],HolidaysCalc[@rule])

Nth Weekday

To determine nth weekday, I again turn to a blank grid to work out the possibilities. To begin, I take stock of what I know: there will always be four of every weekday in any month, some months will have a fifth of some weekdays, and the nth of any weekday depends on which weekday begins the month.

Based on this, I build a grid with 7 rows for "weekday of the first of the month" and 35 columns for "nth (1-5) weekday (1-7)". If the fifth weekday spills into the next month, I'll handle that later.

Table 26: Nth Weekday Holiday Logic

	Nth	1	1	1	1	1	1	1	2	2	...
	Wd	1	2	3	4	5	6	7	1	2	
Weekday of the first of the month	1	1	2	3	4	5	6	7	8	9	
	2	7	1	2	3	4	5	6	14	8	
	3	6	7	1	2	3	4	5	13	14	
	4	5	6	7	1	2	3	4	12	13	
	5	4	5	6	7	1	2	3	11	12	
	6	3	4	5	6	7	1	2	10	11	
	7	2	3	4	5	6	7	1	9	10	

I start filling the grid by just counting. For example, US Labor Day is the first (Nth=1) Monday (Wd=1) of September. If September 1 is a Wednesday (3), we can count off the days to find that Labor Day will be September 6, as outlined in the table above.

Very soon, patterns emerge that are hard to intuit without this kind of brute-force method. For one thing, it clearly depends on the difference between the two weekdays, the sought-for one and the first-of-the-month one.

Finally, I arrive at the following steps:

1. Get the date of the first day of the month (FoM)
2. Add input weekday minus FOM weekday (NWd_1)
3. Calculate Nth weeks, minus a week if input weekday >= FOM weekday (NWd_2)
4. Add step 2 + step 3 + offset day if defined (NWd_3)
5. If step 4 is past the end of the month then subtract 7 (NthWd)

Here are the form 2 calculation stages in descending order. Note the similarity between this table and the "not weekend" table, from the bottom row up; Month is used in both forms, followed by formulas to retrieve par1 and par2. In form 2 though, Nth (par1) is capped at 5, and Wd (par2) has INT applied, in case of a decimal offset, which adds a day via Add.

Table 27: Nth Weekday Calculation

Name	Formula
NthWd	=NWd_3-IF(NWd_3>EOMONTH(FoM,0),7,0)
NWd_3	=NWd_1+NWd_2+Add
NWd_2	=7*(Nth-IF(Wd<WEEKDAY(FoM,2),0,1))
NWd_1	=FoM+Wd-WEEKDAY(FoM,2)
Add	=10*MOD(INDEX(HolidayRules[par2],HolidaysCalc[@rule]),1)
FoM	=DATE(HolidaysCalc[@year],Month,1)
Wd	=INT(INDEX(HolidayRules[par2],HolidaysCalc[@rule]))
Nth	=MIN(INDEX(HolidayRules[par1],HolidaysCalc[@rule]),5)
Month	=INDEX(HolidayRules[month],HolidaysCalc[@rule])

Holiday Rules Table

The HolidayRules table auto-increments the rule index by =N(Above)+1, and the user maintains the description and the four parameters. Data Validation is used in each column to guide and control entries. Allowed values are whole numbers for months (1-12); form (1-2); and par1 (1-31); decimal for par2 (1.0-7.9). Entry-point guidance is essential due to the obscure logic, and the Input Message is perfect for this.

Holidays Input Table

The rules established are not sophisticated enough to calculate all holidays, such as those based on lunar cycles. The easy way around the exceptions is to enable manual entry of holiday dates. The downside is that they must be maintained for each year, the upside is flexibility.

The HolidayInput table is situated below HolidayRules and with the same number of columns. It has just two input columns for name and date. Other columns are not really necessary, except [err], which checks for conflicts with weekends and calculated holidays. By making the tables the same width, rules can be inserted or deleted and the lower table will keep its distance.

Holidays Calculation Table

The result of all the Name Manager and HolidayRules table setup work is the HolidayCalc output table. This table is in its own column group, so that it can be extended as long as needed and viewed by the user as desired. The objectives are to start with the current year based on input date, and automatically update when rules are added or deleted. The table has five columns.

Table 28: Holiday Calculation Table Columns

Column	Formula
Year	=IF(N(Above),IF([@rule]>1,Above,Above+1), MIN(YEAR(Calendar[Su])))
Rule	=IF(N(Above)=MAX(HolidayRules[rule]),1,N(Above)+1)
Name	=INDEX(HolidayRules[holiday],[@rule])
Date	=Holiday
Err	=IFERROR(VALUE(MID(WkString,WEEKDAY([@date],2),1))+ 2*COUNTIF(HolidayInput[date],[@date]),0)

The year starts with the minimum year of the calendar Sunday column, and then increments when rule 1 comes up next. The rule starts at 1 in the first row, and starts over after the last rule number is reached. Name looks up the holiday name, and Holiday is the final output formula, choosing NotWe or NthWd as described earlier.

```
Holiday = IFERROR(CHOOSE(INDEX(HolidayRules[form],
    Holidays[@rule]),NotWe,NthWd),"")
```

The [err] column is to flag holidays that conflict with weekends. This wouldn't make sense, but can occur while setting up the sheet. In case of error, the table row turns red. The user must then adjust either holidays or weekends as needed.

A cell above the table header checks both HolidayCalc and HolidayInput tables and reports if any error is found. It also checks if HolidayCalc horizon is less than the Calendar horizon, prompting the user to extend the horizon by copying the bottom row down.

```
=IF(SUM(HolidayCalc[err],HolidayInput[err]),"errors",
    IF(MAX(Calendar[Mo])>MAX(HolidayCalc[date]),"extend",""))
```

Highlighting

Now that I have user inputs and configuration defined, it's time to return to the Calendar to set up Conditional Formatting. This is a chance to play artist. First, let me review what it is that I'm highlighting.

I've defined four types of input dates; date ranges, discrete dates, annual events, and cycles. I've configured two other types of dates; weekends and holidays. Finally, I want to highlight the current date. I have a total of seven conditions to format.

The next task is to decide the type of format for each, and the order. I think that most of the time, most of the date types will not overlap, but of course it will happen, and I'll handle it as best as I can.

Condition Order

When multiple conditions are applied to the same range, consider the order in which they apply. If the conditions are mutually exclusive, then they can't overlap and order doesn't matter. For example, the first Monday and the second Wednesday of each quarter can never conflict.

If they are not mutually exclusive, they apply in the order listed. That's why there are buttons to move conditions up and down in the list. If the formats themselves are not mutually exclusive, they accumulate top-down, unless "stop if true" is ticked.

For example, if you have two or more conditions that can overlap, say a birthday and a holiday on the same day, and they both set fill color, the top one wins. But if one sets fill color and the other sets bold font, they can both show.

I work out a reasonable balance of formats and order based on importance. Later, I'll add conditions to show overlaps. The six initial format types and their inputs are listed here, and explained in order from bottom up.

Table 29: Date Highlighting Types

Type	Input	Example use	Format	Order
Today	=TODAY()		Bold	1
Cycle	Start date and cycle length	Payday		
Date list	Discrete dates	Events	Fill	2
Annuals	Dates irrespective of year	Birthdays	Fill	3
Holidays	Configuration input	Days off	Fill	4
Date range	From and to date pairs	Vacation	Fill	5
Today	=TODAY()		Fill	6
Weekend	Configuration selection		Fill	7

Weekend

As described above, WkString is a seven-character digital string. The condition formula inWeekend then picks out the character of the string representing the weekday of the current cell's date. Because the weekend string format is Monday to Sunday, WEEKDAY type 2 identifies the character. VALUE converts the character to a number, 1 = TRUE for weekends.

```
inWeekend =VALUE(MID(WkString,WEEKDAY(This,2),1))
```

I give this condition a dark gray, thin diagonal crosshatch pattern, very visible but not thick enough to obscure the numbers or the alternating month color.

Current Date

The current date is the easiest one to do directly in Conditional Formatting. If the date is today, flag it. Note, if start date is blank, today will always be in the top row, and if start is in the future, of course today will not be visible!

Format condition formula for the current day:
=This=TODAY()

This is given a fill color, but as a low priority. It is later combined with Cycle to set bold font, in case the fill is covered by another condition.

Date Ranges

DateRanges table has key columns [from] and [to]. The condition formula is in two steps.

Step 1 finds the [from] date that indicates that This is in a defined date range. This calls for MATCH type 1. I create the name From, which finds the equal or nearest lower [from] date to This, or IFNA returns 0 if none found. This type of matching requires that the [from] column be sorted ascending.

Step 2 then uses INDEX to find the [to] date in the same row as From; AND collects the dates that are between [from] and [to], inclusive.

From = IFNA(MATCH(This,DateRanges[from],1),0)
Format condition formula for date ranges:
inRanges = AND(From,This<=INDEX(DateRanges[to],From))

Data Validation rules are set to ensure the two requirements.

Valid: [from] is sorted ascending	=M10>N(Above)
Valid: [to] >= [from]	=N10>=M10

Holidays

As explained previously, holidays can come from either HolidayCalc table or HolidayInput table. The condition is the sum of two COUNTIF functions against each table, equivalent to logical OR.

COUNTIF(HolidayCalc[date],This)+COUNTIF(HolidayInput[date],This)

Annual Events

Annuals are meant to highlight birthdays, anniversaries, and so forth that occur on the same date every year. Annual events need to be matched based on month and day only, independent of year. To do this I convert dates to "mdd" integers, from 101 to 1231, by 100*Month+Day. MDThis applies to This cell; MDAnnuals returns an array representing the event dates, Annuals[date], converted in the same way. MATCH returns TRUE when MDThis is in MDAnnuals.

```
MDThis = 100*MONTH(This)+DAY(This)
MDAnnuals = 100*MONTH(Annuals[date])+DAY(Annuals[date])
Format condition formula for annual events:
inAnnuals = MATCH(MDThis,MDAnnuals,0)
```

Date List

DateList condition uses COUNTIF as a Boolean "exists or not".

```
Format condition formula for date list:
inList=COUNTIF(DateList[date],This)
```

Cycle

This is intended for a 14-day pay cycle, 91-day reporting cycle, or for any event that occurs with regular frequency. To highlight the cycle in the calendar I define two input cells, First is a reference date and Cycle is the cycle in days. The Cycle cell is formatted "every "0" days", so that the number entered is displayed as a phrase. The condition uses MOD to tell when This is a multiple of Cycle from First.

```
Format condition formula for cycle:
inCycle = MOD(This-First,Cycle)=0
```

User Controls

Adding form controls to a project is a choice to make when it enhances value. Among the simplest opportunities is a checkbox control, it's a nice way to present an option toggle switch. The checkbox will be linked to a cell which will contain its TRUE or FALSE state. This cell is then used in conditional formulas. The general steps to follow are:

1. Name and hide the switch cell
2. Insert a checkbox and link it to the switch cell
3. Add the switch cell as a condition in formulas or formats

Here I want to give the user the option to display or not each of the input types. The switch cells should be invisible – I don't want "TRUE" and "FALSE" all over the screen. This could be done by formatting the cells, or by hiding them in a group, or on a hidden sheet. Within the calendar control panel I name and hide each switch cell. The names follow a convention: ShowAnnuals, ShowCycle, etc. The cells are hidden by format, ";;;".

From the Developer tab I insert a Form Check Box for each switch cell, adjusting size and alignment to make them all fit the row height and look neatly spaced. With a right-click on the control, I select Edit Text to write what it does – "show dates" etc. With another right-click, I select Format Control, and in Cell link, type in the respective switch cell name.

With the Check Boxes formatted and linked to their respective cells, I edit each input table and Calendar format condition, adding "Show..." to the existing one, using AND. Checking each box now toggles the highlight on and off in both the input table date column and the Calendar table. The final conditions for both tables are shown below. For input columns, LEN(This) formats only the non-blank cells.

Table 30: Calendar Formatting Conditions

Input	Input range format condition	Calendar format condition
(none)	=ShowToday	=AND(This=TODAY(),ShowToday)
First, Cycle	=ShowCycle	=AND(inCycle,ShowCycle)
DateRanges[from] and [to]	=AND(ShowRanges,LEN(This))	=AND(inRanges,ShowRanges)
Annuals[date]	=AND(ShowAnnuals,LEN(This))	=AND(inAnnuals,ShowAnnuals)
DateList[date]	=AND(ShowList,LEN(This))	=AND(inList,ShowList)
HolidayCalc[date], HolidayInput[date]	=AND(ShowHolidays,LEN(This))	=AND(inHolidays,ShowHolidays)

Coming back after building the second output table of bucket counts, I needed controls for the exclusion or inclusion of certain days in the work day and cycle count calculations. Additional “count” checkboxes were added, neatly juxtaposed with the relevant “show” controls for cycles, date ranges, date list and holidays.

Process Table

As sometimes occurs when I reach a point of mounting complexity, I felt the need to extract the conditions into a table for better control and visibility of both Calendar and Buckets tables. This was added after Buckets, described in the next section, but needs to be explained now for clarity.

The point of overlapping conditions was like a bug in my ear. I wanted some way to flag such cases. Combining conditions would quickly become overly complex and was out of the question. On top of that, the calculation of bucket counts was cumbersome, with multiple ranges of dates to subtract from working days. I tried various ways, finally settling once again on a process table. It had to be granular, to expose daily conditions that could then be counted. I decided on a reference table named Days, hidden in another column group.

The first four columns are Y, M, W and Day, with appropriate duplicate hiding as used before. The first row lines up with the first row of the Buckets table, to ensure that counts will be accurate.

```
[Day] =IF(N(Above),Above+1,IF(Bucket="W",Monday,
    EOMONTH(EDATE(Start,-1),0)+1))
```

Show Conditions

Following [Day] are four columns of conditions for the four main "show" options; Annuals, Ranges, List and Holidays. Weekend, Today and Cycle are not needed. Each column uses the logic as described in the previous section, but instead of being based on This, each condition is based on [@Day]. These four columns, [isAnnual], [isRange], [isList], and [isHoliday], each determine if [@Day] is their type, and return 1 if so or 0 if not. The logic can be reviewed in the Highlighting section, here's an example:

```
[isList] =IF(COUNTIF(DateList[date],[@Day]),1,0)
```

Conditions are modified in Name Manager for each type, to look in its own Days column and return TRUE if 1 is found. Conditional Formatting rules are unchanged. Example:

```
inList =INDEX(Days[isList],MATCH(This,Days[Day],0))
```

To identify days with multiple conditions, it must be based on the user's selections of whether to display them or not. For convenience, above the header of each column I retrieve the setting thus:

```
=IF(ShowAnnuals,1,0), etc.
```

These four cells are formatted to display "show" if 1 and blank if 0, and the four-cell range is named DaysShowSwitches. The next column [Highlights] counts the selected conditions by multiplying two binary four-cell ranges.

```
[Highlights]
    =SUMPRODUCT(DaysShowSwitches,Days[@[isAnnual]:[isHoliday]])
```

Now I can find overlapping conditions by creating two more Name Manager formulas.

```
inTwo =INDEX(Days[Highlights],MATCH(This,Days[Day],0))=2
inThree =INDEX(Days[Highlights],MATCH(This,Days[Day],0))>2
```

There's not a lot of options left for formatting that will show through the fill, but I manage to find two types that have an adequate effect; Number format "+"d, combined with Font format single underline for inTwo, and double underline for inThree.

Count Conditions

The second purpose of Days is to help with counts. Annuals are not relevant, so there are three more columns, [CtRng], [CtList] and [CtHols]. The respective "count" checkbox values are retrieved, and hybrid-named = DaysCountSwitch, absolute row and relative column in which they lie. Each column has a simple formula to retrieve the condition already established, if the count is turned on, returning 1 or 0.

```
[CtRng] =[@isRange]*DaysCountSwitch, etc.
```

The final column collects all the selected off days by multiplying the max of the three columns (0 or 1) by [@Day]. This single column can now be used as the "holidays" argument in the workdays calculation to come next.

```
[OffDays] =PRODUCT(MAX(Days[@[CtRng]:[CtHols]]),[@Day])
```

Bucket Counts

The primary Calendar output is ready, and I've defined several inputs to enhance its usefulness. Now there's the other output table, to summarize weekly or monthly counts of workdays and cycles.

Workdays are used for capacity planning, and this will be useful in other projects. Even with weekends alone and no holidays, months range from 20 to 23 workdays, a 15% difference. Add holidays and the gap widens, add special days and it widens further. Output expectations and work assignments need to consider capacity based on working days available.

For cycles, a common payday example is every 14 days, 26 per year. Most months have two, and two months per year have three. For monthly budgeting it's nice to know which months have three paydays. For longer cycles, it helps to know in which buckets it occurs.

It can be important to have counts for both weeks and months. Above the table is a selection cell named Bucket with two options, M or W. The Buckets table has five columns, with formatting to display either months or weeks.

The middle column [bucket] is the key. This is a date value, =Monday if week (the same formula used in Calendar), or else the first of the month.

```
[bucket] =IF(Bucket="W",Monday,EOMONTH(IF(N(Above),Above,
    EDATE(Start,-1)),0)+1)
```

[num] converts [bucket] to either week number or month number, and [year] is just the year of the bucket (what a time to be alive!).

[bucket] format is "dd mmm", appropriate for week buckets, with two conditions; for weeks within the same month, "dd" to remove month, and for month buckets, "mmm" to remove day.

Work Days

Column [work] uses the international function NETWORKDAYS.INTL with all four arguments. I can use [@bucket] as the start argument, because it is always the first day of the bucket. For the end argument, another name is used:

```
EoBThis =IF(Bucket="W",Buckets[@bucket]+6,
    EOMONTH(Buckets[@bucket],0))
```

WkString is the weekend argument, and Days[OffDays] is the holiday argument.

```
[work] =IFERROR(NETWORKDAYS.INTL([@bucket],EoBThis,
    WkString,Days[OffDays]),0)
```

Cycles

To count cycles requires knowing the date of the first occurrence of the cycle within the bucket, if any. The initial steps are as numbered below and are defined in a formula named FirstCoB

1. Get the last day of the previous bucket
2. Subtract the portion of cycle passed as of then
3. Add cycle

```
FirstCoB = Buckets[@bucket]-1-MOD(Buckets[@bucket]-1-
    First,Cycle)+Cycle
```

Using this to get the count, if FirstCoB is beyond the end of the bucket, the count is 0, otherwise, count the cycles remaining in the bucket, and add 1 for the first.

```
[cycles] = IF(FirstCoB>EoBThis,0,IFERROR(ROUNDDOWN((EoBThis-
    FirstCoB)/Cycle,0)+1,""))
```

These two output columns, [work] and [cycles] have a small range of values, and the extremes are what is interesting, so I use data bars on each column separately to visualize them.

Horizons

With any project, especially one with so many interdependent tables, it's important to have a governance strategy. I've built in error handling with Data Validation and special red-flag formulas and messages. A more subtle risk is the chance that supplying tables run out of data before the receiving tables. This might be called a domain mismatch, or since we're working with dates, a horizon mismatch.

Calendar table shows every day, but in seven columns, so a row is one week. Days table is one row per day. An obvious concern is that, in order to cover the same horizon, it will need seven times as many rows as Calendar.

Days is an intermediate supplier, input tables are the primary suppliers. HolidayInput, DateRanges and DateList of course are dependent on the user to maintain as far into the future as needed and possible. Days adds no value beyond the user input horizon. The risk is uncertainty, that the user could input dates that don't show or are not counted as expected.

The three input tables noted are each added another rule, to turn the font red if a date is beyond the Days table horizon. An accompanying message appears above each table to alert the user.

It is not necessary to extend Days to cover Calendar and Buckets output tables, as long as it covers the input table horizons. However, for transparency, I also add output table formats to show where the Days horizon ends, with a gray cross-hatch similar to weekends. The message is not to rely on the output that far out.

There might be a touch of overkill in all these conditions. Most of the user time spent on this sheet will be on the first screen. It's a matter of integrity to account for the rare, even unexpected use so as never to misinform.

A final note on horizon maintenance is that it is incumbent on the user to delete the past occasionally.

Tweaks and Tips

Data Validation messages are attached to several symbols in row 1, one for Calendar Help and the others as column group headers.

The column group labeled "Settings and Inputs" is the main dashboard of user interaction, and I expect it will normally be open. If closed, the checkbox controls will remain visible, which is not desirable. A tip in Calendar Help is to hide controls by Ctrl+6. When done, also hidden is a rectangle that hides text, saying "Ctrl+6 to show controls". It is more important as a reminder how to turn them on again than to turn them off.

A fourth column is added to each of the input tables in this section, and the non-table settings range at top is adjusted to match. The column [until] calculates days until the next date, capped at ±999:

```
[until] =IF([@date],MIN(MAX([@date]-TODAY(),-999),999),0)
```

For Annuals and for Cycle it is modified to return days until the next occurrence.

The Calendar can be used to pick a date, then copy and paste where it's needed. The target cell should have an appropriate date format, and the paste should be the value only. Paste values via right-click or from the quick access toolbar, or by one of the shortcut methods shown earlier. This technique can be practiced by copying a date from the calendar and pasting it as a value to the StartInput cell.

Controls Sheet

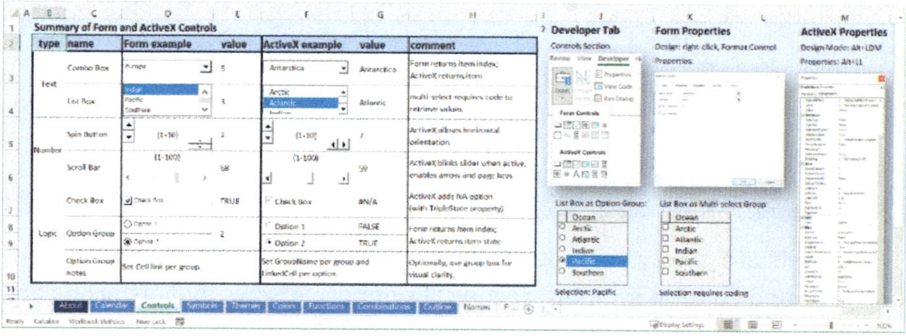

Controls can be confusing as a group and individually. Should I use Form controls or ActiveX controls? How do I create an Option Button group? How is a Combo Box different from a List Box? How can I get back the control's value? What is Triplestate? MultiSelect?

This sheet is a visual companion to the Controls section in Chapter 3, which explains the two families and gives some detail about each control. Here the six main controls are grouped as Text (List Box and Combo Box), Number (Spin Button, Scroll Bar) and Logic (Check Box, Option Group). To aid familiarization, the two types are shown side by side with comments about the usage and differences.

Symbols Sheet

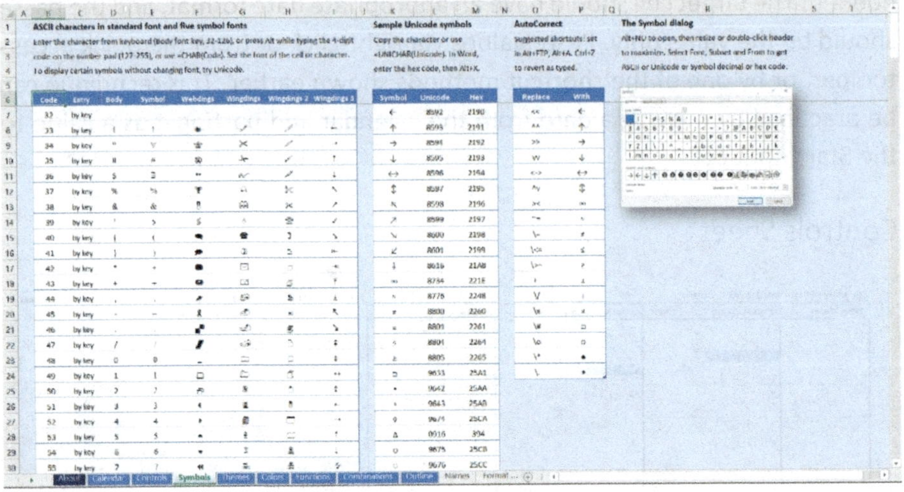

Symbols are a way to enhance text with graphic detail, including many linguistic and cultural symbols, technical symbols, arrows, bullets, icons and emoji. They can be used alone or in the middle of a string. They fit and wrap with other text and can be processed as text. For some purposes there is no substitute. To learn how to use them requires a little background.

ASCII and Unicode define different character sets that you can choose from in any given font. Think of ASCII as basic, Unicode as enhanced. Initially, ASCII used 7 bits, which allows $2^7 = 128$ characters, 95 corresponding to the keyboard and the rest for program controls. Later, an 8th bit was added, doubling the set to 256. The added range is used for modified Latin letters used in some languages, and a small set of currency, legal and technical symbols. As computer use expanded globally in the 1980's, the need for more characters grew exponentially. Unicode was introduced in 1988 and now has over a million characters, including many different alphabets and an enormous range of symbols.

There are way more symbols than you'll ever need, so start with some exploration. Open the Symbol dialog, Alt-N,U. Double-click the header to make it full screen, you'll need it. First, at bottom right, select ASCII (either decimal or hex), then at top left select the font picklist, and starting at the top of the list, scroll through the fonts with the down arrow. Notice that most fonts have mostly the same characters, just different looks. If you keep scrolling, eventually you'll find some fonts with musical notations, or other strange symbols. If you look at the bottom right you may notice that from: is no longer ASCII, but Symbol. This indicates a symbol-dedicated font.

Keep scrolling fonts, holding down the down arrow to go fast, or type a letter to jump. Stop to review Symbol, Webdings and the three Wingdings fonts. Note that each of them has a loosely-defined theme. The table on the Symbols sheet shows the ASCII set of these five symbol fonts (they have no Unicode extensions) side by side with the normal body font for reference.

Next, go back to the top of the font list (normal font), buckle your seat belt and select Unicode in the from: box. Before changing the font, scroll down the character grid to get a feel for how many different types of characters there are. Make a mental note that you may want to return here to collect some favorites in the normal font, for reasons explained later. Notice that the new Subset: picklist at top right changes as you scroll. Open it to view the subsets, and scroll the list to jump to the beginning of each group.

Now go back to the font list and scroll down it again, noting that some fonts have only the short ASCII list, while others have thousands of new characters. It's worth checking out the new symbol sets in at least the following fonts: Segoe MDL2 Assets, Segoe UI Emoji, Segoe UI Symbol.

The point of this exercise is to help you to filter out the thousands and find the few that are useful to you. Think about how you will use the symbols. Probably you'll use them in a cell by themselves, or combined with normal text. You might also want to use them as inputs to formulas, or pivots, or slicers, or format conditions. These don't care about the font, only the characters, and if it's Unicode, it may or may not display as expected.

To see how a symbol will be passed, view it in the formula bar. Below is a string of symbols from four different fonts, each group separated by a space. In cell 1, each set is formatted with its own font. The formula bar shows that some of them are passed exactly, some approximately, some as their undisguised self, and some are incognito. Cell 2 is Calibri (Body) font, in which some look like the formula bar, some like cell 1, and one symbol has disappeared entirely.

Figure 1: Symbol Appearance and Content

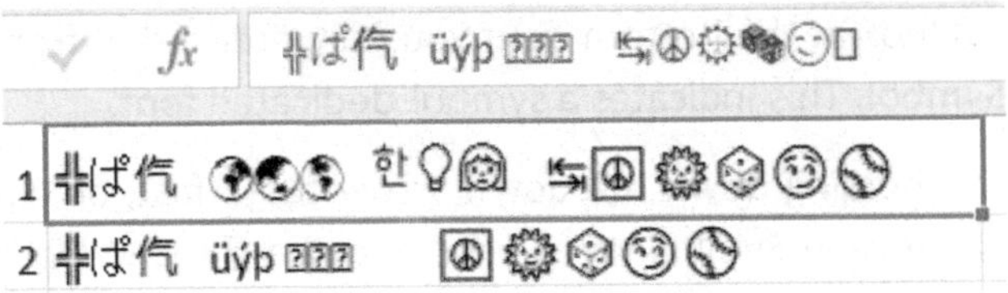

The lesson? Symbols are not always "what you see is what you get," but it's easy to tell by checking the formula bar. Avoid fonts and symbols that don't pass well, if that matters. You can set symbol font on part of a constant cell, but of course a formula cell can only have one font. If you set a formula cell to a symbol font, you can no longer edit-in-cell. Instead, use the formula bar.

Now to introduce the Symbols sheet, which has two tables for ASCII and Unicode.

In the ASCII table, column [Code] lists the ASCII codes, 32 to 255 (1 to 31 are non-printable control characters). This is followed by the method of entry, and the code's character in six different fonts, the standard Body font and five symbol fonts. The six font columns all contain the same value, =CHAR([@Code]); only the font differs.

In the Unicode table, a small set of useful symbols is shown in the Body font. This is converted to the Unicode value, =UNICODE([@Body]), and its hexadecimal equivalent, =DEC2HEX([@Unicode],4).

Interesting note: I can use =CODE(symbol) to return the ASCII code of a symbol, and =CHAR(code) to return the character of a code. So if I do =CHAR(CODE(symbol)), I should get the same symbol, right? For codes within the ASCII range, this works. If the symbol is outside the ASCII range, it returns "?" (code 63). However, =UNICHAR(UNICODE(symbol)) always returns the same symbol, because nothing is outside the Unicode range.

A third table gives another way to enter symbols, via AutoCorrect. Go to File-Options-Proofing, Alt-F,T,P, then Alt+A, to set AutoCorrect Options as shortcuts. Set them up from any Office program and they are available in all, but may work a little differently. Word and PowerPoint are text-based, so to them, + or – or = are just characters. In Excel these invoke the formula syntax, so symbol replacements don't work. For example, standard arrow shortcuts "-->" = →, "==>" = ➔, etc. do not work in Excel.

Table 31: Symbol Entry Tips

code	entry methods
any	insert from Symbol picker
32-126	Keyboard
127-255	Alt+0+code (number pad)
ASCII	=CHAR(code)
Unicode	=UNICHAR(Unicode)
any	copy cell (character and font)
any	copy character only

Replacement symbols improve text appearance, but can break an Excel formula, for example, if you replace ">=" with "≥". Watch as you type, and if you get an unwanted symbol, Ctrl+Z immediately to undo the substitution and continue with the characters as typed. If you don't catch it while typing you will have an error. To avoid this, set up AutoCorrect characters that you'll never use in a formula, or simply choose to avoid such AutoCorrect sequences.

The final shortcut to mention is to use Word to create a Unicode symbol by typing the hex code followed by Alt+X. For example, 25CF followed by Alt+X = ●. Symbols can thus be entered in Word and copied to Excel.

Themes Sheet

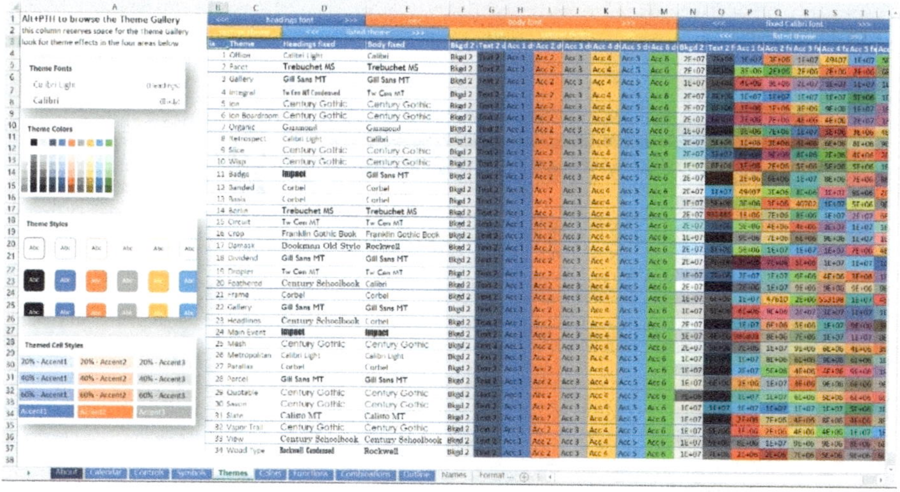

Themes, I think, are under-appreciated. They need some marketing to show them off and explain their benefits. Here they are laid out in a way that as you scroll the Theme Gallery, you see the sheet change and learn the scope of what elements are linked to the Theme.

Themes are composed of selected colors, fonts and effects. Of course, these and all other formats are individually customizable, but these three can also be set as groups. You can select a different color set, font set, or effect set, or a different theme which combines all three. Most users don't give a care whether they are using a theme-dependent format or not, but as a developer it's something you should be aware of. Choose elements consciously with the following considerations.

- If you stay within the themed elements, they will change if a user selects a different theme. They will maintain appropriate contrast and balance, but may change window size, cell wrapping, etc.
- If you want the project to be user-theme-independent, use non-themed elements, or control it in VBA.
- Avoid mixing themed and non-themed elements.

If you consider setting theme in code, record it to find the path. I found some theme files in one folder path, and others in a completely different path. If you are distributing the Excel file, consider distributing the theme file with it, and be aware of different versions.

Colors Sheet

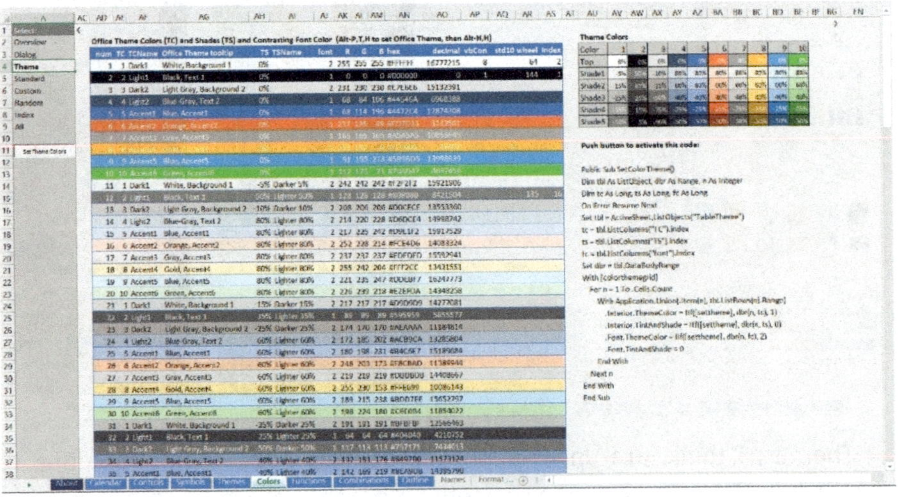

Color Selection

Aren't colors wonderful? They are simple and obvious, yet complex and mysterious. Most users interact with them visually with no thought to the numbers behind them, and most only ever use a few, or several colors, picked for contrast or emphasis. Excel can display over 16 million colors! This needs some breakdown and some VBA examples on different ways to set colors.

The user interface simplifies color options, stepping in with four stages of increasing complexity. Here I have ordered them and given each a catchy name.

Table 32: Color Selection Four Ways

Selection	Display
Crayon Box Color Dialog – Standard 10 standard colors	
Ensemble Color Dialog – Theme 10 theme colors x 6 shades = 60 colors	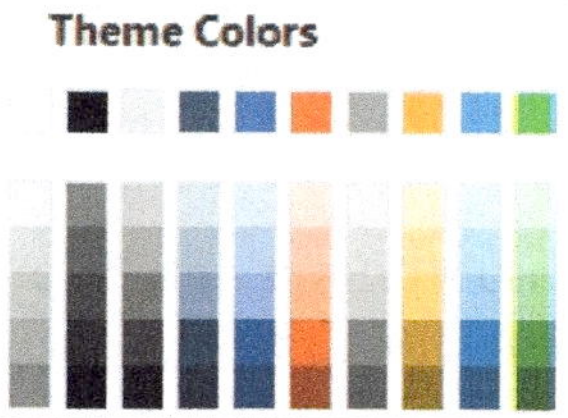
Designer Set Color Dialog – More Colors – Standard 2^7 = 127 colors + 2^4 = 16 grays	

Selection	Display
Rainbow Heaven Color Dialog – More Colors – Custom 2^8 Red X 2^8 Green X 2^8 Blue = 2^{24} = 16,777,216 colors	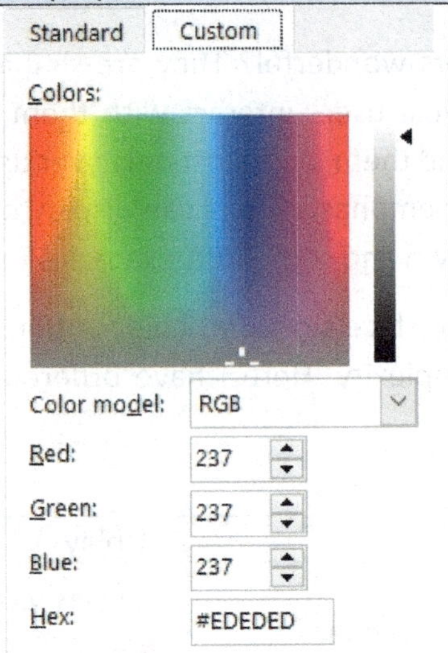

VBA Color Numbers

Excel colors are visual, VBA is not. Color numbers are used in VBA to read and write Excel colors. There is a decimal value of each color, from 0 to 16777215, that is only used in VBA. But who wants to derive or interpret 16 million color numbers? Like Excel, VBA has simpler ways to select colors and know what you're getting.

When you record a macro while setting a color, you get the property statement like .Color = 256, or, if you select from the theme color palette, something like .ThemeColor = xlThemeColorAccent1. Within VBA there are other ways to select color that are not recorded. This means you have to know what they are, but once you do they are a great convenience.

The simplest selection, like the crayon box, is a set of eight color constants: vbBlack, vbBlue, vbGreen, vbCyan, vbRed, vbMagenta, vbYellow, vbWhite. If your needs are that simple, there's little to memorize. In the VBA Object Browser (F2) you can see the list and their decimal and hex values.

Next up the scale is .ColorIndex, with 56 values. This is a default palette that can be customized at workbook level. One way to see them is to create a list or grid from 1 to 56 and write a macro to set .Interior.ColorIndex = .Value.

Table 33: VBA Color Properties

Property	Range	Comment
.Color	RGB(r,g,b), each 0 to 255, or decimal 0 to 16777215	VBA records decimal value, Custom dialog displays RGB and Hex values
	8 color constants, vbBlack to vbWhite	These are the permutations of none (0) and all (255) of R,G,B
.ColorIndex	1 to 56	Workbook.Colors to customize palette
.ThemeColor	By name or 1 to 12	View 12 theme colors at Alt-P,T,C,C
.TintAndShade	-1.00 to +1.00 dark to light	Modifies any color property

Finally, the RGB function can express any color as a combination of red, green and blue. It's a lot easier to envision a scale of 256 values for each of three colors than a scale of 16 million. You'll learn that RGB(255,0,0) is red, RGB(0,0,255) is blue, and RGB with three equal numbers is a shade of gray. RGB values are visible in the Excel custom color picker, but are not recorded.

You will also see or read about a hex value. Since hex is base 16, a two digit hex number, 00 to FF, can represent decimal numbers from 0 to 255 (=16^2). Thus an RGB color value can be expressed as a concatenation of three two-digit hex numbers, like #RRGGBB, from #000000 for black to #FFFFFF for white.

Curiously, the decimal value used in VBA is in BGR order of significance, while the hex value is in RGB significance order. In Excel and VBA, you do not need to be concerned with hex values. In Excel you select visually, or by entering RGB values in the custom color dialog. In VBA you record and set the decimal, or use one of the methods above to select by name, index or RGB. Hex codes are used in web design and may come into play in other programs.

If you're uneasy about the reversed significance, do an exercise to clarify this for yourself. Record a macro while setting three cells to true red, green and blue. Then, open the custom color picker on each cell, and compare the hex value there to the recorded decimal value in VBA.

You would expect that the color value would be the same number, whether it's expressed in base 10 or base 16, but when the decimals are converted to hex they are the reverse of the hex color value.

Table 34: Hex vs. Decimal RGB Significance

Color	R	G	B	Hex	Decimal	DEC2HEX(Decimal,6)
Red	255	0	0	#FF0000	255	0000FF
Green	0	255	0	#00FF00	65280	00FF00
Blue	0	0	255	#0000FF	16711680	FF0000

This odd logic is a feature. Just know that if you ever have need to use hex color codes, they are in RGB order. The VBA decimal is the one that's out of order. This is not a concern because the decimal is not meaningful in itself, we use the methods noted to give it meaning.

Sheet Interface

The VBA methods to select colors by name or number help in development, but don't give you any visual preview of the colors. This needs to be laid out and exposed. I want a reference showing the various color selection methods for both user and programmer. I want to see fill and font colors together, for best readability. And, I want some code samples that I can copy to other projects as needed.

To keep it handy and compact within Startup, I'll use column groups on a single sheet with tab-like controls to simulate sheets-within-a-sheet. This is another prototype technique as an example of how user interface can be managed.

Column A is a menu of sections. The entire column is shaded darker than the rest of the sheet. When a menu item is selected, it activates code via the Worksheet_SelectionChange event, which is limited only to the menu range. Each section is in a named column group, and the event will use a Select Case group on the menu items to do three things:

1. Highlight the selected cell, and reset the rest of the menu
2. Display the related column group, and hide the rest of the columns
3. Display any related controls and hide all others

In each step, the first action is to hide or reset everything, followed by the specific action to unhide or highlight the selected element. Thus, it appears that each menu item is opening a different page.

Sheet Sections

The menu has seven sections, each focused on a certain scope or technique to envision, maintain and program colors, as summarized in the table.

Table 35: Color Sheet Sections

Section	Scope	Controls	Control Action
Overview	8 vb Color Constants		
Dialog	10 Standard Colors		
Theme	60 Theme Colors	Toggle Button	Set/unset the colors
Standard	142 More...Standard	Toggle Button	Set/unset the colors
Custom	2^{24} More...Custom	3 Scroll Bars	Set RGB values
Random	20x20 random colors	Command Button	Randomize the colors
Index	56 ColorIndex Colors	Toggle Button	Set/unset the colors

Each section has a helpful table with color name if available, decimal, hex and RGB values, and reference to other color selection methods. Those with controls have a copy of the VBA code on the sheet. The sheet is thus a comprehensive reference for color selection, color values, and color coding.

Functions Sheet

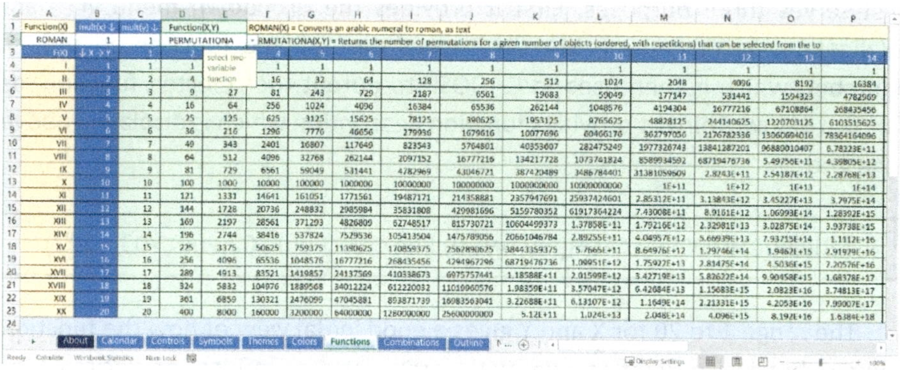

Function descriptions and help are good and important ways to get to know what the functions do and how to use them. Sometimes I need to see examples, and I thought of a multiplication table. I can make a grid of x and y values, then pick a function from a list to display the result f(x,y).

I went through all the functions and made a list of interesting ones. Then I realized that several of them have only one operand, so I made two lists; one of single-operand functions, the other of multi-operand functions. My design was to lay out the sheet to show me a range of results of whatever function I select from each list.

The layout is a 20x20 grid, X going down the rows in column B and Y going across the columns in row 4. In column A is the single-operand column. The f(x) range and the f(x,y) range are independent of each other and colored differently for visual separation. Name Manager then defines each input, lookup and output.

Table 36: Functions Sheet Names

Type	Name	Refers to
Input	X	= $B5 (relative to cell C5)
	Y	= C$4 (relative to cell C5)
Lookup	FX	Cell containing the selected f(x)
	FXs	Range containing the list of f(x)
	FXY	Cell containing the selected f(x,y)
	FXYs	Range containing the list of f(x,y)
Output	FunX01... up to FunX13	=DEC2BIN(X)... etc.
	FunXY01... up to FunXY21	=GCD(X, Y)... etc.

The function lists are off to the right of the formula grid. The function name list serves three purposes. First it provides the dropdown menu via Data Validation. Second, using MATCH it gives the selected function an ordinal number, which is then used in CHOOSE to output the selected function, as shown below. Third, it provides function description which is displayed above the grid.

```
=IFERROR(CHOOSE(MATCH(fxy,fxys,0),FunXY01,FunXY02,FunXY03,...),"")
```

The range 1 to 20 for X and Y gives a good initial view of how the function works, but I also want to play with inputs, use negatives, or decimals, or multiples of 100 just to see what happens. X and Y each have a multiplier cell, mx and my. Then the 20 actual X values and 20 actual Y values are calculated.

```
20 X inputs = IF(N(mx),mx,1)*(ROW()-ROW(Y))
20 Y inputs =IF(N(my),my,1)*(COLUMN()-COLUMN(mx))
```

I'll add some code to this sheet for the Worksheet_Change event, which is activated only for the pick list cells and the multiplier cells, collectively named "controls". Whenever one of these four cells is changed, the columns are autofit. However, this looks weird if the columns end up very different widths. Cell merging is used where the function name or description would cause an autofit column to be too wide. To set a minimum column width, I page down to pick a row and enter =REPT("_",8) in all the output display columns. The string of eight underscores defines the minimum autofit column width.

Combinations Sheet

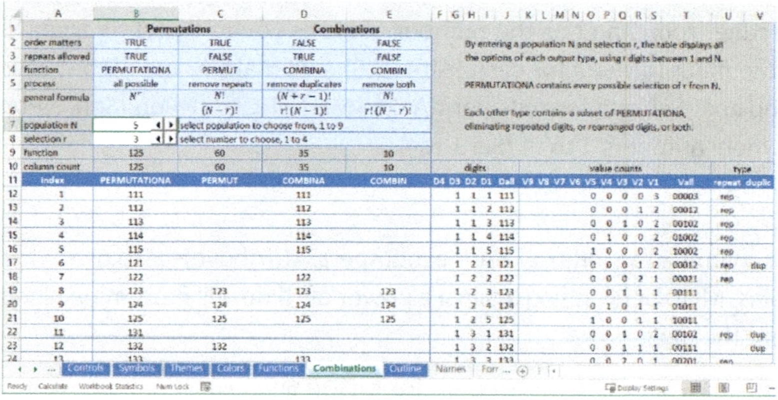

Combinations and permutations are hard to understand and remember how they work. Each one has two variants, with or without repetition. There are four Excel functions with decent help text, but Excel will not teach you everything you need to know. You need to understand the concepts. What better way than to lay them out in a reference sheet?

In the process of creating this sheet, I learned and became more comfortable with the four types. I started by manually working out lists of permutations with repetition using r digits between 1 and N. These are the easiest to understand because repetition of digits is allowed, and rearrangement of the same digits is allowed. In other words, there are no limitations. This is like a padlock with three dials from 0 to 9, which has 10^3 = 1000 ways from 000 to 999 (call it a "permutation lock"?).

Each of the other three functions eliminates some items from this initial list. Combinations eliminate items from permutations, by not allowing the same set of digits to be rearranged; chocolate and vanilla is the same as vanilla and chocolate, order doesn't matter. Combinations and permutations without repetition remove those items with any repeating digit; choosing unique items from a jar, you can't choose the same item twice. By setting up a table with the four lists in columns, it's easy to see the attrition of items by applying the logic of each type.

I listed out example data using numeric digits. Once I got the manual logic, I started working out the calculation logic digit by digit. The strategy is to calculate the permutations with repetition, and use columns to identify repeats and duplicates to be eliminated from the others.

Notation of these formulas in math texts uses N as the population count you're selecting from, and r as the number of items you're selecting from N. I'll display the math formula for each (Alt-N,Z,S), and make N and r input cells named NPop and rSel, and formula PermA=PERMUTATIONA(NPop,rSel). NPop will allow whole numbers 1 to 9, rSel 1 to 4.

Table

The first column is an index of ordinal numbers, =N(Above)+1, to use in the digit formulas. MOD of [@index] against a power of NPop will determine when to increment the digit.

The first digit from the right is easy; use MOD([@index],NPop) unless it is 0, then use NPop. The first phrase hides values that are outside the set.

```
[D1] =IF([@index]>PermA,"",IF(MOD([@index],NPop),
     MOD([@index],NPop),NPop))
```

For the remaining digits, each value needs to repeat until the next power of NPop. Here I want to use the number from the column headers in row 11 in formulas by picking the right character, then VALUE to convert it to a number.

```
HdrVal =VALUE(RIGHT(F$11,1))          with active cell in column F
```

By referring to the header, the formula for digits 2, 3 and 4 is the same.

```
[D2], [D3], [D4] =IF(OR([@index]>PermA,rSel<HdrVal),"",IF(N(Above),IF(
    MOD([@index],POWER(NPop,HdrVal-1))=1,
    IF(Above=NPop,1,Above+1),Above),1))
```

The four digits are concatenated to create the item, which is also used in the PERMUTATIONA column.

```
[Dall] =CONCAT(Combinations[@[D4]:[D1]])
```

The next step is to identify the items to be removed from the other sets. These are two types, repeats and duplicates. Repeats are whenever the same value is in multiple output digits. Duplicates are when the same values are used in a different order. Both require a count of the values in each item.

There can be up to four output digits, but they can have values from 1 to 9, by my arbitrary rules. So next are nine columns, each doing COUNTIF on the 4-column digit range, for the value 1 to 9.

```
[V1], [V2], etc. =IF(OR([@index]>PermA,NPop<HdrVal),"",
    COUNTIF(Combinations[@[D4]:[D1]],HdrVal))
```

Repeats occur when the max of these nine COUNTIF columns is greater than 1. Another column checks this and flags “rep” all that match.

```
[repeat] =IF([@index]>PermA,"",IF(MAX(Combinations[@[V9]:[V1]])>1,
    "rep",""))
```

Duplicates uses another CONCAT, this one of the nine COUNTIF columns, to identify items with the same number of the same values; 112 and 121 both have one 2 and two 1’s; the CONCAT will be the same.

```
[Vall] =CONCAT(Combinations[@[V9]:[V1]])
```

The trick now is only to flag the second and subsequent duplicates, not the first. This is done by using an OFFSET range to look in, starting from the row above and up to the header. This flags "dup".

```
[duplic] =IF([@index]>PermA,"",IF(COUNTIF(OFFSET([@[Vall]],-1,0,-(ROW()-
    ROW(Combinations[#Headers]))),[@Vall]),"dup",""))
```

With NPop 1 to 9 and rSel 1 to 4, the maximum number of rows required is then 9^4 = 6561. Once all columns were defined, I copied them down to 6561 rows.

Header

Above the table are two rows, one with the four functions, the other with a count of items in the four columns, COUNTIF(data column,">'0'"). The function result and the column count should always match, providing validation of the math. This sheet is a good visual and logical reference.

Outline Sheet

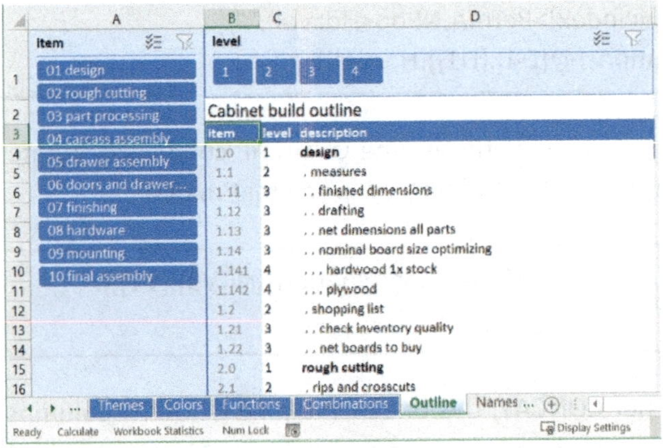

Purpose

Most attempts I have witnessed to create an outline in Excel have ended badly. It is clumsy to promote, demote and rearrange a hierarchical list of items, and to keep them enumerated logically.

I built a tool years ago, one of my early VBA projects, that creates row groups based on a column of level numbers. Groups are good for collapsing and expanding levels, but they're designed for data summarization, not outlining. To get users to adjust, or to protect them from needing to, is probably more effort than the benefit you or they get back.

Word is a far superior tool for outlining. It is simple and intuitive. It auto-increments with Enter and auto-indents with Tab. You can cut and paste and it auto-adjusts. You can define different formats for each level and can easily switch and combine letters, numbers, roman numerals and bullets.

I could stop this effort before it starts by declaring Word as the go-to outline tool. Let's start by clarifying the purpose. If you intend to write paragraphs, the first question is why? – it's an outline! – but if so, Word is the obvious choice. If you just need a quick ordered list of short phrases as a guide for some project, you might choose Excel. This enables you to combine it with other sheets and calculations, or to program an interactive interface.

You might end up with an unintentional outline, as you start listing items and realize later that some are subordinate, and that the list needs to be ordered.

This project will serve to demonstrate some formula and table techniques, and a little cool math. I'll use a table to auto-generate outline numbers, with whole numbers at the top level, and each lower level adding a decimal place.

The Math

First, create or imagine a single-level numbering table. Two columns, one auto-generates ordinal whole numbers, the other is for whatever text you want to list. With relative name Above defined, the numbering formula is Item = N(Above)+1.

Whatever you do to this table – add rows at the bottom, insert rows at the top, drag rows up and down – they will always stay in numerical order. You wouldn't want that with data, but we're not talking about data, we're just listing items. The list keeps itself straight, like a Word outline.

Now, to make this multi-level with decimals, I add another column for level. Level is a manual entry, starting with 1 at the top and increasing with each level. Like priority, level numbers go up as levels go down in significance.

Now, levels see-saw down and back up, and down again. So I have two requirements:

1. When the level number increases, add a decimal digit to the previous item number
2. When level number decreases, remove a decimal and increment the previous level item

Fun challenge! First point, increasing levels. Working inside out, I start again with N(Above). Instead of adding 1, I add $10^{(1\text{-level})}$. Starting at level 1 it means adding $10^{(1-1)} = 10^0 = 1$. Level 2 will add $10^{(1-2)} = 10^{-1} = 0.1$, and so on. This can be notated 10^(1-[@level]) or POWER(10,1-[@level]).

Second point, now I need to handle decreasing levels. To remove decimals is to round, and I want to round down. The number of digits I want to end up with is [@level]-1. This gives me 0 decimals for level 1, 1 decimal for level 2, etc.

```
=ROUNDDOWN(N(above)+ POWER(10,1-[@level]),[@level]-1)
```

I confess to a geek thrill upon discovering this formula. Later in testing, I modified the formula to protect against missing level:

```
=IF(N(Above),ROUNDDOWN(N(Above)+POWER(10,1-
    MAX([@level],1)),MAX([@level],1)-1),1)
```

I would still go to Word to write an outline. This one is limited to nine consecutive items at each level except the top, and is harder to format and harder to read than Word. But to play out the use case we've defined let's embellish a bit, while illustrating some other points.

Slicers

If you have a long list of items in a table you can scroll it, or you can manually filter by one of the columns, but this is where it's nice to slice. A table slicer is really nothing more than a shortcut to a column filter, with some key advantages. One advantage is that it presents the unique values in the column as buttons, which can be sized and arranged in a vertical, horizontal or rectangular configuration. Another advantage is that it can expose the values from hidden columns. This means that you can create and set up columns especially for this purpose.

As previously described, the disadvantage of Slicers is the space they consume. This is weighed against the advantages to provide utility without clutter. Layout can be a bit like making a jigsaw puzzle. Slicers are objects like shapes or pictures, and can easily be hidden in the Selection Pane or by Ctrl+6 while building. Once positioned they can be locked in place by selecting "Disable resizing and moving" in the Position and Layout format section.

I decide on two slicers. First I'll slice by the top-level items. For this I'll create a slicer column, first, to group the items by their parent level-1 title, and second, to sort the slicer buttons logically. The objective is to build the slicer button text from the whole-number item and its description. To do this I'll round down the item number, convert it to two-digit text, and concatenate the description.

```
=TEXT(ROUNDDOWN([@item],0),"00")&" "& INDEX([description],
    MATCH(ROUNDDOWN([@item],0),[item],0))
```

Now that I have a group column to slice, I add the slicer. With the active cell in the table, I click slicer on the Table Design tab, and select the group column. I've left space to the left of the table for it, and I start stretching it out to fill the space.

The slicer need not be too tall, but as long as there's space I'll use it. In fact, the screen looks better with the slicer covering the visible screen height, about 30 rows. It hides the useless space beneath, like tucking in your shirt. In most cases this will also avoid the scroll bar that appears when the slicer fills up.

The second slicer is a small one for level. This will mostly be used to collapse the outline by selecting level 1, or levels 1 and 2, etc. It wouldn't make sense to collapse to level 2 without level 1 – unless it's used together with the item slicer.

Since level is a numeric column there's no transformation needed, I add the slicer directly. This one will be horizontal at the top, and I give it ten columns. I'll probably never use more than four levels, but the buttons are small and I have the space. I adjust the height together with the row height, just tall enough for the header and buttons with no cropping.

Slicer formatting can be customized. First see if the slicer style gallery has one you like. To change, right-click the style in the gallery and select Duplicate... This opens a window of options to format every element of your custom copy. Once saved, to make further changes, right-click it in the gallery and select Modify...

To complete the layout, I lock both slicers in place as described above, turn off the table filter, and hide the group slicer column.

Conditional Formatting

I'll use Conditional Formatting here to bold level 1, and to indent level>1 with a dotted leader. I could create a Name Manager alias such as Level = Outline[@level], but in this case I'll just use unstructured reference to [level] in column C. I select [description], then create four rules

1. When $C4=1 set bold font
2. When $C4=2 set number format " . "@
3. When $C4=3 set number format " . . "@
4. When $C4>3 set number format " . . . "@

Chapter 5: Keyboard Trainer

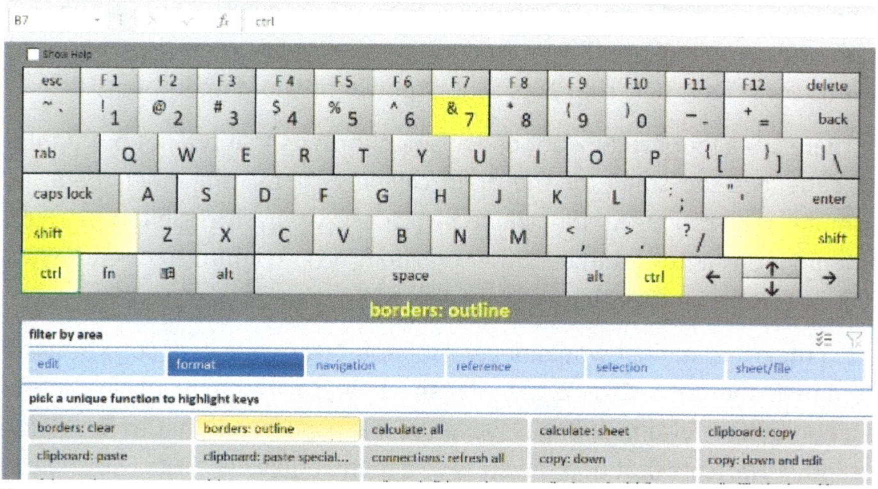

Purpose

With modern devices offering touch and voice controls, the keyboard approach might seem a bit old school. Remember Star Trek 4 from 1986? After traveling back in time from the future to the 1980's, Scotty attempts to command a computer by speaking into the mouse. When directed to the keyboard he famously quips, "ah, a keyboard – how quaint!"

This view of the keyboard is not unjust. The QWERTY layout dates from 19th century typewriters, when it was designed to avoid jamming the mechanical arms. Yet as quaint as it may be, there are still advantages to keyboard navigation over mouse or touch. In theory, the more you learn to do with the keyboard, the less you'll be switching back and forth and the more productive you'll be.

Further, computers have allowed programmers to build in key combinations to perform common tasks efficiently – with no risk of jamming! The more feature-rich the program, the more plentiful and useful are keyboard shortcuts. Being less visual, the keyboard takes more memorization to become proficient, but they are usually designed mnemonically or spatially to be easy to remember, and even menu paths can be deftly unfolded by key sequence.

Consider the purpose of the modifier keys – Shift, Ctrl, Alt – what are they for? Like QWERTY, Shift descends from the typewriter, still used for capitalization but now with some superpowers. Ctrl and Alt evolved from early computing uses and now are known for their superpowers. These three keys, singly and combined, modify letter and special keys in more ways than you'll ever use or remember. That puts a lot of power at your fingertips.

There are a lot of redundant or esoteric shortcuts that are not profitable – the benefit is too small for the brain cells it cost to remember them. For example, you can print the sheet by Ctrl+P, or by Ctrl+Shift+F12. I can remember Ctrl+P for print, the other one no way, and I print so rarely anyway I just don't care enough to memorize a shortcut.

On the other hand, I would never use mouse for undo, cut, copy or paste, when their shortcuts, Ctrl+ Z, X, C, V respectively, are all so neatly juxtaposed to be hit by the left index finger while the left pinky is on the Ctrl key. There are some shortcuts that don't even have a menu equivalent, like copy down – Ctrl+D – and copy right – Ctrl+R.

For menu browsing in the ribbon, with the mouse each tab is a click, whereas with the keyboard, once you have a tab selected (Alt or /), arrow keys let you surf from tab to tab or item to item (left/right, tab) or from tab to items (up/down). Hold down the keys to accelerate, and Alt+Down to open drop-downs, or tab to move on.

KeyTips jump through menu paths when you forget the shortcut or there is none. For example, to toggle headings, Alt-W,V,H. To hide the window, Alt-W,H; Alt-W,U to unhide. There's no need to try to remember a lot of paths, because the signposts are always there. If you find certain paths useful, with practice you will add them to your repertoire as hotkey sequences.

To be pragmatic you must find the right methods that are comfortable for you. The point is not to neglect free tools that can make you more productive. Immerse yourself enough to become fluent. Remember when you learned to type words? Learning to type commands is not much different. I encourage you to master all that the keyboard has to offer, and refresh yourself often. After years of power-using Excel, I still need to update my keyboard skills periodically, and I can still be pleasantly surprised to rediscover shortcuts I can use.

In my need to relearn, I bookmarked online lists and made cheat sheets. I methodically tested every combination. Eventually the opportunity matured into a project. The bonus is that the finished project will help tone up your basic Excel skills.

The concept is to simulate the keyboard on the screen, provide a means to select functions, and highlight the keyboard to visually link the key combination with the function. This will be a great use for slicers; they're intuitive, visual and can be arranged on screen with the keyboard. There will be no need for the data itself to be visible.

This tool nicely illustrates three programming stages: Input via four Slicers; Process via hidden Table and PivotTable; Output via on-screen keyboard highlighting.

Keyboard

The keyboard is meant to look as realistic as possible. When you look at a keyboard, the rows of keys are offset by about a third of a key. To mimic this I made the column widths small and made each key three columns wide by merging cells. I give the whole sheet a dark gray fill, and each key has a gradient fill effect with two shades of gray to give it a slight shadow.

F1 to F9 have a space in the middle (e.g. F 1), so that all 12 F-keys sort correctly in the slicer. F1-F12 keys do not include their alternate (fn) functions such as volume and brightness, since these have no relevance to Excel. For the purpose of this project, the F key is the default, so the fn key is not included. Depending on the computer, this default may be set with hardware (fn lock), software (configuration utility) or the BIOS setup utility.

Font sizes are adjusted for realism. Single-character keys are size 16, multi-character keys are size 12. Combination keys are made with the first character superscript font 20, and the second normal font 16. Letter keys are padded with a space on either side, sorting the alphabet together in the slicer and retaining the center alignment; likewise the special character and punctuation keys.

Arrow keys are copied from the Symbol picker, Alt-N,U, from the Unicode set, using the same Calibri font as the other keys. Wingdings 3 font has many more arrow symbol options, but that only changes the appearance of the character in the cell to an arrow, not the character itself. Here I want the character itself to be an arrow, so that the slicer will display it as an arrow, so I use what arrows are available in Calibri. See the Startup Symbols Sheet for symbol examples.

The keyboard layout is based on an hp envy with a separate number pad. The number pad does not have special functions, but offers alternate ways to call the same functions. The trick is to be proactively aware of the num lock key status. It is important to be fluent with whatever keyboards you may use – work, home, external. The tool can be interpreted or modified for use with any keyboard.

Table

The table and its pivot will be hidden off to the right of the keyboard. Column [Key] is based on the keys in the keyboard, exactly copied. This means the content must match, not the format. Many keys have two characters, or spaces, and the keys are made of merged cells. If you copy and paste directly you will copy the format including cell merging.

If you paste values, the target cells will not be merged, but will be overwritten, so use a safe range. The safest way is to edit the merged cell to copy only the value: **F2** to edit, **Ctrl+A** or **Shift+↑** to select all, **Ctrl+C** to copy. Then it will safely paste into a single cell.

There are two modifier key columns, [Mod1] and [Mod2], allowing for none, one or two together. These plus the [Key] column are used to highlight the keyboard. [Key] is also a slicer, explained later.

[Area] is a function category to help the search, and supplies the first slicer. I carefully name and assign the values to end up with a handful of areas, each with a reasonable number of functions. This serves as roughly an order of magnitude zoom out on the detail function list.

[Function] is the description starting with the most likely sought-after keywords, with sort also in mind. For example, clipboard functions start with "clipboard" so they will stay together, like another grouping level. Following this is a succinct description. This feeds the second and main slicer, and can be used with or without the other slicers.

[Way] provides for multiple ways to do the same function, feeding the third slicer. For any multi-way function the ways are numbered, beginning with the one I think is the easiest or most likely to be remembered and used. Single-way functions are all assigned way 1, avoiding blank value in the slicer.

[Numlock] passes on or off status to the format condition, for those records where it matters, that is, for any of the dual-function keys in the number pad. For all other keys it is blank.

Pivot

The first step to add the slicers is to create a pivot table. But I can add slicers to the table directly, so why do I need a pivot table? A table slicer will display the selected record just as a pivot slicer will. The difference is in how filtering works, as explained below.

Table 37: Table Slicer and Pivot Slicer

Behavior	Slicer
All rows but the selected one are hidden, but they are still there. The selected function is in D7, but there is no way to reference it.	**Table Slicer** 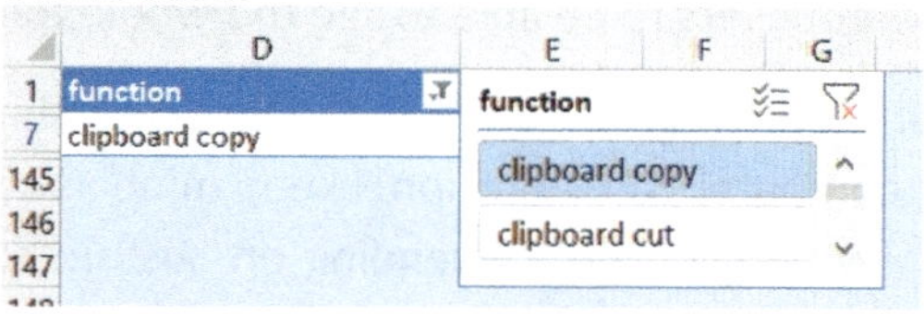
The data are filtered as the selected record is retrieved. The pivot only contains the selected record. The selection can be referenced as A2.	**Pivot Slicer** 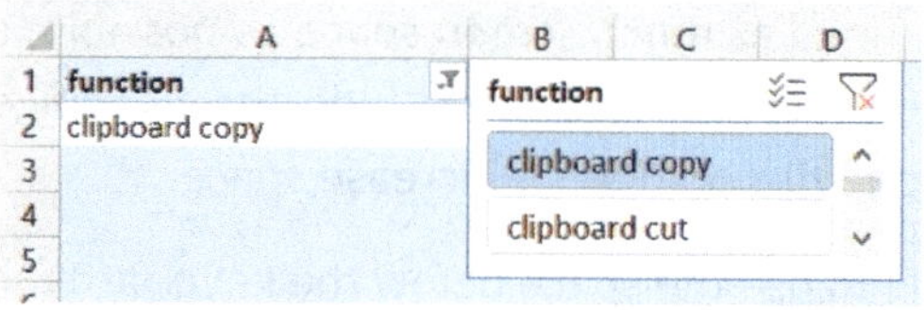

Thus I am using the pivot only to pass the selection from the slicer on to the subsequent process, in this case, Conditional Formatting. In the example shown, I would reference A2 to get the selected function, and use it to look up the keys to highlight.

Using a pivot here is even easier than passing on a lookup value. The pivot has all the table columns at its disposal. Some are used for the slicers and some are used for the formatting.

All seven table columns are included in the pivot, though they don't have to be in the same order. They're all placed in the rows section of the pivot. With totaling removed and report layout set to tabular form, the pivot looks a lot like the table itself.

Next, I create names for the top row of values so they can easily be referenced. With the pivot header and the row below it selected, and practicing using keyboard functions, I hit Ctrl+Shift+F3 to create names from the top row. Now the top data row, which will have the unique selected record, is named by the field headings. Mod1 and Mod2 names become Mod1_ and Mod2_, since otherwise they would conflict with cell addresses.

Slicers

I begin by looking at the keyboard sheet to see what kind of space I have to work with and how best to use it. The keyboard takes up about half of the vertical space and about two thirds of the horizontal space on my 15 inch screen. I want users to be able to see the whole thing, keyboard and slicers.

At work, the great majority of people I'd be sharing with probably have a standard computer configuration. I keep mine as standard as possible so that they will see what I see. Depending on custom screen size and resolution, some may have to zoom out, or minimize other features. I can't please everyone but I will try to give tips for adjustment.

Since I need as much screen space as possible, and the columns and rows of the sheet are not relevant, I hide the headings, Alt-W,V,H. Later I'll add some helpful tips on how to increase space.

I decide to use the space below the keyboard for Area and Function, which have longer text length needing wider buttons. Way will be small and easy to fit in. I'll use the space to the right for Key. With the cursor in the pivot, I select Insert Slicer from the pivot menu, and select the four selection fields.

The first slicer is Area. I ended up with six areas, so I give the slicer six columns for a horizontal layout. I duplicate the format in the gallery, then modify it to fit the sheet color scheme. In Slicer Settings I change the caption to “filter by area”, and uncheck “Show items with no data last”. This will keep the areas in constant position.

The second slicer is for Function. This takes a little more careful thought. There are a lot of values, so there will be a scroll bar, and the function texts vary in length. I need a button width that allows a lot of buttons to show but minimizes truncation of the description. I line up the slicer width with the total width of the keyboard and number pad. Tweaking the number of columns, I arrive at six. Setting the height to use the space with the ribbon minimized gives me eight rows of buttons. The full list is a little more than two full pages within the slicer.

This time I leave the option on to “Show items with no data last”. With so many buttons, I want the selected group to collect at the top. As a general rule, if there’s a scroll bar, I leave this option on to avoid hiding buttons that may be filtered by another slicer. If there’s no scroll bar then nothing is hidden, and it’s easier on the eye to keep the buttons in place by turning the option off.

The third slicer is a tiny one for Way. It will have just four buttons labeled 1 to 4. I give it five columns leaving a space at the end, and making it the same height as Area.

Carefully jockeying these three slicers into position, I fit them all neatly into the space below the keyboard. Snap-to-grid alignment gives a sharp look, but sometimes it requires tweaking column width or row height to work it out just right. A trick to manage row height is to pick an empty cell and increment font size until the height is just right. This ensures it will not revert to the default height.

The final slicer is Key. Key selection is added to help memorization by position, and to learn function groupings. For example, F6 has four functions with different modifiers, all related to navigation between panes and windows. This represents a different learning approach, and so is logically separated from the other slicers, filling up the right side of the screen.

The Key slicer has the same height as the keyboard plus other slicers. At this height, all the keys fit with four columns, eliminating the scrollbar. Then I adjust the width for a comfortable button size. With no scrollbar to deal with, I turn off the “Show items with no data last” option.

Slicer order determines the selection cycle when tab navigation is used. The right-click menu has Bring to Front and Send to Back, or with multiple objects I go to the Selection Pane to arrange order, Alt+F10. Use the arrow buttons with selected objects to set the depth. Tab navigation goes from bottom to top: Area, Function, Way, Key. The Selection Pane is useful to select, order and hide some or all objects.

Trying out the slicers, the Area slicer filters the Function slicer as desired, and the pivot's top data row always has the unique function and way selected. If there are multiple ways and none is selected, they are sorted and the top row is by default way 1.

When I so carefully arrange slicers or other objects, I want them to stay in place. To lock them from inadvertent slips, right-click → Size and Properties → Position and Layout → Disable resizing and moving.

Formatting

Now before I get to formatting, there are preconditions to define. I don't want the highlighting to turn on until there's a unique function selected. Otherwise, the first function would be marked even when none is selected. I need a way to tell if a specific function is selected, not just an area.

The number of rows in the pivot changes with each slicer button. A single-way function button has one row. A multi-way function can have several, probably not more than four. With no function selected, an area button will have as many function-ways as are assigned to it. Checking each area, I find the minimum is thirteen. I pick seven as a number that is between four and thirteen, then count the blanks in the top seven cells of the Function pivot column. There will be zero blanks if no function is selected, and a positive number if one is selected, whether it is single or multi-way. This provides a Boolean "is selected" condition. In addition, I check that it's either way 1 of a multi-way function, or a single row. This eliminates- any confusion that might result if, for example, two functions are selected.

```
IsSelFunc = AND(COUNTBLANK(OFFSET(Function,0,0,7)),
    OR(AND(OFFSET(Function,1,0)=Function,Way=1),
    ISBLANK(OFFSET(Function,1,0))))
```

Now with the entire keyboard selected, active cell B2, the formatting formula to highlight the keys in yellow fill:

```
=AND(IsSelFunc,B2=Key)
```

Next, a similar condition is applied to the modifier keys. Because they each have two keys, left and right, I want to highlight both, but of course not suggest that they are both required. They get a gradient fill as a subtle hint to use one or the other. This is only applied to the three modifier pairs, Shift, Ctrl, Alt, and the two Enter keys, and works on top of the first condition. The keys are selected carefully, first the left set then the right set with opposite gradients. For the left set, active cell is B6:

```
=AND(IsSelFunc,OR(B6=Mod1_,B6=Mod2_))
```

Finally, when the Key slicer is used to pick a key that has multiple functions, I want to show that differently, using a pattern to say "has multiple functions". When this happens, the Function slicer shows and sorts the possible functions to the top to aid retention. Once one of the functions is selected, the clear highlighting turns on with the relevant modifiers. This uses a similar check as above, with the condition that the first two pivot rows have the same key:

```
IsSelKey = AND(COUNTBLANK(OFFSET(Key,0,0,7)),OFFSET(Key,1,0)=Key)
format condition formula: =AND(IsSelKey,B2=Key)
```

The num lock key has two special conditions, formatted white for on and black with white font for off. This only applies for the dual-function number pad keys which are never way 1, so require a single record.

```
"on" condition =AND(IsSelFunc,Numlock="on",ISBLANK(OFFSET(Key,1,0)))
"off" condition =AND(IsSelFunc,Numlock="off",ISBLANK(OFFSET(Key,1,0)))
```

Now to practice! Try this: scroll the Function slicer to find "select: objects", click it, then execute the highlighted key combination (Ctrl+Alt+5). This should select the Area slicer. With a watchful eye on the slicer features – the slicer edge, the multi-select button, the unfilter button, the button area – hit Tab repeatedly to see how the focus moves. Keep going until you're on the Function slicer with the focus on a function button. Use arrow keys to move the focus, and space or enter to select other buttons.

If you still prefer the mouse, note that to use the scroll wheel to scroll up and down the Function slicer, first select the slicer. Clicking a button in the slicer or dragging the scroll bar does not select the slicer. Click somewhere on the header or edge of the slicer. When the whole thing is outlined with a white border it is selected, and you can scroll the buttons. When you use mouse click to select buttons, use Ctrl+click to unselect.

When using slicers or any filters, remember to unfilter all or level by level. If you select Area → Function → Way, then unfilter in reverse. Unfilter Way before selecting another Function, and unfilter Function before selecting another Area. Also, whenever you update the source table you need to refresh, which you can do either from the pivot or the slicers.

Watch out if you are using tab and arrow key navigation in the slicers, that some of the actual functions won't work as long as the focus is on the slicer. Hit Esc to return focus to the sheet if this happens.

For a clean screen I hide the table and the pivot. These are initial setup, rarely edited, and would detract from the appearance. There are various ways to hide data or parts of a workbook. Here grouped columns make the most sense.

The table and the pivot each have seven columns and are separated by a small blank column. Practicing keyboard skills, I select the seven full-worksheet columns covering first the table then the pivot, and hit Alt+Shift+→ to create a group. Then, Data → Outline → Settings → uncheck "Summary columns to right of detail". Finally, I collapse the groups, and hit Ctrl+8 to hide the outline symbol.

By hiding the + group symbol, I regain about two rows of space and remove clutter. The groups can easily be opened and closed multiple ways, as shown in the section on Grouping in Chapter 3 Formatting section.

To identify the group header, I usually use a single letter or symbol. Here I use P for pivot and T for table, which are revealed only when the help is turned on.

Help is provided in several grouped cells in row 1 that each contain a single word with a Data Validation input message explaining the topic. The cells are hidden until the "Show Help" check box is set. When help is turned on, each grouped cell is made to appear like a button with gradient fill. When help is turned off, the information is still there, but only the check box is visible on the sheet.

Ribbon KeyTips

Figure 2: KeyTips

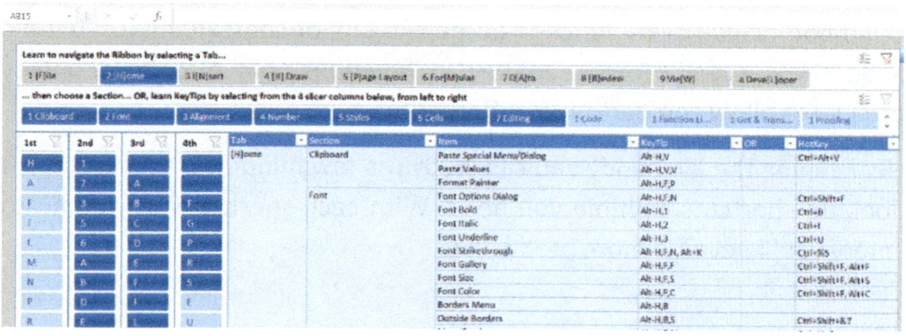

Ribbon KeyTips are too numerous to include in the keyboard simulator, and are worthy of their own training tool. The KeyTips sheet does not have a graphic model, but otherwise has similar structure to the KeyBoard sheet. It starts with a table and ends with a pivot controlled by several slicers. Without graphic, the pivot itself is the output, and only the table is hidden.

In place of a graphic ribbon, the main slicer at the top of the sheet is horizontal, simulating the main tabs. It is sized to avoid tab name truncation and to avoid a scroll bar, and the setting "Show items with no data last" is cleared so the buttons remain in constant position. Each tab is prefixed for sorting, and its KeyTip is enclosed in square brackets, as in "2 [H]ome".

The second slicer contains the tab sections. These are also prefixed for sorting, but have no KeyTip. The setting "Show items with no data last" is set so that as a tab button is selected, the sections for that tab are shown appropriately. The most sections on a tab is eleven on the Insert tab, so the slicer is set with eleven columns.

The table lists every tab, section and function in the ribbon with the KeyTip sequence. The KeyTips are then separated out into four columns of single characters, KT1 to KT4, which appear in sequenced slicers, like a KeyTip spelling primer. Finally there are two columns for alternate methods, one for a second KeyTip and one for a keyboard shortcut. For example, the ribbon sequence for outside borders is Home, Borders, Outside; the KeyTip is thus Alt-H,B,S, and the shortcut is Ctrl+Shift+7.

The four vertical slicers are narrow, with no room for the heading. To label them 1st through 4th, I use small shapes overlaying the headers but not covering the Clear Filter buttons. Then, to lock the labels in place I protect the sheet, with Use PivotTable checked, allowing the slicers to work.

I did not include every function in the File tab, or contextual tabs, but did include some specific extended KeyTip functions that also have hotkey shortcuts, to allow comparison of different methods.

By keeping the file handy you can study it a few minutes a day, and use it to look up shortcuts anytime you need. With each shortcut you commit to memory you'll become more productive.

Chapter 6: Gantt Chart

Figure 3: Gantt Chart

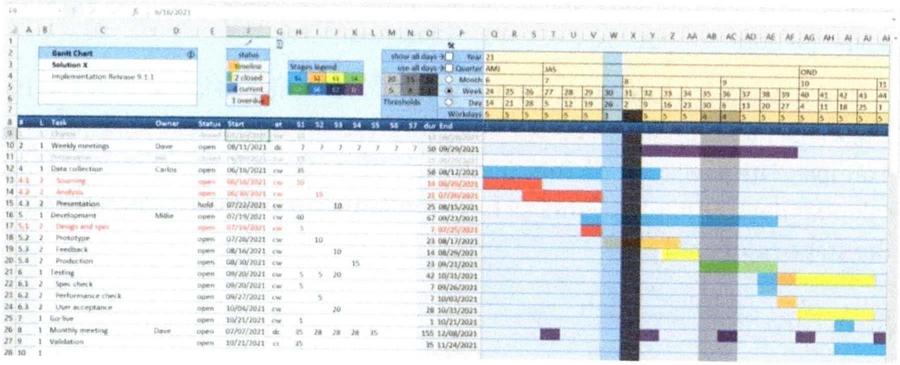

Purpose

A Gantt chart is a common tool for managing project tasks and milestones. If you're familiar with Gantt charts you might ask, "why another Gantt?" Certainly if you use MS Project or similar tool you don't need to build one in Excel. If your need is occasional and simple, there are plenty of nifty Gantt templates to choose from. This project incorporates the Calendar sheet from the Startup File project, and introduces some uncommon features that serve to illustrate some advanced date and format techniques.

- **Capacity**: set custom work week, holidays and other down days
- **Zoom**: four column bucket options, from day to month
- **Stages**: up to seven sequential stages in different colors
- **Events**: up to seven discrete instances per repeating task

Failure to plan capacity is the downfall of many projects. Of course, many wise managers will build in additional time to account for peak holidays and probable vacation periods. For a day or two here and there it is close enough, but having a clear list of non-working dates adds transparency. Custom down days and weekly patterns support unique project scenarios. Duration is set in either workdays or calendar days per task.

Zoom enables the manager to adjust to the audience, with daily bucket detail for weekly team meetings, and weekly or monthly bucket overview for management review.

Stages allow for sequential related tasks on a single row, in up to seven different colors. An example is a change release, with multiple changes going through standard stages of design, build, test, pilot, rollout and validation. Listing each stage for each change as separate rows would take a lot of space, while not adding value.

Discrete events such as monthly reviews can be entered like stages, but the length is the separation between events rather than their duration. For example, Nth weekday of the month can be separated by either 28 or 35 calendar days. Discrete events all have the same color which is different from the stage colors.

Structure

The structure of a Gantt is a transposed calendar with a horizontal time scale. The vertical dimension comprises the tasks of the project, which appear in the timescale columns as bars, the width of duration. They are listed in more or less chronological order, so that the bars appear like a somewhat uneven staircase going diagonally down from top left to bottom right.

A common challenge of project management is the scale of the time dimension. The granularity of daily columns support detailed task management, but often need to be manually converted to weeks or months to provide the full horizon view to management. This Gantt makes that conversion with the click of an option button to select month, week or day periods.

The task list is formatted as a table named Project, convenient for insertion, deletion and extension of rows, and for referencing. There are three calculated columns, and many more named formulas that reference the table. The graphic side of the table has no contents, it is only formatting, for which the calculation is performed via names.

Period Headers

The time column headers are six rows not including the table header. The period is represented in five units; Year, Quarter, Month, Week and Day. The sixth row serves two purposes. With Day columns, it gives the weekday number, counting from 1=Monday. With Week or Month columns, it gives the number of workdays in the period.

The Day row of the header calculates the date from which the other rows are calculated. The period size selected is represented by an index number 1 to 4; 1 =calendar days, 2 =workdays, 3 =weeks, 4 =months. PerAll is a checkbox to "show all days", and PerOpt is the linked cell of the 3-button option group: Month (1), Week (2), Day (3).

```
PerIndex =IF(AND(PerAll,PerOpt=3),1,5-PerOpt)
```

The date is one formula for the first period, and another for all the other periods. The first column indexes to the first day of the period in which the project starts.

```
PerDate =IF(ISTEXT(Left),PerFirst,PerRest)
PerFirst =CHOOSE(PerIndex,ProjectStart,ProjectStart,ProjectStart-
    WEEKDAY(ProjectStart,WdType)+1,
    DATE(YEAR(ProjectStart),MONTH(ProjectStart),1))
```

The other columns use a relative name Left =the cell to the left, similar to how I have used Above in vertical tables. Uncon is another checkbox to "use all days", to see the unconstrained schedule. WkString and Days[OffDays] are from Calendar.

```
PerRest =CHOOSE(PerIndex, Left+1,WORKDAY.INTL(Left,1,
    IF(Uncon,"0000000",Wkstring),
    IF(Uncon,0,Days[OffDays])),Left+7,EDATE(Left,1))
```

The Workdays formula returns weekday for Day bucket (PerIndex 1 or 2), and workdays for Week or Month bucket. This uses NETWORKDAYS.INTL from PerThis (this column's date) to PerNext (next column's date). The IF(PerNext statement accounts for the last column not having any PerNext value by making an equal jump from PerPrev (previous column's date).

```
Workdays =IF(PerIndex<3,WEEKDAY(PerThis,WdType),
    NETWORKDAYS.INTL(PerThis,IF(PerNext,PerNext,PerThis+(PerThis-
    PerPrev))-1,IF(Uncon,"0000000",Wkstring), IF(Uncon,0,Days[OffDays])))
```

Configuration

Configuration of holidays, other down days, week pattern and date format is done in the Calendar Sheet, which is copied from the Startup project. Dates with a "count" checkbox apply here as different ways to maintain project downtime. That includes date ranges, date list, and calculated or entered holidays.

Calendar highlights each date type differently and can be used to document the down periods, while the project schedule simply considers them all equally down, if their "count" checkbox is set, corresponding to Calendar's Buckets table count of workdays.

Date format is the combination of date order and date separator settings. Work week selection is one of seven 5-day weeks, or a custom string of seven binary digits to define working and non-working days. These are described in more detail in Chapter 4 Startup.

The Plan sheet has two areas of configuration, the first is the stage legend. This is simply a range of small cells numbered S1 to S7, plus D for discrete, where each cell is the color of the stage on the chart. Stages are optional and work best for well-known stages that can be described by acronym or abbreviation. By assigning a different color to each stage, the chart conveys information graphically without the need for explanation. The legend is a shorthand reference; the cells are in small font and limited to four characters.

The second Plan sheet configuration is capacity thresholds. These apply to week and month buckets, when selected, to shade in three levels of gray those buckets with limited capacity. For example, a week with fewer than five workdays is lightly-shaded; fewer than four, medium shaded; fewer than one (full week down), dark shaded.

Shading of low-capacity buckets alerts the manager and team that there can be even lower capacity, if members take vacation when the work schedule is already short. These thresholds can be customized and are for display only. Scheduling of task end dates takes down days into consideration based on other settings.

Inputs

The first input is the project title, with some additional space provided for descriptive notes. These cells are white and lined, like a notepad. The cells just to the right of these input cells have an apostrophe character. This is invisible, yet occupies the cell so that text does not spill outside the input range.

The table of tasks has thirteen input columns. The first four columns are about the task; level, description, owner and status. Level [L] is a choice of 1 =main task or 2 =sub-task. A sub-task adds a decimal to the calculated task number, and highlights the chart with stripes. The decimal is added using the formula from the Startup Outline, and is limited to nine sub-tasks per task.

```
Task # =IF([@L],ROUNDDOWN(N(Above)+POWER(10,1-[@L]),[@L]-1),"")
```

Description and owner are free text, and status is a picklist of open, hold, and closed. Hold and closed turn the row gray, and closed turns the font a darker gray, still legible but different from hold.

The remaining nine columns are about the scheduling of the task, beginning with the start date, followed by a picklist column of indicators, labeled "et" for event type, then seven duration columns.

Column [et] combines two indicators; one to select continuous or discrete event, the other to select workday input or calendar day input.

Table 38: Gantt event type and input type

et	Event type	Input type	Days of
cw	Continuous	Workdays	Duration
cc	Continuous	Calendar days	Duration
dw	Discrete	Workdays	Separation
dc	Discrete	Calendar days	Separation

Data Validation limits the entries and provides the picklist, but does not require an entry. If [et] is not filled, the default is cw = continuous in workdays. Most tasks will be defined in workdays, otherwise defining non-workdays is pointless. The default is set by IF:

```
TypeDay =IF(RIGHT(Project[@et],1)="c","c","w")
TypeEvent =IF(LEFT(Project[@et],1)="d","d","c")
```

A common use for calendar day input is for discrete events that occur on the same weekday every so many weeks, with the days entered as multiples of 7. It is important to choose [et] carefully for the intended effect and to avoid confusion.

Of the remaining seven columns, one of them must contain a duration for a continuous event to show on the chart. Normally a stand-alone task is entered in S1, but any of S1 to S7 can be used. The task can thus be given a different color by entering its duration in a different column. A task with two stages can be entered in any two columns, etc. However, if colors correspond to particular activities, then the same columns should be used for all tasks that share those activities.

With continuous stages, S1 is the duration of stage 1, S2 is the duration of stage 2, etc. With discrete events, the first one is on the start date, the second is S1 days later. Thus there can be eight discrete events on a single row, or a single event with no entries in S1 to S7. Discrete events are all the same color, so there is no reason not to use columns S1 to S7 from left to right.

The primary fields of a task record are description, start date and duration, and the chart will begin to form with nothing else. Understanding and using the nuances of stages, continuous vs. discrete events and workday vs. calendar day entry can be learned and adopted over time.

True project management software includes relationships between tasks. This is out of scope for this Gantt, other than the implicit finish/start relationship between stages. Relationship between tasks is by manual maintenance of successor start dates.

Controls

In addition to the task inputs, there are three controls; two checkboxes, and counting a three-button option group as one control. These are all aligned in a vertical stack just to the left of the period headers, above the End column. The linked cells are hidden within plain sight in the header.

The first checkbox "show all days" is relevant only when the Day bucket is selected; it displays down days with dark shading, otherwise, only workdays are displayed. The second checkbox "use all days", turns off down days and shows what an unconstrained schedule would look like. This answers the question, "what if we work through weekends and holidays?" to give the earliest possible end date of tasks. This is meant to be a quick look, not a tactic. The strategy is to maintain realistic durations and downtimes, with tactical compromises.

The option group has three buttons lined up with the three buckets, Month, Week and Day. Changing the selection has the effect to expand or collapse the periods. With workdays display, that is, Day without "show all days", there is no column shading because all columns are workdays. With Week or Month, shading takes effect once the low-capacity thresholds are crossed.

When period columns collapse into a larger bucket, the cell displays the stage color in effect at the end of the bucket. Stages that occur within the bucket are lost. This is the natural effect of zooming out.

Formatting

Use of Conditional Formatting here is unique in that there is no data in the chart cells. The chart appears to have colored shapes, which are cells formatted by the intersection of task and period data. Good Name Manager practices of naming convention and documentation is important to establish and audit the logic.

The logic must reference the stage milestone dates from the row and compare them to the period dates based on whichever bucket is selected. To accomplish this, relative names are defined for the current column period, PerThis, and the next column period, PerNext.

Stage Start

First, the task row's milestone dates must be determined. The start date of each stage is required for both continuous and discrete events. Stage 1 begins on the manually-input task start date, and each successive stage's start is offset from there by the previous stages' duration.

```
TaskStart =Project[@Start]
TaskStartStage2 =WORKDAY.INTL(Project[@Start],Project[@S1],
    IF(OR(Uncon,TypeDay="c"),"0000000",Wkstring),
    IF(OR(Uncon,TypeDay="c"),0,Days[OffDays]))
```

Each stage accumulates previous stages, replacing Project[@S1] with SUM(Project[@[S1]:[S2]]), etc., and the last stage has an end date.

```
TaskEnd =IF(Project[@Start],WORKDAY.INTL(Project[@Start],
    SUM(Project[@[S1]:[S7]]),IF(OR(Uncon,TypeDay="c"),"0000000",
    Wkstring),IF(OR(Uncon,TypeDay="c"),0,Days[OffDays]))-
    IF(TypeEvent="d",0,1),"")
```

Continuous Stages

For continuous stages, the condition to highlight the stage must be true for the duration of the stage, that is, until the next stage starts. Stage 1 to 7 each has a Boolean formula to turn on its color. The condition relies on the intersection of two date inequalities.

The first inequality is when the next column period's start date, PerNext, is greater than the start date of the row's current or "nth" stage, TaskStartStage"n". That means that "stage n has begun". The first column that meets this condition is the stage start period, and the stage continues as long as the next condition is true.

The second inequality is when the current column period's start date, PerThis, is less than the start date of the row's next or "nth+1" stage, TaskStartStage"n+1". That means that "stage n has not ended", or more accurately, "stage n+1 has not begun".

The intersection of these two inequalities is where "stage n has begun and stage n+1 has not begun", which is the duration of stage n.

Two more criteria are added to the condition: that [Sn] is not blank or 0, and that [et] is set as a continuous event type. The final stage uses the task end date to turn off the condition.

```
ContinuousStage1 =AND(PerNext>TaskStart,
    PerThis<TaskStartStage2,Project[@S1]>0,TypeEvent="c")
ContinuousStage2 =AND(PerNext>TaskStartStage2,
    PerThis<TaskStartStage3,Project[@S2]>0,TypeEvent="c")
...
ContinuousStage7 =AND(PerNext>TaskStartStage7,
    PerThis<=Project[@End],Project[@S7]>0,TypeEvent="c")
```

Discrete Events

For discrete events, the condition to highlight the chart must be true for a single period at a time, requiring a change to the logic. The first inequality is the same as "stage n has begun". The second inequality is when the current column period's start date, PerThis, is now less than or equal to the start date of the row's current or "nth" stage, TaskStartStage"n". There is no reference to the next, "n+1" stage. The condition thus means that the discrete event date occurs within the current period.

There are eight discrete event formulas, each with the two inequalities and the [et] discrete event criteria. For the chart, all discrete events are the same format, so a single formula combines the eight instances into one with OR.

```
DiscreteEvent1 =AND(PerNext>TaskStart,
      PerThis<=TaskStart,TypeEvent="d")
DiscreteEvent2 =AND(PerNext>TaskStartStage2,
      PerThis<=TaskStartStage2,TypeEvent="d")
...
DiscreteEvent8 =AND(PerNext>TaskEnd+1,
      PerThis<=TaskEnd,TypeEvent="d")
DiscreteEvent =OR(DiscreteEvent1,DiscreteEvent2,...,DiscreteEvent8)
```

Other Formatting

The stages and events described above set cell formats. There are also full-row and full-column formats.

Column formats have five conditions in two types. The first type is the gray shading based on Month and Week capacity thresholds, as described in Configuration, with three levels from light gray to dark gray. The configuration cells are named like CT.. for capacity threshold. The formulas use PerIndex and are entered directly in Conditional Formatting. The dark formula also shades down days, when calendar days are displayed (Day with “show all days”).

```
Dark =CHOOSE(PerIndex,DownDay,0,PerDays<CTWk3,PerDays<CTMo3)
Medium =CHOOSE(PerIndex,0,0,PerDays<CTWk2,PerDays<CTMo2)
Light =CHOOSE(PerIndex,0,0,PerDays<CTWk1,PerDays<CTMo1)
```

These shades are patterns, so they can overlap and not obscure the task formats. They extend from the Weekday / Workdays row down all table rows.

The second type of column format is to show two key milestones, the current period and the project end. These use similar criteria to the discrete events, and set a light pattern blue for now and green for end. Vertical bars extend from Year through all period header rows and down the table rows. These two indicators are like goalposts showing the zone of action and what work remains to be done or caught up.

```
FormatEnd =AND(PerThis<=ProjectEnd,PerNext>ProjectEnd)
FormatNow =AND(PerThis<=TODAY(),PerNext>TODAY())
```

Row formats have several conditions. Some are applied across the entire table, some are separated between the text columns and the chart columns.

The first is for subtasks, which can be identified by level =2, or by =MOD(Project[@['#']],1). The task description is indented, and the chart is striped. Second, [Status] flags two formats that apply across the whole table. Status "hold" and "closed" both set the fill color gray, "closed" also sets the font gray. Finally, the implicit status "overdue" is determined and flags the row.

For text columns, if the status is not closed and the end date is in the past, all columns are set red font.

```
TaskLateText =AND(Project[@Status] <>"closed",Project[@End]<TODAY())
```

For the chart, the entire task, all stages are filled red.

```
TaskLateChart =AND(Project[@Status]<>"closed",
    Project[@Start]<PerNext,Project[@End]>=PerThis,
    Project[@End]<TODAY(),Project[@dur]>0)
```

Monitoring

Monitoring project progress is the whole point of having a Gantt Chart. The intent is to expose schedule status, delays and risks, and to support proactive adjustments to stay on track, or reactions to get back on track or to "recalculate" the plan.

The header has a status pane with four cells, each with a different color Data Bar format. At a glance these give a high-level view of where the project stands.

The first is the current date, displayed as “timeline”, with the Data Bar min and max set by the formula option to the project start and end dates. This is simply a progress bar of how far along the timeline the project is.

The second status cell has the number of closed tasks, =COUNTIF(Project [Status],"closed"). The Data Bar max is the count of all tasks with duration>0.

Third, current tasks are counted, defined as status=open, start before today, and end after today. These are the tasks that need to be worked on now. This bar’s max is the count of open tasks only.

```
Current tasks =COUNTIFS(Project[Start],"<"&TODAY(),
    Project[End],">"&TODAY(),Project[Status],"open")
```

The fourth status bar is tasks that are overdue, that is, in the past and still open. This bar is red, and goes from right to left, opposite the others for emphasis. The max is the count of open tasks.

```
Overdue tasks =COUNTIFS(Project[End],"<"&TODAY(),
    Project[Status],"open")
```

Maintaining overdue tasks is fundamental. If the task is completed, the status should be closed. If not, the end date should be rescheduled to a realistic date by extending the duration.

Some Gantt templates include a % complete, but in real life I have not seen that used. Some people manage their tasks fairly evenly, others wait until the day before they’re due.

Project management is part science and part politics. It involves teasing out information and influencing behavior to accomplish the objective. The Gantt provides the transparent tool for the manager to monitor the big picture and “make the rounds” to get the details – “We have two weeks left in stage 3 of task xyz. How’s it going? Any help needed?” The successful manager is one who can convince members to be truthful, even when the obstacle is self-imposed.

Chapter 7: Team Calendar

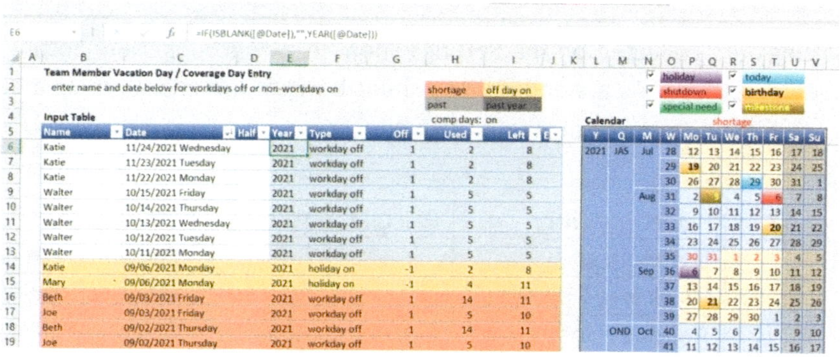

E6 =IF(ISBLANK([@Date]),"",YEAR([@Date]))

Team Member Vacation Day / Coverage Day Entry

enter name and date below for workdays off or non-workdays on

shortage | off day on | past | past year

comp days: on

Input Table

Name	Date	Half	Year	Type	Off	Used	Left
Katie	11/24/2021 Wednesday		2021	workday off	1	2	8
Katie	11/23/2021 Tuesday		2021	workday off	1	2	8
Katie	11/22/2021 Monday		2021	workday off	1	2	8
Walter	10/15/2021 Friday		2021	workday off	1	5	5
Walter	10/14/2021 Thursday		2021	workday off	1	5	5
Walter	10/13/2021 Wednesday		2021	workday off	1	5	5
Walter	10/12/2021 Tuesday		2021	workday off	1	5	5
Walter	10/11/2021 Monday		2021	workday off	1	5	5
Katie	09/06/2021 Monday		2021	holiday on	-1	2	8
Mary	09/06/2021 Monday		2021	holiday on	-1	4	11
Beth	09/03/2021 Friday		2021	workday off	1	14	11
Joe	09/03/2021 Friday		2021	workday off	1	5	10
Beth	09/02/2021 Thursday		2021	workday off	1	14	11
Joe	09/02/2021 Thursday		2021	workday off	1	5	10

holiday | shutdown | special need | today | birthday | milestone

Calendar shortage

Y	Q	M	W	Mo	Tu	We	Th	Fr	Sa	Su
2021	JAS	Jul	28	12	13	14	15	16	17	18
			29	19	20	21	22	23	24	25
			30	26	27	28	29	30	31	1
		Aug	31	2	3	4	5	6	7	8
			32	9	10	11	12	13	14	15
			33	16	17	18	19	20	21	22
			34	23	24	25	26	27	28	29
			35	30	31	1	2	3	4	5
		Sep	36	6	7	8	9	10	11	12
			37	13	14	15	16	17	18	19
			38	20	21	22	23	24	25	26
			39	27	28	29	30	1	2	3
	OND	Oct	40	4	5	6	7	8	9	10
			41	11	12	13	14	15	16	17

Purpose

There are several reasons for having a robust team calendar. HR usually provides either formal or informal team calendars to ensure that managers are accountable for their team's vacation entitlements. Managers also have a need to manage staffing around peak demand periods, and the "hockey stick" effect of end-of-year vacations.

For capacity, we are concerned with routine work that requires a certain level of staffing to operate machines, answer phones, etc. There may also be special needs to cover weekends and holidays, or promotional periods when full staffing is required. Finally, there might be occasional shutdowns that are considered mandatory vacation days. The manager should have control of such events, and visibility to staffing shortages.

This should be a transparent, interactive tool for team members to enter their vacation days, sign up for non-workday coverage, and track their own balance. It must also serve the manager to track individual and overall team days off and coverage requirements.

Structure

There are four sheets, each with a purpose; Input for member entry of vacation and coverage days, Report for management tracking of staffing needs and coverage, Analysis for pivot-chart views of member and team days, and Settings for configuration. The Startup File Calendar is not copied in, but several elements of it are reapplied. For these I will briefly describe them here, refer to the Startup Calendar for detail.

Settings

Settings are collected on the Settings sheet in two groups, Date Settings and Team Settings. As a standard, the sheet background and all calculated cells are shaded, so only entry cells are white.

Table 39: Team Calendar Settings

Section	Selection/entry	Calculated result	Where used
Date Settings	Date format		Full date cells
	Work week pattern		Input, Report, Calendar, Special
	Holiday rules	Calculated holidays	
	Manual holidays		
Team Settings	Controls		Input, Report
	Vacation policy	Milestone anniversaries, vacation days granted	Team
	Team members and dates		Input, Calendar

Calculated holidays and vacation day entitlements are given for the current plus the next four years.

Date Settings

Date settings are mostly one-time setup. There are two column groups to hide them when not in use. The first column group includes individual selection cells, followed by three stacked tables, all with the same number of columns to enable insertion and deletion of rows. These are HolidayRules, HolidayCalc and HolidayInput.

The second column group contains the Weeks table, which is a static lookup table used for workday selection and formulas.

Date Format (see Startup Calendar Date Format)

Date format is set by two indicators, DateOrder and DateSeparator. DateOrder is one of {dmy,mdy,ymd} and DateSeparator is one of {.,/,-}. The nine possible formats are applied to all full dates.

Work Week (see Startup Calendar Work Week)

Work week is selected from the Weeks lookup table. A standard five-day work week can start any day of the week, or a custom weekly pattern can be defined. Whether standard or custom, the week is defined by the seven-binary-digit string format used in international workday functions. This string is then dissected to find out if the reference date is on a weekend.

```
(is a weekend) = ... VALUE(MID(WkString,WEEKDAY([@date],2),1)) ...
```

This can be used as a date type index (1=weekend) or as a Boolean (is weekend).

Holidays (see Startup Calendar Holidays)

Holidays can be calculated from rules, or entered in a table, or both. Manually entered holidays must be entered for each year. Then a holiday is identified if the reference date exists in either the HolidayCalc table or the HolidayInput table, here as example applied to the Report table:

```
(is a holiday) = OR(COUNTIF(HolidayInput[date],
    Report[@date]),COUNTIF(HolidayCalc[date],Report[@date]))
```

Now with Booleans for both weekend and holiday, they are combined in a date type formula for each table.

```
Date Type (general form): =IF(is a weekend, 1, IF(is a holiday, 2, 0))
```

Date Type then evaluates as a Boolean itself, "is a non-workday", and also +1 as an index for CHOOSE.

```
Boolean example =IF(OR(DateTypeReport,ScheduleShutdown),0,StaffMin)
Index example =CHOOSE(DateTypeReport+1,
    "workday","weekend","holiday")
```

Holiday tables have error checking that flags the unlikely condition that a holiday falls on a weekend. This can occur during configuration when changing week or holiday selections, but once they are set up correctly will not recur. It is a matter of principle to alert the user of any error that can occur based on their input.

Team Settings

Controls

The first group of team settings is a set of management controls. The term "controls" is used here in its general sense; there is only one checkbox as an actual "form control".

Table 40: Team Calendar Controls

Label	Cell name	Validation
Alert start	AlertStart	Jan,Feb,Mar,etc.
Alert level	AlertLevel	1% to 99%
Comp days	CompDays	Checkbox
Min staff	MinStaff	1% to 99%

Alert start and alert level work together to flag the risk of low vacation usage. Report[Used] is the % days taken of days entitled for the team as a whole. If vacation usage is on track, the value will approach 100%. If it is low, there is risk of an end-of-year spike, which should prompt the manager to remind members to take their vacation. The result of these settings is presented in the Report table section.

The third control setting is for comp days. If a member works on a weekend or holiday, comp days means they are compensated with a day of vacation. This setting is displayed on the Input sheet and is used in the calculation of days taken and remaining, making it transparent to the user.

The fourth control cell MinStaff is to set a minimum staff level as a percent of the total roster. A certain percentage of the team is expected to be off work at any time. To allow for such normal absences, MinStaff sets the level below which the manager is alerted of a shortage. This can occur due to special requirements or due to vacations.

Vacation Policy

The policy table is two columns for years of service and vacation days granted. Some years do not change the days granted, but are used to define milestone anniversaries. For clarity, [Service] is formatted 0" y", and [Days] is formatted 0" d".

Team Table

Figure 4: Team Table

	new	future	leaving											
Team Milestones and Vacation Days				Milestone		Now		2021			2022	2023	2024	2025
Name	**Birthday**	**Start**	**End**	**Anniv**	**Next**	**Service**	**Days**	**Add**	**Yr0**	**Left**	**Yr1**	**Yr2**	**Yr3**	**Yr4**
new hire		03/01/23				-2 y	0 d		0 d	0 d	0 d	5 d	10 d	10 d
new hire		06/01/21		06/01/22	1 y	0 y	5 d		5 d	5 d	10 d	10 d	10 d	10 d
Beth	01/13/77	08/03/01		08/03/21	20 y	20 y	25 d		25 d	11 d	25 d	25 d	25 d	25 d
Bob	02/14/95	06/11/20		06/11/25	5 y	1 y	10 d		10 d	6 d	10 d	10 d	10 d	10 d
Jane	08/20/80	06/14/04		06/14/24	20 y	17 y	20 d		20 d	13 d	20 d	20 d	25 d	25 d
Joe	03/15/85	03/05/10		03/05/25	15 y	11 y	15 d		15 d	10 d	15 d	15 d	15 d	20 d
Juanita	09/21/97	10/01/17		10/01/22	5 y	4 y	10 d		10 d	9 d	10 d	10 d	10 d	10 d
Katie	05/17/95	05/09/18		05/09/23	5 y	3 y	10 d		10 d	8 d	10 d	10 d	10 d	10 d
Mary	04/16/90	06/17/11		06/17/26	15 y	10 y	15 d		15 d	11 d	15 d	15 d	15 d	15 d
Paul	06/18/66	07/01/90	12/31/21	07/01/25	35 y	31 y	30 d	5 d	35 d	19 d	0 d	0 d	0 d	0 d
Walter	07/19/90	09/03/13		09/03/23	10 y	8 y	10 d		10 d	5 d	10 d	15 d	15 d	15 d
Total									**155 d**	**97 d**	**125 d**	**135 d**	**145 d**	**150 d**

The Team table serves two purposes. First, it gives the vacation days due each member, based on their start date and the policy. This is used to determine and track the usage of vacation days, at the member level in the Input table, and at the team level in the Report and Analysis sheets. The second purpose is to determine milestone anniversaries, and provide these and birthdays to the Calendar.

Inputs are Name, Birthday, Start date, and End date if known, such as a planned retirement date. Outputs are years of Service, now and at the Next milestone, the date of the next Milestone, and vacation days granted, this year (Yr0) and for the next four years.

```
[Service] =IF([@Start],ThisYear-YEAR([@Start]),"")
```

The policy is implicitly based on the calendar year in which the service milestone is reached, not full years. Days granted is then indexed to the policy.

The default MATCH type finds the largest Policy[Service] value which is less than or equal to the Team[@Service] years, which returns the days granted.

```
[Days] = IFERROR(IF(AND([@End]>0,ThisYear>YEAR([@End])),0,
   INDEX(Policy[Days],MATCH([@Service],Policy[Service]))),0)
```

Another input column [Add] allows adjustment for carry-over days, which are added to the current year.

```
[Yr0] = [@Days]+[@Add]
```

The five-year horizon is for planning purposes. Table headings cannot be formulas, so above the column headings Yr0, Yr1, etc. are the actual years, hybrid C$R name VacYear. For each future year, as members reach a new milestone, their days granted are indexed to the policy. If [@End] is given, there are no more days due as of the year after that.

```
[Yr1], [Yr2], etc. =IFERROR(IF(AND([@End]>0,VacYear>YEAR([@End])),0,
     INDEX(Policy[Days],MATCH(VacYear-
     YEAR([@Start]),Policy[Service]))),0)
```

The next milestone years of service uses exact MATCH to find if a milestone occurs this year, then adds 1 row if it has already passed. If this is not a milestone year for the member, exact match will return #NA. In that case, the default “less than” MATCH type is used as with Grant, and adds 1 row to get the next milestone row.

```
[Next] =IFERROR(INDEX(Policy[Service],
     IFNA(MATCH([@Service],Policy[Service],0)+IF(StartMDD<
     TodayMDD,1,0),MATCH([@Service],Policy[Service])+1)),"")
```

StartMDD and TodayMDD are defined in Name Manager as =100*MONTH(date)+DAY(date), to determine if a date in the current year has passed yet. This logic is also used in the Startup File.

Finally, the date of the next milestone is determined for display on the Calendar.

```
[Anniv] =IFERROR(EDATE([@Start],12*[@Next]),"")
```

Member exits are highlighted in red fill. New hires can be entered as placeholders with future start dates. These are highlighted in two fill colors, green for the current year, as imminent or recent hire, and blue for future years. The future vacation days are calculated based on the start year entered.

Lastly, to the right of the Team table is a single hidden column, with a single formula in the cell named Active. This will provide the list of active members to the Input sheet, filtering out any future placeholders.

```
Active =FILTER(Team[Name],Team[Start]<=TODAY()).
```

Input Sheet

The Input sheet is the retail shelf of the tool, where the team members interact with it. The Input table has three data entry columns, each with an Input Message. Calculated columns give feedback to the user and feed the Report table. Error checking and Conditional Formatting are applied. To the right of the table is copy of the Calendar from the Report sheet.

Input Columns

Required entries are minimal, just Name and Date. Name is a Data Validation list using the source **=Active#**, which returns the spilled array from the FILTER formula above. Note, for the list to reject invalid names, there cannot be any blank names in the Team table.

Date is as described above; entry format is per computer setting, display format is per DateOrder and DateSeparator settings as one-time settings. If the team members are in different countries with different conventions, take care to avoid confusion.

The third entry column is optional, to enter a half day. Lower case **x** cuts the day in half. The implicit policy is that half day is the smallest increment for days off.

Calculated Columns

There are six calculated columns; two are for process control, four give user feedback. Except for [E] for error tracking, each formula begins by displaying blank until a date is entered. This is a way of being kind to the user.

```
=IF(ISBLANK([@date]),"", etc.
```

[Year] of course can be derived from [Date], but is explicitly displayed as the basis for vacation tracking. If someone begins entering vacation for next year, it is tracked against next year's vacation.

```
[Year] =IF(ISBLANK([@Date]),"",YEAR([@Date]))
```

[Off] is not helpful in itself, but exposes the key input to [Used] and to the Report[Have] column. It is the product of two conditions. First, DateTypeInput is the Input table's version of the DateType logic discussed above, resulting in 0 (FALSE) for workdays and >0 (TRUE) for non-workdays, specifically 1 for weekend and 2 for holiday. The first IF statement assigns -1 to non-workdays and +1 to workdays. The second condition is to allow half-day increments. Any entry in [Half] multiplies the first conditional result by 0.5.

```
[Off] = IF(DateTypeInput,-1,1)*IF(ISBLANK([@Half]),1,0.5)
```

Remaining columns give feedback to the user. [Type] displays the date type of the entry, and helps clarify the +/- value of [Off] by adding "off" or "on".

```
[Type] =IF(ISBLANK([@Date]),"",CHOOSE(DateTypeInput+1,"workday
    off","weekend on","holiday on"))
```

[Used] calculates how many days have already been recorded for the member for the [Year]. The first step sums the positive [Off] days. The second step adds the sum of negative [Off] days, if CompDays is enabled.

If CompDays are enabled, the day is subtracted (the -1 day is added) from Input[@Used], for tracking the individual's days, and from Report[Used], for tracking team usage. If CompDays are disabled, there is no effect on usage.

```
[Used] =IF(ISBLANK([@Date]),"",SUMIFS([Off],[Off],">0",
    [Name],[@Name],[Year],[@Year])+IF(CompDays,
    SUMIFS([Off],[Off],"<0",[Name],[@Name],[Year],[@Year]),0))
```

If CompDays are disabled as a policy yet certain individuals are due comp days, the Team[Add] column can be used to adjust the days per member for the current year.

[Left] finds the days due the member for the input year and subtracts [Used]. Here INDEX looks in the full table for MATCH on both row and column. VacationYears is the range one row above the Team table headers that contains the actual years.

```
[Left] =IF(ISBLANK([@Date]),"",IFNA(INDEX(Team,MATCH([@Name],
    Team[Name],0),MATCH([@Year],VacationYears,0))-[@Used],""))
```

Error Tracking

Possible errors are not always obvious while building the tool, but hopefully are exposed as you begin to use it. Here I track three types of error; date with no name, duplicate entry, and days over policy (negative [@Left]).

Data Validation is a great way to prevent errors and give helpful feedback. It might not be the most practical method to trap every error. For example, some errors are based on the combination of two fields. This is worth a brief elucidation.

How would you trap a duplicate entry? In a single column, duplicate entries can be prevented by Data Validation rule. In this example, the value in each column must be unique. The same value can exist in the column A range and the column B range, but not within the same column.

```
Allow: Custom
Formula: =COUNTIF(relative column range,relative cell)=1
Example: =COUNTIF(A$2:B$21,A2)=1
```

Here, a duplicate Input record is when two rows have the same name and the same date. Theoretically, this could be checked with COUNTIF, by concatenating the two columns into one, or by COUNTIFS, as shown below. This can become a messy point to design around, and to get the table and Data Validation to play well together.

The method I use here is the "traffic cop": let the offense occur, identify it by formula, and expose it to the user on the sheet. I use the small column [E] to flag errors, assigning them each a number:

1. Name is blank and Date is not
2. Name and Date are duplicated
3. [@Left]<0.

```
[E] =IF(AND(ISBLANK([@Name]),NOT(ISBLANK([@Date]))),1,
    IF(COUNTIFS([Name],[@Name],[Date],[@Date])>1,2,IF([@Left]<0,3,0)))
```

The column is formatted to hide zeroes (0;;). Conditional Formatting turns error rows red font, and a conditional message appears above the table, only for the current year. Two adjacent cells deliver the message in red font:

```
=IF(COUNTIFS(Input[E],">0",Input[Year],ThisYear),"Errors found:","")
=IF(COUNTIFS(Input[E],1,Input[Year],ThisYear),"Err 1: missing name;
    ","")&IF(COUNTIFS(Input[E],2,Input[Year],ThisYear),"Err 2: duplicates;
    ","")&IF(COUNTIFS(Input[E],3,Input[Year],ThisYear),"Err 3: over
    policy","")
```

This is a "soft validation" and is a reasonable and adequate solution for the need.

Conditional Formatting

Conditional Formatting is always a key element of elegant user feedback. Here, in addition to the nine date formatting conditions and the red font error condition, there are four conditions that set fill color for the entire row.

First, previous years are shaded dark gray, and past dates in the current year are lighter gray. Records must be kept until the year is closed out, that is, any days left at the end have been recorded as carryover days in the Team table. This is a January maintenance task.

Past dates should not be deleted until the year is closed out. At the end of the year, the manager and member align that all days due were taken, with comp days if relevant, or that there are unused days to carry over to the next year. Once all carry days are recorded, the old year's records can be deleted. They don't need to be, but they have no value once the new year has begun.

Then there are two user-relevant conditions.

When a member wants to take a vacation, it may be approved or denied based on the needs of the team. This feedback of possible denial is given immediately. When the manager diligently maintains staffing requirements, then as vacation requests are entered, the Report table determines which days will be short-staffed. This condition then shades the Input rows for those dates, and the team has to work it out to maintain capacity. Name Manager defines the condition:

```
ShortInput =INDEX(Report[Net],MATCH(Input[@Date],Report[Date],0))>0
```

There may be an implicit expectation of "first-come, first-served", but in reality the table cannot tell which entry first caused the shortage. Thus, resolution is by honor system, voluntary compromise, or seniority.

Finally, another color highlights non-workdays. This gives added exposure to the secondary purpose of the table, to track non-workday coverage. The condition is =DateTypeInput.

There is one condition that cannot be shown on the Input table. The Report table has every date, so when there are too many people working, it shows there. The Input table only has the dates entered, so over-staffing is not visible. This can occur in a shutdown or slow-down scenario. The manager then needs to work it out with the team to take mandatory vacation or some other measure.

Calendar Copy

Next to the Input table is a linked image of the Calendar (see Camera Tool in Chapter 3, Formatting). The actual Calendar table resides on the Report sheet. Display of special dates on the Calendar is co-controlled by two sets of checkboxes, one on each sheet, linked to the same cells. Here members use the Calendar to see upcoming events as they plan and make their entries.

Report Sheet

The Report sheet is mainly for the manager, and may occasionally be of interest to members. The sheet has one selection cell, StartSelect, to set the start date of the table. There are three start date options: This year, Today, Next year. This short list is maintained in Data Validation, and in Name Manager as the array StartList for use in defining the start date:

```
StartDate =CHOOSE(MATCH(StartSelect,StartList,0),
    DATE(ThisYear,1,1),TODAY(),DATE(ThisYear+1,1,1))
```

Most of the time, starting today is most useful for tracking the immediate future. Occasionally it may be necessary to start from the beginning of this year or next year.

Special Table

Special is an input table in which the manager can list any special event requirements for either plus or minus staffing. It has three input columns; [Date], [Need] and [Comment]. Positive [Need] is for non-workday coverage, or special events when the full staff is required. Negative [Need] is for workdays that are shut down or reduced staff. This can be used to balance days that are short, such as the day before a holiday. When [Need] is 0 it indicates a shutdown.

[Type] labels the entry with one of four strings based on DateType described earlier. The difference from other tables is when it's a workday, if [Need] has a value it is called "± help", and if it's blank or 0 it calls it "shutdown".

```
[Type] =IF([@Date],CHOOSE(DateTypeSpecial+1,IF([@Need],"±
    help","shutdown"),"weekend","holiday"),"")
```

[Net] then goes to the Report table to see if the need has already been met or not. This will be described in the next section.

```
[Net] =IFERROR(INDEX(Report[Net],MATCH([@Date],Report[Date],0)),"")
```

Conditional Formatting shades rows gray to be ignored when they are in the past, or when there is no [Net] requirement.

Report Table

The Report table summarizes the work requirements and staffing day-by-day. This is a list of every date from the selected start date for about a year and a half, and can be extended as needed by copying the bottom row down.

```
[Date] =IF(N(Above),Above+1,StartDate)
```

Date header columns to the left of [Date] give the [Wk], [Mo] and [Year], formatted to hide duplicates as previously demonstrated. To the right of [Date] is [Type] = workday, weekend or holiday.

The heart of the table is the next four columns which present the staffing numbers.

[Min] is the base staff requirement for normal days. For weekends and holidays (DateTypeReport = TRUE) or if there is a shutdown defined in the Special table, [Min] is 0. For workdays, [Min] is StaffMin, based on StaffFull, (the current roster) and MinStaff (the % configured in Settings).

```
StaffMin =ROUND(StaffFull*MinStaff,0)
StaffFull =COUNTIF(Team[Start],"<="&StartDate)-
    COUNTIF(Team[End],"<="&StartDate)
[Min] =IF(OR(DateTypeReport,ScheduleShutdown),0,StaffMin)
```

[Extra] is the plus or minus [Need] from the Special table.

```
[Extra] =SUMIF(Special[Date],[@Date],Special[Need])
```

[Have] is 0 for non-workdays and full staff for workdays, minus days off entered in the Input table. Because Input[Off] is negative on non-workdays, this becomes a positive in [Have].

```
[Have] =IF(DateTypeReport,0,StaffFull)-
    SUMIF(Input[Date],[@Date],Input[Off])
```

[Net] then compares demand and supply and shows how many more are needed. Net requirements can occur when a lot of people take off, or when there are special needs. The short condition is when there's not enough staff, [@Min]+[@Extra]>[@Have]. The over condition is when there's unneeded staff on non-workdays, or staff during shutdown or above slowdown requirement. In any of these cases, the difference is given. On normal workdays if there is more staff than required, [Net]=0. [Flag] converts any non-zero [Net] to text.

```
[Net] =IF(OR([@Min]=0,[@Extra]<0,
    [@Min]+[@Extra]>[@Have]),[@Min]+[@Extra]-[@Have],0)
[Flag] =IF([@Net]>0,"short",IF([@Net]<0,"over",""))
```

The final column [Used] is for the purpose of tracking total vacation days taken versus days entitled. Days taken is the sum of Input[Off] for the year, reduced by comp days if CompDays is turned on. Entitled days is the sum of the current year's column in the Team table.

```
[Used] =IFERROR((SUMIFS(Input[Off],Input[Off],">0",
    Input[Date],"<="&[@Date],Input[Year],[@Year])+IF(CompDays,SUMIFS(
    Input[Off],Input[Off],"<0",Input[Date],"<="&[@Date],Input[Year],[@Ye
    ar]),0))/INDEX(Team[#Totals],1,MATCH([@Year],VacationYears,0)),0)
```

The alert condition to turn the font red in Report[Used] is the product of three conditions; ① the month of the date is greater than or equal to the alert start month, ② the cell value is below the alert threshold level, and ③ the date is in the current year.

```
=①AND(MONTH($E6)>=MATCH(AlertStart,Mons,0), ②$L6<AlertLevel, ③
    $B6=ThisYear)                (active cell in row 6)
```

This formula uses cell references because it is entered directly into Conditional Formatting, and thus cannot use structured references.

In theory, each quarter should have about 25% of the total vacation days, but in reality there are peak seasons, and the procrastination effect. The more days off a person has, the more likely they will take days at the end of the year because they have to "use them or lose them". When people leave many days unscheduled until late in the year, it poses the risk of an empty workplace.

Above the Report table are six informative cells in three groups.

Table 41: Team Calendar Info Cells

Group	Cell	Formula
Staff	Full	=COUNTIF(Team[Start],"<="&StartDate)- COUNTIF(Team[End],"<="&StartDate)
	Min	=ROUND(StaffFull*MinStaff,0)
Vacation days	Due	=INDEX(Team[#Totals],1, MATCH(@StartYear,VacationYears,0))
	Used	=SUMIFS(Input[Off],Input[Off],">0",Input[Year], StartYear)+IF(CompDays,SUMIFS(Input[Off], Input[Off],"<0",Input[Year],StartYear),0)
Shortages	Days	=COUNTIFS(Report[Flag],"short", Report[Date],">="&TODAY())
	Next	=IFERROR(INDEX(Report[Date], MATCH("short",Report[Flag],0))-TODAY(),"")

Analysis Sheet

The Analysis sheet presents two sample pivot tables and accompanying charts.

The first pivot is sourced from the Input table. [Name] is in the Rows area, [Used] and [Left] are in the Values area, renamed "taken" and "due" respectively, [Year] is in the Columns area, filtered for this year. The chart shows the team members with how many days they have taken and how many they have left as horizontal stacked bars. The manager can use this to remind certain individuals to schedule their days off.

The second pivot is sourced from the Report table, with [Wk] in the Rows area and Average of [Used] in the Values area, Year in the Columns area and filtered for this year. The chart shows the total team days taken as a percent line graph over the weeks of the year, or remainder of the year, if StartSelect is today. This highlights how big the hockey stick risk is.

Chapter 8: Project Tracker

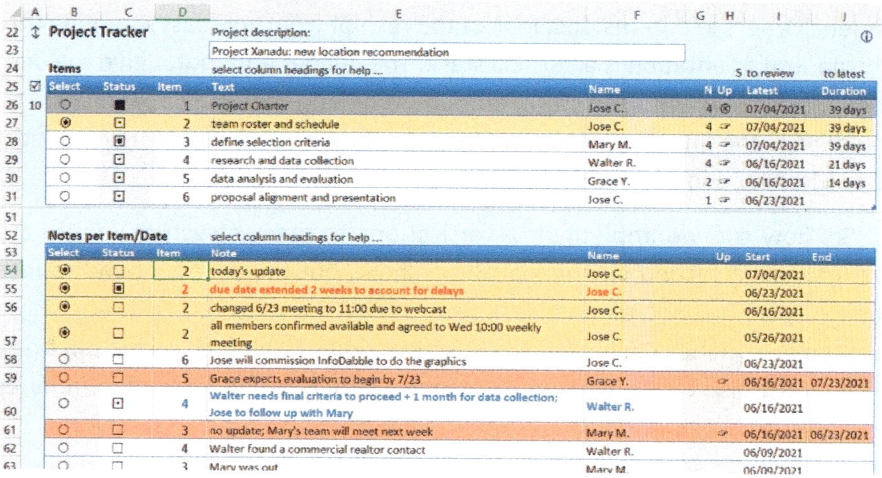

Purpose

Business projects commonly span several months and even years, with weekly status meetings tracking a seemingly endless list of tasks and updates. When Excel is used as a tracking device, it's usually thrown together with little forethought or design, setting the stage for spreadsheet abuse.

An ad-hoc project sheet might look something like this: a few columns on the left containing a few words describing the main item, and a column on the right snowballing weekly updates. The "details" cell has dates and names mingled with long, wrapping text, consuming the screen height and unbalancing the left and right sides of the screen. Add disregard for alignment and you have a candidate for the ugliest spreadsheet award.

Functionality is also lost. The only way to update notes is to edit the monster cell, and use strikethrough or bold or font color to add or remove emphasis. Dates and names are lost in the text and cannot be used. Team members struggle to grasp the real status or to look up their to-do's. Team leaders struggle to convey the project status and hold members accountable. No doubt there exist formal tools to manage this, but they are unknown or inaccessible to many managers. This case is ripe for a solution.

Structure

The two-tier structure of headings and details brings to mind common relational database examples: Accounts and Transactions; Customers and Orders; Orders and Items. Just look at the receipt from your last shopping trip. The natural orientation is a vertical stack. The header and footer give the one-record sale view, with the store, amount, date and method of payment. The middle has the linked variable-length view of items. You would never expect to see header and detail side by side.

So, how can we implement a vertical one-to-many structure? There are ways to use a second view or to split a sheet, but the user is bound to lose their way trying to scroll and track records between the two. There must be two tables dynamically linked to focus attention on selected records in both. There must also be simple, intuitive controls that can be learned in minutes and executed in seconds. This is definitely a good case for a VBA project.

To begin the design, I define and separate the levels as two tables, naming them "Items" and "Notes". The key field "Item" will be a number connecting the tables with a many-to-one relationship from Notes to Items. As the primary key, Items[Item] must be unique; each Item has one and only one row. Notes[Item] is the foreign key; it must exist in Items[Item], but there can be many Notes for the same Item. Automated insertion will obey these rules, and Data Validation will enforce the law in case of manual maintenance.

After considering some display options, I decide to split the sheet into top and bottom panes for the two tables. As I list the fields of interest in each table, several are common and can be passed between them: a selection indicator should be set in Items and passed to Notes; Status should be set in Notes and reflected in Items; dates are set in Notes and summarized in Items. The structure should reflect the purpose of balancing attention between two levels, while minimizing data entry.

The two tables will have the same number and types of columns so that the width and formatting will look natural in both. This is important for visual balance, and to ensure that as records are inserted and deleted in the top table, the bottom table is shifted down and up, maintaining the separation between them.

User input will be limited; text descriptions, names of team members, and target due date if known. Other columns will be set by formula, or by a VBA mouse event. Symbols and Conditional Formats will be used to help minimize the need for interpretation.

VBA Techniques

Worksheet Events

This is a case where the user needs to interact with individual records and get a relevant program response. Using controls to run the code would be clumsy at best. To enable context-sensitive execution, I look at worksheet events that capture the target cell. For example, when the user selects or right-clicks or double-clicks a cell, these are all separate events that can be programmed based on the cell address.

Event procedures are pre-defined. With the Sheet selected in the VBA Project Explorer, the code pane has two drop-down lists. In the first, select Worksheet, then open the second to see all the events. To review how they work, I write simple programs for the most interesting events. Then I return to the sheet and play around to trigger the events. Here's an example, with test code:

```
Private Sub Worksheet_BeforeDoubleClick(ByVal Target As Range,
Cancel As Boolean)
MsgBox "BeforeDoubleClick target = " & Target.Address
Cancel = True
End Sub
```

Some interesting behaviors noted:

- BeforeDoubleClick and BeforeRightClick replace the default action with the custom action when Cancel = True, and precede it when Cancel = False or omitted
- BeforeDoubleClick Target is a single cell

- BeforeRightClick Target can be single or multi-cell
- Change captures the new value, after the change
- Change captures multi-cell change via Ctrl+Enter (but cannot return .Value)
- SelectionChange does not capture active cell change within a selection (via Tab or Enter)

The SelectionChange event would appear useful to run code with a single left click. However, it can be confusing to click the same cell again and nothing happens. Further, it is triggered by any navigation – arrow key, page up, home, etc. It can be programmed to run only on certain targets, of course, but I want the commands to be intentional and not triggered inadvertently. For these reasons I decide not to use SelectionChange.

After some more experimentation, I assign general usage categories by event:

Table 42: Project Tracker VBA Worksheet Events

Event	Arguments	Use
BeforeDoubleClick	Target and Cancel	"Hard" commands
BeforeRightClick	Target and Cancel	"Soft" commands
Change	Target	Cleanup actions

When the Target address is used as a program condition it provides contextual functionality. The code will react based on the location of the target cell. If the user double-clicks in the Select column it will do one thing, if they double-click in the Item column it will do another. Thus, the event procedure needs to first determine where the target cell is relative to reference ranges, then have multiple paths based on the result.

The pre-named event routines are the gateway to the sheet module and provide the means to direct the program without user controls. For simple actions they contain the direct commands, and for more complex or reusable actions they call other subroutines.

Contextual Paths

My first task in establishing contextual paths is to determine the context. Target gives the interacted cell. To find what table and column it's in, I need a range variable representing each column's data range. There are many, here is one example using a naming convention of I=Items, C=Column, Sel=Select, Rng=Range: ICSelRng is the data body range of Items[Select].

```
Dim Tracker As Worksheet
Dim ITable As ListObject, ICSelRng as Range
Set Tracker = ActiveWorkbook.Sheets("Tracker")
Set ITable = Tracker.ListObjects("Items")
Set ICSelRng = ITable.ListColumns("Select").DataBodyRange
```

I use the Application.Intersect method to tell if Target is within the range. Here I've made a Boolean function to simplify, since I use this a lot.

```
Private Function Within(Target, Rng) As Boolean
If Application.Intersect(Target, Rng) Is Nothing _
Then Within = False Else Within = True
End Function
```

Then, within the BeforeDoubleClick and BeforeRightClick Subs, I create multiple segments, each headed by a go-to location name and where each operates independently, like a Select Case block. For example, if Target is within ICSelRng, it will call a subroutine, cancel the default action, and exit. If Target is not within ICSelRng, it goes to the next segment header, runs Within on the next interactive column, and so on.

```
target1:
    If Not Within(Target, ICSelRng) Then GoTo target2:
    Call Sub...
    Cancel = True
    Exit Sub
target2:
    If Not Within(Target, ICItmRng) Then GoTo target3:
...
```

This gives clean separation of the code applied to each column or other action range.

Faux Controls

Controls such as checkboxes and option buttons are good when they have a stable range to live in. When you want them to appear at the record level you can simulate their appearance with symbols, creating what I call "faux controls", text characters that look like controls that you can manipulate and format as desired within the cell. Using mouse events the symbols can be modified and used in both program logic and sheet formulas and formats.

“Symbol” fonts, Symbol, Webdings, Windings, etc., have a lot of good options to choose from. They can be selected such that they sort up or down in a way that makes sense to the user, if necessary. If they’re used as a toggle, like Selected and Unselected, then sort order is no matter. If they form a series, test to be sure how they will sort before settling on the symbols.

Each set of symbols is proprietary to the column it’s used in, and each character is defined in Name Manager as a constant, for example:

```
Selected = CHAR(158)
```

The table below lists characters used with the symbols in Wingdings 2 font.

Table 43: Project Tracker Symbols

Location, Sort	Code	Body font	Wingdings 2	Name
[Select]	158	Ž	◉	Selected
Descending	153	™	○	Unselected
[Status]	169	©	▣	SquareHi
Descending	167	§	⊡	SquareLo
	163	£	□	SquareOpen
	162	¢	■	SquareDone
[Up]	63	?	☞	UpToDo
Ascending	79	O	×	UpDefault (hidden)
	80	P	✓	UpToday
	86	V	⊗	UpDone
SplitSet (cell)	82	R	☑	SquareCheck

As an interesting watchout when working with symbol fonts, beware that the symbol is evaluated by its value, not its appearance. The name UpToDo appears as a hand pointing right in Wingdings 2, but is actually a question mark character when viewed in the formula bar. When I wrote a formula to count the remaining “UpToDo’s”, it returned the full number of records in the column, not just those with the UpToDo character. I was puzzled until I realized that “?” is a wildcard. To get the count of actual “?” characters, it must be preceded by a tilde character, as in

```
=COUNTIF(Items[Up],"~"&UpTodo)
```

I had to trick the [Up] column symbol set into sorting UpToDo at the top, followed by the default records. Originally I left the default blank, which sorted them first. To sort as intended, the UpDefault character code has to be between 63 and 80. I chose 79 for the sort, and used Conditional Formatting on the column to hide the value when it is UpDefault.

I use the same names in Name Manager and in VBA, but a little differently. In Name Manager, the names refer to CHAR(Code), and are then used in formulas as both input and output:

```
Items[Up] =IF([@Status]=SquareDone,UpDone,IF(COUNTIFS(
    Notes[Item],[@Item],Notes[Up],UpToday),UpToday,UpTodo))
```

In the VBA module, the name is a constant that refers to the code value. This is then used to read (via Asc function) and write (via Chr function) the character. The following segment unselects all Item records, then selects the target record.

```
Const Unselected = 153, Selected = 158
...
Set TmpRng = Tracker.Cells(Target.Row, ICSelRng.Column)
If Asc(TmpRng) = Unselected Then
    For Each c In ICSelRng.Cells
        c.Value = Chr(Unselected)
    Next
    TmpRng.Value = Chr(Selected)
End If
```

The split-screen feature uses the same symbol toggle technique, combined with an action routine. There is a checkbox-like cell SplitSet for the toggle, and a numeric cell SplitRow to set the row number to split on. SplitSet is toggled upon DoubleClick, which triggers the Change event, which calls the SplitWindow routine. A change in SplitRow also calls SplitWindow.

I also need a Boolean to tell me if the screen is split or not, and to keep the symbol aligned to the state. To convert the value of the SplitSet symbol to a Boolean, I create the name SplitFlag, TRUE when SplitSet has the SquareCheck symbol.

```
SplitFlag =SplitSet=SquareCheck
```

Sort Table

The tables have the filter buttons turned off. Selection acts like a filter, and I pre-define logical multi-column sorts. The RightClick event on any column header activates the custom sort. The Sub first uses Within to tell if Target is in the table header, then Select Case Target.Column to tell which column.

Table 44: Project Tracker Sort by Right-Click on Header

Table	Column	Items Sort	Notes Sort
Both	[Select]	Select D, Up A, Item A	Select D, Start D, Status D
Both	[Status]	Status D, Up A, Item A	Status D, Up A, Start D
Both	[Item]	Item A	Item A, Status D, Start D
Items	[Text]	Text A, Item A	
Notes	[Note]		Note A, Item A
Both	[Name]	Name A, Item A	Name A, Item A
Both	[Up]	Up A, Status D, Item A	Up A, End A, Item A
Items	[Latest]	Latest D, Item A	
Notes	[Start]		Start D, Status D, Item A
Items	[Duration]	Dur D, Item A	
Notes	[End]		End A, Status D, Item A

Some double-click actions also perform a sort. For example, when Items[Item] is double-clicked, a new Note record for the Target Item is inserted; then both tables are sorted by [Select] first, then by two other columns to call appropriate attention.

Split Window

It is important to maintain the split window well. The split is the key to the dual-table interaction, so it is refreshed whenever a record is inserted or selected, as well as when the SplitSet or SplitRow cells are changed. It is also called by the Calculate event, which checks that the Split property equals the SplitFlag setting, in case Split was manually removed. Sub SplitWindow() uses ActiveWindow properties .SplitRow, and .ScrollRow with .Panes(1) and .Panes(2) to maintain screen balance.

Set Date Format

Date format options are important for international users. As in other projects, I use two picklists to select date order and separator, each with three options, defining nine total formats. These could be done with Conditional Formatting, but the code method is more secure. SetDateFormat() is triggered by the Change event in either DateOrder or DateSeparator. It uses nested Select Case statements to set one of nine values to the .NumberFormat property of Range("Items[Latest],Notes[[Start]:[End]]").

Conditional Formatting

Conditional Formatting can get messy when ranges are deleted or copied and pasted, etc. They are also hard to extract for documentation. In VBA I can make them easier to maintain and protect them from errors in code. It is easiest to record while setting, but once the pattern is known the logic of the dialog can be copied and edited, considering the sequence and StopIfTrue setting.

Most Conditional Formats involve fill and/or font colors. The themed color palette has ten colors with six shades each. The tooltips show the color names and the shade as a percent lighter or darker than the standard color. In VBA, the color is a name or number from the xlThemeColor enumeration, and the shade is a decimal value, positive if lighter, negative if darker. The Colors sheet in the Startup File project explains more and gives enumerations.

Sub FormatItems() applies five rules to the Items table:

Table 45: Project Tracker Conditional Formatting

Formula1	Name meaning	Format
=HasNoNotes	=Items[@N]=0	Accent2, Shade 0.4
=ItemToday	=Items[@Up]=UpToday	Accent6, Shade 0.6
=ItemDone	=Items[@Status]=SquareDone	Accent3, Shade 0
=ItemSelected	=Items[@Select]=Selected	Accent4, Shade 0.6
=ISFORMULA (ThisCell)		Accent3, Shade 0.8

Sub FormatNotes() similarly applies rules to the Notes table.

How It Works

The first step is to enter the items as the main tasks or deliverables of the project. Fill in the blank rows, then double-click on an item text to insert the next number.

Start adding notes for each item by double-click on the item number in either table to insert a new note for that item, with today's date.

To set note status, right-click the status cell to cycle between empty square (low), small square fill with blue font (medium) and large square fill with red font (high).

To flag a note as complete, double-click the status. Double-click again to reset.

To conduct a regular review, double-click the first item in the Items table. This creates today's note, which is flagged green. Enter text in the note, flag status and set end date as needed. Double-click the next item, and repeat. You will see the remaining items to be reviewed until you reach the end and all items have an update today. If there is no update today for an item, you can choose either to record that with a note, or skip it.

Support

If the user follows the normal process there should be few problems, but they can manually change things that can cause inconsistencies. One of these is orphan notes. Items and notes are like parent and children. If the item is deleted, the notes become orphans. These are flagged with dark red and a message appears above the Notes table. There is a small column in both tables that counts the corresponding records from the other table. In Items, it's the "N" column. In Notes it's called "It" but is hidden. There can only be one item per note, or 0 if the note is an orphan. The user doesn't need to see this, its only use is to count orphans, which is displayed above the table.

The cells labeled ↕ are DoubleClick toggles to expand and collapse the row group at top for more information. This contains some settings, a color legend, an action and symbol legend, and space for header notes about the project.

Chapter 9: MRP Demo

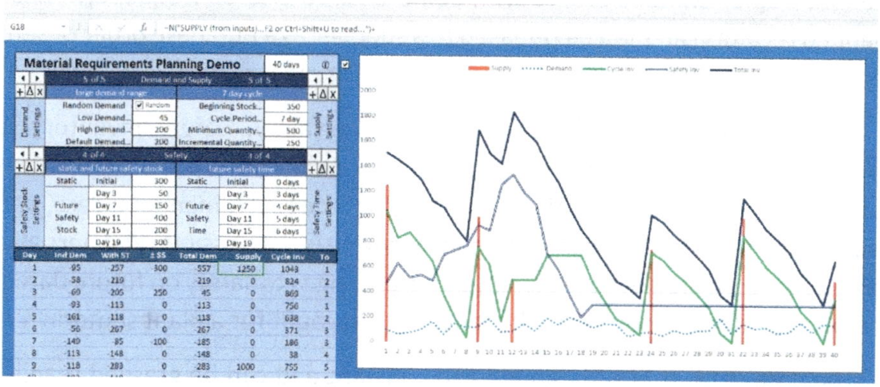

Purpose

MRP stands for Material Requirements Planning. It was an early application of computers in industry, replacing manual inventory card files. It plans replenishment of manufacturing materials and parts as they are received, moved, produced, inspected, approved and consumed in production of finished goods.

Good planning balances the economics of production run quantities with inventory holding costs, and accounts for constraints. Derivation of the parameters to drive an optimal plan would be a significant project in itself. My scope here is to illustrate how such parameters are used to calculate replenishment orders, resulting in the plan. Having worked and taught in this area for many years, the topic is near and dear, but I chose it as a project because it affords an excellent self-learning opportunity.

There are two general levels of MRP. At the top is the finished product level, which plans production to meet demand from customers, called independent demand. This level is referred to as Master Production

Scheduling or MPS. Below that is MRP for everything that goes into production, where demand can be calculated and is called dependent demand. This project will simulate independent demand, with the option of constant or randomized demand. Both MPS and MRP use the same logic and are often both referred to simply as MRP.

MRP plans future receipts to meet known or estimated requirements, and to maintain an inventory balance. It starts with beginning inventory and some supply parameters, is fed a series of requirements, and it calculates a series of planned replenishment orders with some desired size or frequency. These planned receipts can then be released to a supplier as a purchase order or sent to another operation or plant as a work order for manufacture.

To account for demand and supply uncertainty, safety inventory is commonly used as a buffer. The replenishment calculator plans to maintain safety as the minimum. The planner knows that the real minimum is zero, and uses safety to meet demand when replenishment is not possible. Planners also have ways to manipulate the plan by adding changes to safety on future dates, for example, for extraordinary demand, or to account for a plant shutdown.

The core logic of MRP is simple and constant and can be grasped readily. Yet, there are so many complex connections of products, parts, locations and parameters that even smart analysts are sometimes challenged to explain the result. If there is one small error in one link of the chain, it is amplified by those interdependencies with a bullwhip effect.

Planners and managers make better decisions when they clearly understand how each parameter and each type of plan manipulation works and will impact inventory levels. Despite the apparent simplicity of MRP, the combination of options makes this is a good opportunity for a demo. This is in no way intended as an actual MRP model and is purely for instructional value.

Logic

MRP logic considers three types of inputs; demand, inventory and parameters. To logically organize the project I break these out to four areas; demand, supply (inventory and lot sizing parameters), safety stock and safety time. For the purpose of explaining net requirements, inventory is considered here with demand.

Net Requirements

Net requirements means that the initial inventory balance at the end of today is yesterday's ending balance minus today's demand, including safety. If there was enough inventory left yesterday to cover all of today's demand, then there is no net requirement for today. If not, the difference between inventory and demand is the net requirement.

Net requirement tells us whether or not to place a replenishment order. There should be a supply order on each day that has a net requirement. If the order exactly covers the net requirement quantity, there will be an order on each day that has demand. It is most often the case, due to logistical constraints or economics, that there is a minimum order quantity or period that exceeds daily demand, resulting in a sawtooth replenishment pattern.

The concept of net requirement is a bit elusive because it does not appear in the plan, since the plan is always to replenish in time to prevent it. It is a hidden calculation. The net requirement date tells us when to order, and the net requirement quantity feeds the replenishment order calculation. As each planned order adds to inventory, the next net requirement date is determined, and so on.

Planning usually involves a firm period in which orders can only be changed by a planner. Within this zone, if replenishment is not in time, the inventory balance can go negative, revealing unintentional net requirements. But, not all negative inventory is bad. If the plan includes safety as part of the total demand, then negative inventory means it is below safety. The planner must judge how much safety remains, if any, to determine what interventions are needed. The demo will not have a firm zone; its purpose is only to show how the MRP calculations work, so there will never be negative inventory.

Safety Stock

Safety stock that is entered as a part parameter is static – effective now and always. Statistical models are used to determine the amount based on service level desired, demand and supply variability and other factors.

Static safety is subtracted from current inventory, creating in effect a false floor for the plan, like pretending you have less than you really do, or like a reserve gas tank. The plan always calculates supply to maintain inventory at or above safety.

Safety stock can be entered to take effect on future dates. This is usually done for two general reasons; abnormal demand such as promotions or seasonality, or to prepare for supply constraints. It is driven by strategy versus statistics, and is temporary. Once the abnormality is passed, the strategy is to return to normal statistical safety.

As a temporary strategy, what goes up must come down. In effect what it is doing is not adding demand to the plan but leveling it. It borrows demand from a constrained period to put it in an earlier, less constrained period. This looks like a fake demand in the early period and a fake supply in the later period, providing relief to the constraint. When the plan is recalculated, it moves the real supply plan to match the manipulated demand plan, resulting in inventory prebuild.

The mechanism used to effect future changes to safety is to introduce a plan element – a placeholder with a date, and a quantity that can be either negative or positive. In the demo the amounts entered are absolute targets, increasing from static safety to the peak, then returning to static safety or other desired level. The program determines the plus or minus incremental amount to place in each period.

The demo is too simple to include constraints or firming, but does show the effect of mitigation measures. The user can pretend to balance a constraint as they experiment, and see how production and inventory would be impacted. A particularly revealing lesson can be learned by changing safety stock and supply parameters when there is no demand. The point often learned the hard way is that safety stock generates supply orders even with no actual demand.

Safety Time

Safety time is like safety stock in most regards. It can be either a statistically derived static parameter, or a profile of strategic ups and downs on future dates. What makes it different is the mechanism and the effect. Where safety stock is pretending you have less than you do, safety time is pretending you need it sooner than you do. It advances demand by the set days. This creates a false floor not as a constant quantity, but as a constant days of coverage. As demand goes up or down, the safety amount follows it.

When a safety days increase or decrease is set to take effect on a future date, demand is offset by the new number of days beginning on that date. This has a ramping effect as some dates have double demand and some have none.

A key advantage of safety time over safety stock is that if there is no demand, there is no safety to generate supply. For this reason it is the preferred strategy at end of product lifecycle, or when demand is very uncertain.

Lot Sizing

Once all demands are considered and netted to inventory, it's time to create a supply order. Lot sizing is about following logistical rules. Logistics is about respecting the reality of how material is procured, packaged, shipped, handled, stored and used.

Consider how you buy food. When you eat out or take out, you purchase to your immediate need, called lot-for-lot procurement. When you go grocery shopping, you probably buy more than just your next meal. Some things you buy in large packages so that you don't need to buy it again soon, like toilet paper or cereal. Others you buy in the minimum package, perhaps because of shelf life, like eggs. Each item causes you some mental math, even subconsciously. You know the more you buy, the cheaper the unit cost, but the higher the probability of waste. Meanwhile, you are also doing net requirements calculations based on what's still in your refrigerator or pantry at home.

The demo includes three lot sizing parameters; cycle, minimum quantity and incremental quantity. Cycle refers to the replenishment frequency. If the nearest store is an hour away, cycle is likely a larger factor in your shopping behavior than if it's around the corner. Minimum is the least you can buy. If it's a low-use item, the minimum drives frequency because the package lasts longer than one shopping cycle. Order quantity must always be at least the minimum, and must be a multiple of the incremental quantity.

Formulas

A demo is likely to be viewed and analyzed by some very smart and curious people. For this reason, I pay special attention to making the formulas easy to read and understand, with structured references and named input cells.

Formulas can thus be read without reference to the sheet. In fact I can turn off sheet headings for a clean screen.

There are a total of fourteen columns that I divide into two sets. The main set of columns lines up with the user input section, leaving clean lines and space for the chart. These are the columns of primary interest. Additional columns are used to break down the long calculation chain into intelligible steps, to retrieve the safety inputs, and feed outputs to the chart. Being of secondary interest, they are hidden when the chart is displayed, and revealed by toggle when the chart is hidden.

Formula notes

Formulas are self-documented with N("text"), beginning with a brief description and a shortcut tip to either call edit mode or expand the formula bar, and including a plain English version of the formula.

All arguments are named, either as other table columns (with brackets), or as range names (without brackets). OFFSET is used to retrieve (with rows argument) or accumulate (with height argument) other table rows with reference to the current row.

Complex formulas are written with line breaks and indents for readability. The most complex, Supply, has 15 parentheses, 9 lines and 4 indent levels.

Formulas are written to avoid most errors, which might occur if the user enters unexpected values. For example, Supply uses IncQty as a denominator. To avoid a #DIV/0! error, I use MAX(IncQty,1).

Following are the formulas separated into primary and secondary following the sheet structure. Actual calculations are bolded.

Table 46: MRP Primary Formulas

Name	Formula (all first lines include "F2 or Ctrl+Shift+U to read...")
Day	=N("DAY (ordinal)... F2 or Ctrl+Shift+U to read... ")+ **N(Above)+1**
Ind Dem	=N("DEMAND (from inputs)... ")+ N("...if (checkbox, randomize, else default demand...")+ **IF(Random,** **-RANDBETWEEN(N(DemLow),MAX(N(DemLow),N(DemHigh))),** **-N(DemDefault))**
With ST	=N("DEMAND (with safety time offset)... ")+ N("...where [To]=[@Day], sum demand...")+ **SUMIF([To],[@Day],[Ind Dem])**
± SS	=N("DEMAND (± safety stock increment)... ")+ N("...safety stock quantity minus previous day ...")+ **[@SSQty]-N(OFFSET([@SSQty],-1,0))**
Total Dem	=N("DEMAND (total)... ")+ N("...demand with ST offset plus SS increment...")+ **[@[With ST]]+[@[± SS]]**
Supply	=N("SUPPLY (from inputs)... ")+ N("...if (net demand, roundup (max of (netted cycle demand and min qty), divided by inc qty) times inc qty, else 0) ...")+ **IF(MIN(IF([@Day]=1,N(Stock),OFFSET([@[Cycle Inv]],-1,0))+** **[@[Total Dem]],0),** **ROUNDUP(** **MAX(** **-SUM(OFFSET([@[Total Dem]],0,0,MAX(Cycle,1)))-** **IF([@Day]=1,N(Stock),OFFSET([@[Cycle Inv]],-1,0)),** **MinQty)/** **MAX(IncQty,1),0)*** **MAX(IncQty,1),** **0)**
Cycle Inv	=N("INVENTORY (cycle stock)... ")+ N("...beginning inventory, plus demand, plus supply...")+ **IF([@Day]=1,N(Stock),Above)+[@[Total Dem]]+[@Supply]**
To	=N("SAFETY TIME (day to offset to)... ")+ N("...this day minus safety days, with past on day 1...")+ **MAX(1,[@Day]-[@STDays])**

Table 47: MRP Secondary Formulas

Heading	Formula (all first lines include "Ctrl+Shift+U to read...")
STDays	=N("SAFETY TIME (from inputs)...Ctrl+Shift+U to read...")+ N("... get this day, or initial value, or previous day...")+ **IFNA(** **INDEX(STValues,MATCH([@Day],STDates,0)),** **IF([@Day]=1,N(STInitial),Above))**
STQty	=N("SAFETY TIME (in quantity)... ")+ N("...cum demand with ST minus without ST...")+ **SUM(OFFSET([@[With ST]],0,0,-[@Day]))-** **SUM(OFFSET([@[Ind Dem]],0,0,-[@Day]))**
SSQty	=N("SAFETY STOCK (from inputs)... ")+ N("... get this day, or initial value, or previous day...")+ **IFNA(** **-INDEX(SSValues,MATCH([@Day],SSDates,0)),** **IF([@Day]=1, -N(SSInitial),Above))**
Safety Inv	=N("INVENTORY (total safety, for graph)... ")+ **ABS([@STQty]+[@SSQty])**
Total Inv	=N("INVENTORY (total quantity, for graph)... ")+ **[@[Cycle Inv]]+[@Safety Inv]**
Demand	=N("DEMAND (positive, for graph)... ")+ **ABS([@[Ind Dem]])**

Supply formula detail

Supply is the most complex formula, and being the essence of MRP deserves special attention. To understand a complex formula, it helps to dissect it from the inside out. Here, circled numbers in the formula show the start and end of meaningful segments, which are listed and explained below.

```
⑦IF(②MIN(①IF([@Day]=1, N(Stock),
    OFFSET([@[Cycle Inv]],-1,0)) ①+ [@[Total Dem]],0) ②,
⑥⑤ROUNDUP(
    ④MAX(
    ③-SUM(OFFSET([@[Total Dem]],0,0,MAX(Cycle,1))) ③-
      ①IF([@Day]=1,N(Stock),OFFSET([@[Cycle Inv]],-1,0)) ①,
    MinQty) ④/
MAX(IncQty,1),0) ⑤*
MAX(IncQty,1) ⑥,
0) ⑦
```

① Beginning Inventory = **IF([@Day]=1,N(Stock),OFFSET([@[Cycle Inv]],-1,0))**; Stock if day 1, else previous day's cycle inventory. Cycle inventory is the portion incurred due to supply periodicity and lot size quantities, differentiated from safety inventory, which is built into the demand.

② Net Requirements = **MIN(①+[@[Total Dem]],0)**; if ① Beginning Inventory covers today's total demand, then ② Net Requirements = 0, FALSE; else, ② Net Requirements < 0, TRUE; used as a Boolean trigger for ⑥ Supply Order Quantity in ⑦ Supply.

③ Net Cycle Demand = **-SUM(OFFSET([@[Total Dem]],0,0,MAX (Cycle,1)))-①**; cycle demand - ① Beginning Inventory; cycle demand is the negative sum (positive value) of the next Cycle rows of total demand, starting from today. (In rare conditions, today's demand requires a supply order, but cycle demand amount is not enough to cover it. This can occur when a safety stock decrease (positive demand) exceeds actual independent (negative) demand within the cycle. In this case, negative cycle inventory can briefly occur).

④ Initial Quantity = **MAX(③, MinQty)**; maximum of either ③ Net Cycle Demand, or the minimum order quantity.

⑤ Number of Increments = **ROUNDUP(④/MAX(IncQty,1),0)**; ④ Initial Quantity divided by the incremental order quantity, rounded up to the next whole number (0 digits); incremental order quantity is bottomed at 1 to prevent error.

⑥ Supply Order Quantity = **⑤ * MAX(IncQty,1)**; ⑤ Number of Increments * the incremental order quantity is the final answer.

⑦ Supply = **IF(②, ⑥, 0)**; if ② Net Requirements exist, then calculate ⑥ Supply Order Quantity, else 0, no supply needed.

Scenarios

A demo project is intended to be a user-interactive visual demonstration of a tool or process. It should simulate real life, but with data and features simplified and controlled for the educational purpose. A great tool for this is scenarios. With scenarios you can package data ahead of time with exemplary values. A scenario simply saves cell values, allowing them to be restored anytime. Thus you can offer scenarios while still allowing the user to modify the data for experimentation.

Scenario Manager is not difficult to learn, but it's obscure enough to be ignored or forgotten by most users, and even when familiar it has several drawbacks; one, it covers the screen; two, the chart does not recalculate while it's open; three, it only shows one scenario at a time. I can use code to show and manage scenarios, and to display information about all four scenario areas at once. With a few simple controls and macros, I can provide an engaging interface for self-learning.

The elements of a scenario are the name and the range of cells that are stored in it, which can be up to 32 cells. Values can be specified at creation, but normally the cells already contain the values you want to save, so once the range is defined it will by default save the current values. Comment is optional, and may be important depending on the number of scenarios and of changing cells in each. Like it or not, Excel automatically adds the user's name and date of creation or modification to the comment. Handling this is another objective and benefit of coding.

Controls

When you have scenarios to offer, it's nice and elegant to do so in such a way that users can scan them easily while focusing on the data, especially with a chart or Conditional Formatting to show the change. This is a good case for a spin button control. A spin button is a dual-function button that increments and decrements the output value using min, max and step properties, like a scroll bar without the bar. Often this can be done with no code; the linked cell can be hidden or visible, and used to derive outputs. Here I'll do everything through code.

Since I will be programming the buttons, they don't really need to be spinners, any shape will do. But a spinner is intuitive for this case of scrolling up and down through a series of data sets, and already has the up and down arrows. I will use the SpinUp and SpinDown events of each button to drive actions, so the button properties such as linked cell, min and max are irrelevant. I can also make them circular; SpinUp will not stop at the last, but go back to the first, and SpinDown will go from the first to the last.

Each of the four areas will also have a set of three buttons, to create, change and delete scenarios. With the spinners counted as two for up and down, that's five buttons per area, total twenty, which is a lot. I don't want to confuse the user, nor to write lengthy instructions. Design is important; I'll use small controls with intuitive, single-character faces, repeated per area and nested for a functional and uncluttered appearance. A single help cell will give usage tips.

Technically there are two additional controls. One is the demand method checkbox, which sets random or fixed demand. The other is the chart checkbox to manage the screen. As a principle, a demo should fit a single screen, but here it is hard to do so without overlapping the table and the chart, which is inelegant. To address this, the chart checkbox toggles between two views; one with the chart, and just the primary columns showing, the other with the chart hidden and all the columns showing. The checkbox activates a macro to show or hide the chart, and is linked to a cell which feeds the Conditional Formatting of the secondary column set.

VBA Coding

As the coding brainstorm begins to brew, I start with the list of controls. As noted, I have twenty controls to program (plus the chart toggle), and they must each have their own macro. I look for commonality to avoid duplication. Each control macro can call another macro to perform the common actions. To do this I will need to pass and catch arguments between the macros. To support this, I'll build a strong naming convention for all the dependent variables; the scenario name and abbreviation, the scenario range, and the cells to hold the scenario number, count and comment.

Scenario name roots and abbreviations are Demand (Dem); Supply (Sup); Safety Stock (SST); Safety Time (STI). Scenario names are constructed as the name root followed by a space and a number. A maximum number of scenarios is set as a constant in the module, initially at 99. Abbreviations are then used as arguments linking each control with the main action subroutines, and are used in all the related range names.

Four range names are defined for each area using the abbreviation for a total of sixteen. For example, ScenCellsDem is the range of cells contained in each demand scenario.

Table 48: MRP Range Naming Convention Example

Purpose	Name	Sheet
Range of cells in the scenario	ScenCellsDem	Demo
Cell to hold the current scenario number	ScenThisDem	Data
Cell to hold the count of scenarios	ScensCntDem	Data
Cell to hold the scenario description	ScenDescDem	Data

The purpose of the Data sheet is to hold the parameter values generated in the code and displayed on the Demo sheet. The reason for this is to protect the Demo sheet, and enable tab navigation between all the input cells. If the parameters are stored directly on the Demo sheet, then their cells would need to be unlocked, and the tab cycle would include them. One option is to leave them locked and unprotect the sheet at run time. I've chosen the option to move the coded cells to another sheet which is unprotected and hidden, and reference their names in locked cells in the Demo sheet.

Stage 1 macros are assigned to a control. If the control is unique and the code simple enough, this can be the only stage needed, as with the chart toggle which sets the property ".Visible = Not .Visible".

If the control is one of a class, stage 1 calls a stage 2 subroutine by passing the abbreviation argument identifying the class member. For example, there are four controls in the "create" class, each one passes the abbreviated area name to the main routine to create the scenario; CreateDemScenario() calls ScenCreate("Dem"), etc.

Stage 2 macros are the class-level subroutines that perform actions using the argument passed from stage 1. There are four stage 2 macros, one for each action; ScenCreate, ScenChange, ScenDelete, ScenSpin.

Create, Change and Delete are serious actions, and thus start with a message like "here's what I'm going to do, continue?" The message box has OK and Cancel buttons with Cancel as the default, so to proceed with the action requires conscious choice. This is a kind way of informing the user and protecting them from inadvertent actions.

Here's an example of the general steps in the ScenCreate Sub, followed by the actual code:

1. increment the next scenario number and stop if over max
2. prompt to continue with creation
3. prompt to enter scenario description
4. add the new scenario
5. set the scenario number, count and description cells

```
'************************************
'*    Create Scenario Routine       *
'*    called by 4 buttons           *
'************************************

Sub ScenCreate(ScenAbbr As String)
Dim NewCount As Integer
Dim ScenRoot, ScenDesc As String
On Error GoTo oops:
ScenRoot = Root(ScenAbbr)
With Sheets("Demo")

'increment the next scenario number and stop if over max
NewCount = Sheets("Data").Range("ScensCnt" & ScenAbbr) + 1
If NewCount > MaxScens Then
    MsgBox "Maximum " & MaxScens & " scenarios reached.", , _
      "Add Scenario"
    Exit Sub
Else

'prompt to continue with creation
If MsgBox("Add new " & UCase(ScenRoot) & _
   " scenario with current values?", vbQuestion + vbOKCancel, _
   "Add Scenario") = vbCancel Then Exit Sub
End If
```

```
With .Range("Random")
  If .Value Then .Value = 1 Else .Value = 0
End With

'prompt to enter scenario description
ScenDesc = InputBox("Enter a short description " & _
  "for the new scenario" & vbCr & "(max 30 characters):", _
  "Add Scenario")

'add the new scenario
  .Scenarios.Add _
    Name:=ScenRoot & " " & NewCount, _
    ChangingCells:=.Range("ScenCells" & ScenAbbr), _
    Comment:=ScenDesc & ";"

'set the scenario number, count and description cells
  With Sheets("Data")
    .Range("ScenThis" & ScenAbbr) = NewCount
    .Range("ScensCnt" & ScenAbbr) = NewCount
    .Range("ScenDesc" & ScenAbbr) = ScenDesc
  End With
End With
Exit Sub
oops:
MsgBox ("Error " & Err & " " & Error)
End Sub
```

Stage 3 macros are specialized subroutines that further modularize code segments pulled out of stage 1 or 2 code to simplify program logic. These may be reusable or not, sometimes used to manage complexity, like breaking down long formulas into stages. They can be Subs to process steps or Functions to return a result. They are opportunistic and not pre-designed.

Layout and Formatting

The purpose of a demo is to expose and illustrate a process by letting the user change inputs and immediately see the effect on outputs. Input cells, scenarios and controls enable the interaction, and are all neatly organized in a four-quadrant area. The table and chart supply the visual outputs. Good arrangement of these elements is key to a delightful and instructive user experience.

The user is overtly invited to interact with the inputs. First, all input cells and only input cells are white. Second, inputs are clearly and simply labeled.

Third, controls are simple and intuitive. Finally, the output table and chart are attractive, enticing the user to see what will happen when they change a number or click a button.

Other design tips include use of shades of one color versus multiple colors, section headings in merged and rotated cells, visual symmetry, and use of custom number format to display text with numbers. For example, future days are format **"Day "0**, and the safety time values are format **0" days"**.

The Chart

The chart shows five of the table columns in Combo style, all as lines except supply which is a column, or vertical bar style. This illustrates the effect of supply receipts which instantaneously increment inventory once per cycle, while independent demand is continuous, gradually decrementing inventory. Of keen interest are the three inventory lines showing cycle, safety and total. As they scroll and change the scenarios, experienced planners and managers may be surprised and intrigued by the magnitude of inventory relative to demand.

Figure 5: Custom Chart Type

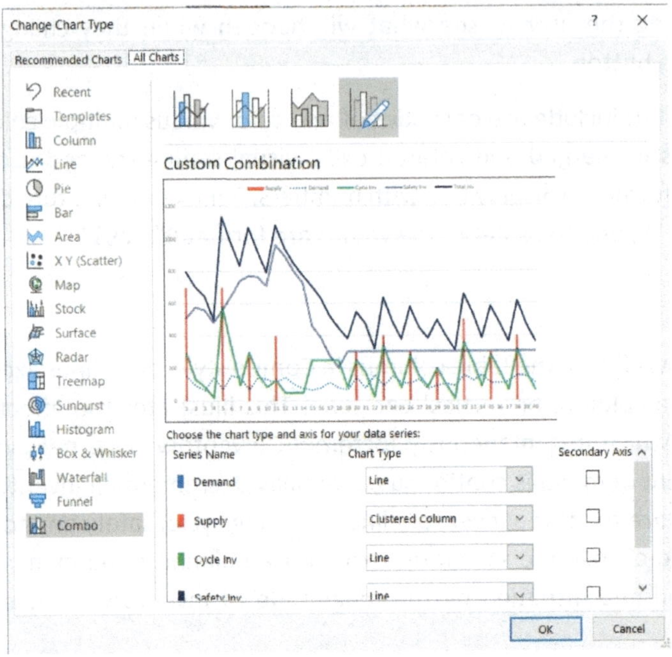

If a picture is worth a thousand words, a demo is worth a thousand pictures. It's more than an introduction for basic training, it's also a great offering for management. Even executives can appreciate relevant elucidation. As such this is an example of how elegant design with purpose can give the designer positive exposure.

Chapter 10: Fun and Games

Purpose

Games can be an addictive distraction, and can also be some of the most effective teaching tools available. My purpose for developing games is as a showcase for interactivity and elegant design. The games are for solo play, but some have two-player competition to add interest and fun. They have compact play areas, tactile controls, and accessible support information. Each has lessons to be learned on design and VBA coding.

Poker

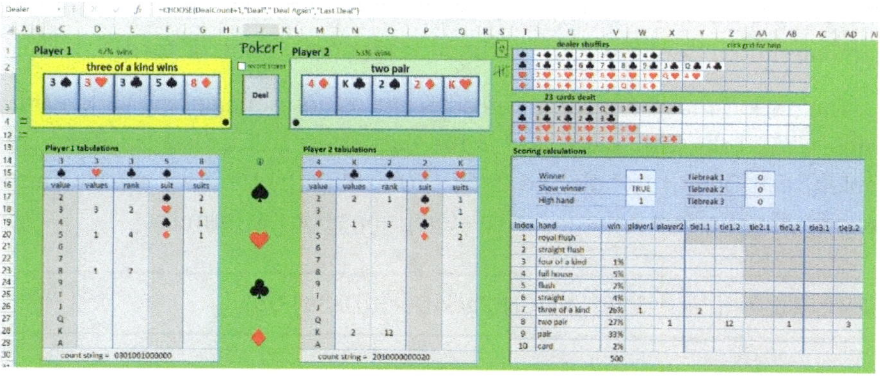

The idea of an Excel poker game raises several intriguing challenges; how to manage the deck as it is dealt out, how to enable discard and replace, how to evaluate hands, and of course, how to design the cards and the table to look good. Without nice looking cards it will not last long, so I'll begin with that.

The Cards

For the card suits, I first looked in the symbol-designated fonts. The Symbol font has the four suit symbols in ASCII codes 167 to 170. To use this font for the cards would make the royal letters Greek, and character-level font setting is not an option. This made me turn to Unicode symbols for the suits. Exploring the Symbol picker, Alt-N,U, I didn't find then in Calibri, but I found them in Arial, Hex codes 2660, 2663, 2665, and 2666. They display nicely in Calibri or any other non-symbol font. So I can paste them into standard font cells and they look great.

Now to create the cards, I make each one three characters, with the value and the suit separated by a space, and substituting T for 10. For hearts and diamonds I use two preset conditions; "Cell Value contains '♦'" and "Cell Value contains '♥'" to turn the font red.

The Deck

The "deck" begins as a "pack" of cards, and I'll use these two terms to distinguish the full pack from the remaining undealt deck. In other words, Pack – Dealt = Deck. The critical point is that there can be no duplicate cards dealt. There must be a list of which cards have been dealt, then a process to eliminate them from the pool for the next randomly selected card.

The deck is maintained in three adjacent columns, beginning with a static range of 52 cells with every card in the pack. Next to that is a single-column table (Dealt[Dealt]) to hold the dealt cards, filled by the deal macro. This is followed by the deck column, calculated using an array formula.

```
Deck =FILTER(Pack,ISNA(MATCH(Pack,Dealt[Dealt],0)))
```

This logic I owe to a post by Keith at extendoffice.com on how to exclude one list from another. It is really quite ingenious, as I'll explain now. (See https://www.extendoffice.com/documents/excel/4076-excel-exclude-one-list-from-another.html)

Normally we are using MATCH to find the index of an item within a list of items, as the arguments suggest: MATCH(*lookup_value, lookup_array, [match_type]*). With match_type 0 for exact match, if the lookup value is not in the array, MATCH returns #N/A.

Here what we are interested in is not the numeric result of MATCH but a Boolean state of the intersection of two arrays, Pack and Dealt. Dealt exists within Pack. What we need is the part of Pack that does not intersect Dealt. This is called a symmetric difference, a.k.a. disjunctive union, denoted as Pack Δ Dealt – just FYI! (https://en.wikipedia.org/wiki/Symmetric_difference)

The MATCH trick is to look up Pack in Dealt. That sounds weird – Pack is bigger than Dealt! To test this, I pick an empty column and enter =MATCH(Pack,Dealt[Dealt],0). This returns an array with all 52 Pack members, with index numbers for those found in Dealt, and #N/A for members not found in Dealt. That set of #N/A Pack members is precisely what I need. FILTER of the Pack for ISNA of the MATCH array then returns the undealt cards.

As an array formula, it is entered in a single cell named Deck and spills down the column. The entire array is referenced as Deck#. A single cell then picks a random card from the deck:

```
NextCard =INDEX(Deck#,RANDBETWEEN(1,COUNTA(Deck#)))
```

For calculation control, I use Worksheet_Activate event to set manual calculation mode. Then in the deal macro, I use the Range.Calculate method to update Deck and NextCard before copying the value.

A bonus feature of deck array management is a display of the dealt and undealt cards by suit as a learning aid. This is done by filtering and transposing the respective columns, presented in the play area via linked image (see Camera Tool in Chapter 3 Formatting).

```
Top grid =IFERROR(TRANSPOSE(FILTER(Deck#,
      RIGHT(Deck#,1)=DeckSuit)),"")
Bottom grid =IFERROR(TRANSPOSE(FILTER(Dealt[Dealt],
      RIGHT(Dealt[Dealt],1)=DeckSuit)),"")
```

Game Play

Two players each have five cards on the table, separated by the Deal button. The cards are covered by transparent shapes that give them a slight 3D appearance, and serve as toggle buttons to hold and unhold the cards.

When a card is clicked, a hold cell is set true and the card becomes shaded. Unshaded cards are discarded and replaced in the next deal, which only calculates Deck and NextCard for unheld cards. The cell DealCount tracks up to three deals, and is reset to 0 when the hand is over.

Processing is done by multiple Subs working together like a dealer team. It begins when the player clicks the Deal button, which calls Sub DealButton(), the team boss. If DealCount is 0, DealButton() prepares the table for a new hand. Think of it like collecting all the cards and shuffling the pack. DealButton() then hands the pack to Deal(dc), along with dc, the DealCount value, before incrementing DealCount.

While DealCount is 0, Deal(dc)'s job is to deal ten cards, one at a time, alternating players. When the initial ten cards are dealt, action returns to the player, who looks at both hands and selects cards to hold.

The implicit rule is that at least one card in the hand must be held in order to replace the others. If none are held when the Deal button is clicked, all holds are set for that hand. If one player has a hold and the other doesn't, the player with the hold can continue to deal. If both players' holds are all set or none set, the hand is over and scored. This governance is performed by DealButton().

Presuming that at least one player has at least one card held, but not all five, Deal(dc) is called in to replace the discarded cards. In this case, the deal is by player precedence. That is, player 1 gets all discards replaced, followed by player 2.

EndHand() is called in after three deals, or if the all-or-none hold condition described ends the hand. EndHand() sets all holds, resets DealCount to 0, and sets the cell ShowHand TRUE. ShowHand enables the scoring formula and winner highlighting to appear. EndHand() in turn calls RecordScore().

RecordScore() is enabled by a checkbox in the play area. If the checkbox is set, RecordScore() will add the result of the hand to the table PokerScores.

These Subs are performing related tasks, and could be combined. Their separation is a convenience. When there are conditional paths in a main Sub, I like to have it call another Sub to focus purpose and for readability. This is similar to how I decide when to use Name Manager to break down complex formulas. The Deal(dc) Sub is shown on the following page.

```
Sub Deal(dc As Integer)
' called by DealButton sub
Dim Player, CardNum As Integer
Dim Calc, Hold, Card As String
Application.ScreenUpdating = False
Select Case dc     'dc passes deal count
  Case 0           'on first deal, deal by card then by player
    For CardNum = 1 To 5
    For Player = 1 To 2
      Card = "Card" & Player & CardNum
        [Deck].Calculate  'refresh Deck = "not dealt"
        With [NextCard]   'NextCard = random pick of Deck
          .Calculate      '(like shuffle)
          .Copy           'copy the random card
        End With
                          'paste random card to card cell
        Range(Card).PasteSpecial (xlPasteValues)
                          'paste same card to Dealt
        Range("Dealt[[#Headers],[Dealt]]").Select
        If Len(Selection.Offset(1, 0)) > 0 Then _
        Selection.End(xlDown).Select
        Selection.Offset(1, 0).PasteSpecial (xlPasteValues)
    Next Player           'alternate players
    Next CardNum          'repeat for each of 5 cards
  Case Else        'after first deal, deal by player then by card
    For Player = 1 To 2
    For CardNum = 1 To 5
      Hold = "Hold" & Player & CardNum
      Card = "Card" & Player & CardNum
      If Not Range(Hold) Then    ' skip if Hold cell is true
        [Deck].Calculate  'same as first deal
        With [NextCard]   '...
          .Calculate      '...
          .Copy           '...
        End With
        Range(Card).PasteSpecial (xlPasteValues)
        Range("Dealt[[#Headers],[Dealt]]").Select
        If Len(Selection.Offset(1, 0)) > 0 Then _
        Selection.End(xlDown).Select
        Selection.Offset(1, 0).PasteSpecial (xlPasteValues)
      End If
    Next CardNum          'next unheld card
    Next Player           'next plyr
End Select
Application.CutCopyMode = False
[Dealer].Select
End Sub
```

Scoring

Traditional poker scoring ranks ten hands, from royal flush down to high card. If one player has a higher-ranked hand, they win the hand. If both players have the same-ranked hand, then tiebreakers come into play. Various methods are used to judge each five-card hand by both value and suit.

Hand Evaluation

The ten ranked hands each have a condition to meet. Pair, two pair, three of a kind, full house and four of a kind are all based on counts of the card values; flush is based on the count of card suits; straight is based on sequential values.

The first step is to parse and tabulate the card values and suits so they can each be counted. This is done for each player by picking the left and right character of each card, creating two arrays.

```
Hand1Values =LEFT(Hand1,1)
Hand1Suits =RIGHT(Hand1,1)
```

These are the basis of the evaluation, which suggests that the five-column range directly below them will be a logical and intuitive data collection area.

The five columns are divided into three for values and two for suits. The first is a list of values from 2 to A, followed by value count and rank columns. For rank, since the values are mixed alpha/numeric, RANK cannot be used; instead, MATCH assigns ascending numeric value to the card values as listed. The last two columns are a list of suits and a suit count.

Most scores use the counts, and the rank for tiebreaking. For example, three of a kind is COUNTIF(Values1,3), a flush is COUNTIF(Suits1,5). The straight requires a different method.

To identify a straight, the value counts are concatenated into a 13-character string. Scoring can then look for “1111*1” for an A2345 straight, or “*11111” for a royal straight, or “*11111*” for any other straight. The string is also used in tiebreaking.

Table 49: Poker Hand Tabulation

Card	J ♣	5 ♣	J ♦	7 ♦	9 ♠
Value	J	5	J	7	9
Suit	♣	♣	♦	♦	♠
Tabulation	Value	Values	Rank	Suit	Suits
	2			♠	1
	3			♥	
	4			♣	2
	5	1	4	♦	2
	6				
	7	1	6		
	8				
	9	1	8		
	T				
	J	2	10		
	Q				
	K				
	A				
count string =		0001010102000			

Hand Scoring

Scoring each of the game hands against the ten ranked hands is a logic exercise. Combined conditions use PRODUCT as AND, and SUM as OR, so that the end result is 0 or 1 in every case. In the table below, hand names are substituted where they have already been defined.

Each COUNTIF evaluation can be only 0 or 1, except pair can also be 2, so one and two pair are converted to Boolean by equalities that return TRUE or FALSE. These are multiplied by 1 in order that all cases return 1 or 0. The final rank is high card, when no other condition is met, similarly evaluated as Boolean and converted to binary.

Some game hands can match multiple rank hands. A royal flush is also a straight flush, a flush, and a straight; a full house is also a three of a kind and a pair. This does not matter because we're only looking for the first MATCH from top down. Here, low score wins because the lower the MATCH result, the higher the rank. SIGN returns -1, 0 or 1, so I use SIGN(difference)+2 as index to CHOOSE among three outputs; player 1 or 2 as winner, or 0 as tie.

High =CHOOSE(SIGN(MATCH(1,Match1,0)-MATCH(1,Match2,0))+2,1,0,2)

Table 50: Poker Ranked Hand Conditions

Rank	Hand	Condition 1	Op	Condition 2
1	Royal flush	COUNTIF(String, "*11111")	×	Flush
2	Straight flush	Straight	×	Flush
3	Four of a kind	COUNTIF(Values,4)		
4	Full house	Three of a kind	×	Pair
5	Flush	COUNTIF(Suits,5)		
6	Straight	COUNTIF(String, "1111*1")	+	COUNTIF(String, "*11111*")
7	Three of a kind	COUNTIF(Values,3)		
8	Two pair	COUNTIF(Values,2)=2	×	1
9	Pair	COUNTIF(Values,2)=1	×	1
10	Card	MAX(the other 9)=0	×	1

Tie Breaking

It's very common to have the same hand rank, and tiebreaks are a routine part of scoring. At the top, a royal flush tie is a deadlock. A straight tie can be won by highest card, and is deadlocked if the straights match. Four or three of a kind cannot be tied. With flush or card, you could still be tied after five tiebreaks, but I'll stop at three.

Table 51: Poker Hand Tiebreaks

Rank	Tie	Tiebreak1	Tiebreak2	Tiebreak3
1	Royal flush	Deadlock		
2	Straight flush	High straight	Deadlock	
3	Four of a kind	High four	Impossible	
4	Full house	High three	Impossible	
5	Flush	High card	Next high card	Next high card
6	Straight	High straight	Deadlock	
7	Three of a kind	High three	Impossible	
8	Two pair	High pair	Next high pair	High card
9	Pair	High pair	High card	Next high card
10	Card	High card	Next high card	Next high card

Most tiebreaks are determined by searching the count string for the relevant marker; a straight is SEARCH(1111,String1), picking up the rank of the lowest card of the straight; four of a kind is SEARCH(4,String1) for the foursome rank. Two pair first finds the rank of the higher pair by SEARCH(2,String1,SEARCH(2,String1)+1), then the lower pair by SEARCH(2,String1).

For flush and card, and for tied pairs and two pairs, individual cards are compared by MAX(Rank1), then by MAXIFS(Rank1,Rank1,"<"&MAX(Rank1)). Pair and two pair use MAXIFS(Rank1,Values1,1) to find the top non-pair value.

Unlike the high hand where lowest value wins, all tiebreaks are highest value wins. Each one is converted to winner = 1 or 2, or 0 = tie, if and only if the higher level is tied. The winner of the hand is then the max of the high hand and three tiebreak cells.

Winning

After DealCount runs out, the winner of the hand is announced and highlighted. Each player's header gives the name of the hand. This is only given at the end of the hand, to help the player learn to recognize the hands while playing. The winner's message adds "wins" after, and "high" before, if result of a tiebreak.

```
Player1 header =IF(ShowHand,CHOOSE(Winner+1,"",IF(High,"","high "),"")&
    INDEX(Hands,IFNA(MATCH(1,Match1,0),10))&
    CHOOSE(Winner+1,""," wins",""),"")

Player2 header =IF(ShowHand,CHOOSE(Winner+1,"","",IF(High,"","high "))&
    INDEX(Hands,IFNA(MATCH(1,Match2,0),10))&
    CHOOSE(Winner+1,"",""," wins"),"")
```

Recording

Table PokerScores records each hand's results with a time stamp, if the checkbox is set. A row above the table is filled with formulas, which is copied and pasted as values into a new table row. This enables some interesting statistics to be displayed in the play area. Winning % per player and per named hand are shown, with the number of hands recorded. This is further education for poker play. Score history is manually reset by deleting table rows. Because the table has some formula columns, it has a message, "to delete history, delete all table rows but one, in that one delete only the white cells."

Design Features

The game includes the play area, calculation areas, documentation and the VBA code all on one sheet. The play area fits neatly within the screen, including the tabulation, scoring, and deck image, and various elements can be hidden for focused play. Subtle icons open and close row groups, and hide and unhide the deck image. Another jumps to the PokerScores table.

There are two types of hiding here. One is within the "home" or play area, where elements directly linked to game play are normally displayed, with buttons to hide them as desired.

The other type of hiding is the processing and recording ranges that are far off-screen, where you wouldn't even know they were there. These have click navigation to avoid clumsy scrolling. One click to get there, and a back arrow button to return home. These areas are placed diagonally below and right of the home, so to be independent of its column and row sizes. DeckZone is accessed by click on the deck image, PokerScores by click on the counting marks icon.

Dice

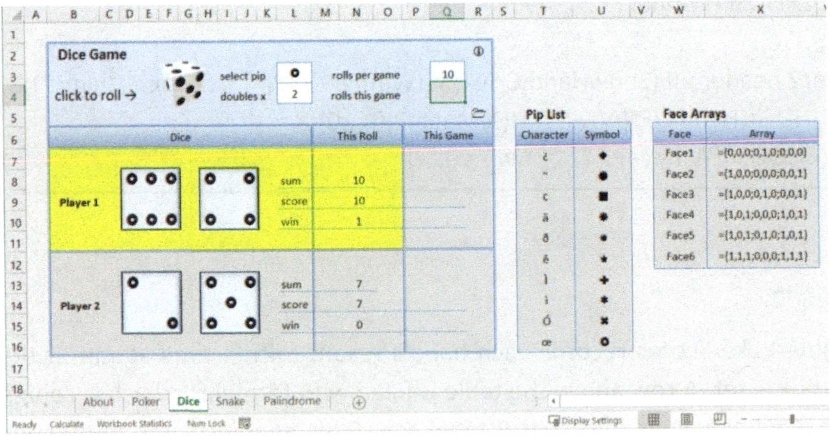

There are many games one could make with dice, from Yahtzee® to craps. This game is none of those, it is just a simple practice game and a demo of how to simulate dice in Excel. To make it somewhat fun, the number of rolls per game can be set, and the "competition" mounts with each roll.

The Initial Answer

The interesting feature of the dice is the face with an array of dots to show the value. As I worked on it I found a number of ways to calculate the dots. In the interest of revealing the development thought process, the graphic below shows how I initially worked out how die value and pip position relate and can be determined mathematically.

Pip	Die dot	Die = 1	Die = 2	Die = 3	Die = 4	Die = 5	Die = 6
1	Die > 1		•	•	•	•	•
2	Die > 5						•
3	Die > 3				•	•	•
4	""						
5	ISODD(Die)	•		•		•	
6	""						
7	Die > 3				•	•	•
8	Die > 5						•
9	Die > 1		•	•	•	•	•
Pip dot (way 1)		Mod(Pip,5)=0	Mod(Pip,8)=1	Mod(Pip,4)=1	Mod(Pip,6)=1,3	Mod(Pip,2)=1	Mod(Pip,7)<4
Pip dot (way 2)		Pip=5	Pip=1,9	Pip=1,5,9	Pip=1,3,7,9	ISODD(Pip)	Pip<4 or >6
Result, with pip numbers:		5	1, 9	1, 5, 9	1, 3, 7, 9	1, 3, 5, 7, 9	1, 2, 3, 7, 8, 9

To combine these conditions into a single formula to display the proper face is possible, but rather messy. Here was my penultimate solution:

> Formula in each of nine cells per die:
>
> =CHOOSE(Die,Face1,Face2,Face3,Face4,Face5,Face6)
>
> Face names as below defined in Name Manager

Table 52: Die Face Formulas

Name	Refers to
Face1	=IF(MOD(Pip,5)=0,Dot,"")
Face2	=IF(MOD(Pip,8)=1,Dot,"")
Face3	=IF(MOD(Pip,4)=1,Dot,"")
Face4	=IF(OR(MOD(Pip,6)=1,MOD(Pip,6)=3),Dot,"")
Face5	=IF(MOD(Pip,2)=1,Dot,"")
Face6	=IF(MOD(Pip,7)<4,Dot,"")

This also required a way to name a cell "Pip" which could represent each of the nine dot positions in turn, which was even more messy. In the end, the trick is to convert a number between 1 and 6 to a 3x3 array, so eventually my mind turned to arrays.

The Final Answer

Each die face is set to an array constant of 0's and 1's where 1 represents the dot positions. Columns are separated with commas and rows with semicolons. Expressing each face is a graphical task; as you look at the arrays you can almost see the faces.

Table 53: Die Face Arrays

Face	Array
Face1	={0,0,0;0,1,0;0,0,0}
Face2	={1,0,0;0,0,0;0,0,1}
Face3	={1,0,0;0,1,0;0,0,1}
Face4	={1,0,1;0,0,0;1,0,1}
Face5	={1,0,1;0,1,0;1,0,1}
Face6	={1,1,1;0,0,0;1,1,1}

Applying the die value is then accomplished by choosing the array corresponding to the value and using **IF(array,Dot,"")**. This returns a 3x3 array where the 0's are blank and the 1's are replaced with whatever character or symbol is defined as Dot. The formula is entered in the upper left corner of the die range.

There are four dice, two per player, each with their own random number generator. The dice are numbered 11, 12, 21, 22 and follow the example shown:

```
DieFace11 =IF(CHOOSE(DieVal11,Face1,Face2,Face3,
      Face4,Face5,Face6),Dot,"")
DieVal11 =RANDBETWEEN(1,6)
Etc.
```

Now I have a cell named Dot in which the user can select from a picklist of symbols. The symbols on the dice are in Wingdings 2 font. This does not translate to the Data Validation picklist, they appear as the raw characters they are. A table lists the characters in both fonts for reference.

The dice are made exact squares by matching the pixel-width of columns to the pixel-height of rows. Some thought is given to what the maximum row height will be. It is usually determined by font size, but can also be affected by styles. Once I settled on 14 pt font for the dice, this gave me a row height of 18 (30 pixels), so I set the column widths to 2.56 (30 pixels).

The Worksheet_Activate event sets manual calculation, and a die icon is used to play the game. The macro tracks the rolls and accumulates the wins and values during the game, resetting them all at game's end.

Conditional Formatting turns the winner's play area yellow. The dice are in the middle of the play area and should remain white, so I give them a white fill format with the condition =TRUE, always on.

A folder icon toggles a column group to show or hide the pip list and the face arrays.

Snake

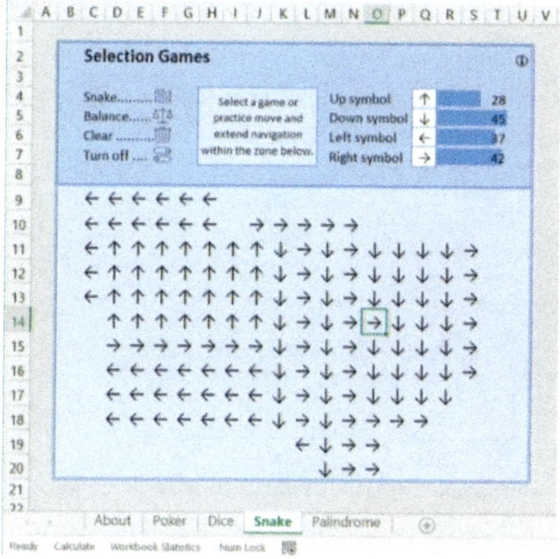

Snake is more puzzle than game. It tracks the SelectionChange event within a defined rectangle, and enters an arrow indicating the direction traveled. Selection can be done one cell at a time by the arrow keys, or extended by holding shift, or by dragging the mouse. If the selection is not entirely within the zone, nothing happens.

The arrows are a learning aid to see how selection works. In extend mode, arrows are like a growing school of fish, all swimming synchronized. The arrows are Unicode symbols 8592 to 8595. The symbols can be changed, but arrows are most intuitive. Next to each directional symbol is a count of how many of them appear in the zone, with Data Bars.

There are two games, Snake and Balance, turned on by icon, or both turned off to just practice. Snake ends when you select a cell that's already filled, reports the % of the zone filled, and resets. Balance waits until the entire zone is filled, reports the balance score, and resets. The balance score is (total – range)/total; if there is an equal number of all four arrows, the balance is 100%.

The code is mainly within the SelectionChange event, with a few other subs for clearing the zone and selecting the games. Hidden cells track the selection column and row number and count. When extending up or left, the selection column and row are changed to the top left corner of the selection. When extending down or right, the selection column and row are not changed. Then, the number of selected columns or rows is used to determine which symbol to put in the selection.

Palindrome

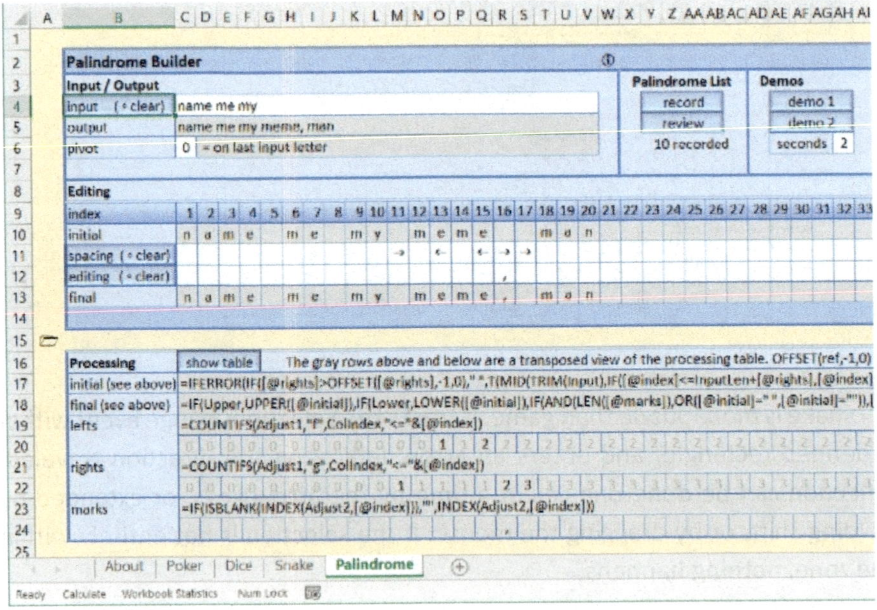

A palindrome is any word or phrase that can be read forwards or backwards, disregarding spaces and punctuation. As you begin to string words together in the front half, in your head, you need to envision a reflection of it, to see if you can form real words from it. This sheet will create the reflection and let you edit the spaces and punctuation until it makes sense, if ever.

Input

The input phrase is entered in a single cell, with no punctuation. Then the pivot point is selected, referring to where the reflection begins. There are two options; 0 means pivot on the last input letter, 1 means pivot after the last input letter. For example, if input= "ref", pivot 0 output= "refer"; pivot 1 output= "reffer".

The editing area is laid out horizontally. The input phrase is parsed and reflected, character by character, into up to sixty columns for editing. Processing of the text is done in a table, PalProcess, and transposed to columns for intuitive interaction. The initial reflection, =TRANSPOSE(PalProcess[initial]), begins the interaction stage.

Below the initial reflection are two rows of white cells for adjustments, named Adjust1 and Adjust2. Adjust1 is for spacing. This row is formatted in Wingdings 3 font, and accepts only f (←) to close a space or g (→) to open a space. The spacing edits must proceed left to right because they accumulate, and must include an extra space for each punctuation mark to be added.

In the left half of the initial reflection, that is the input half, spaces can only be added for punctuation, since the input already has proper word spacing, and is trimmed in processing in case any extra spaces were inadvertently entered. In the right, reflected half, the letters are like Lego parts that need to be separated from one group and attached to another to form words, by entering a series of f= move left and g= move right.

Below the Adjust1 row is the Adjust2 row for capitalization and punctuation, in normal font. Case adjustment is done by entering any of a set of characters for upper and lower case. These characters are maintained in the Case table and can be modified; the initial pairs of (upper, lower) are (u,l), (^,v), ([,]), which do not conflict with likely punctuation. The idea is to let the user pick whichever pair of indicators they can easily remember and use. Punctuation marks can be entered under a space or at the end of the palindrome. Apostrophe (') must be entered twice ('') to show. These edits can be made column by column or after all spacing adjustments are done.

Processing

The processing table begins with an index column, 1 to 60. In the first half, up to the input length, MID picks out each character at the index position. For the second half reflection, the character picked is twice the input length minus the index, plus the pivot. Thus, if the input length is 12 and pivot= 0, the 13th output character is input character number (24-13+0)= 11, the 14th output is input number (24-14+0)= 10, etc. until the 23rd output is input number (24-23+0)= 1, back to the beginning. If pivot= 1, then there will be two of the last input character before the countdown.

```
Up to input length =MID(TRIM(Input),[@index],1)
After input length =MID(TRIM(Input),2*InputLen-[@index]+Pivot,1)
InputLen =LEN(TRIM(Input))
```

The next step is to account for spacing adjustments. This uses a cumulative count of left and right adjustment entries:

```
Lefts =COUNTIFS(Adjust1,"f",ColIndex,"<="&[@index])
Rights =COUNTIFS(Adjust1,"g",ColIndex,"<="&[@index])
```

When there is a right-arrow “g” entered, the cumulative count increases, that is, [@rights]> OFFSET([@rights],-1,0), and a space is output. Otherwise, the output character is offset from the index by subtracting [@rights] in the first half, and by adding [@rights] and subtracting [@lefts] in the second half.

```
Initial =IFERROR(IF([@rights]>OFFSET([@rights],-1,0)," ",
    T(MID(TRIM(Input),IF([@index]<=InputLen+[@rights],[@index]-
    [@rights],2*InputLen-[@index]+Pivot+[@rights]-[@lefts]),1))),"")
```

The final step is to adopt the capitalization and punctuation entries.

```
Upper =AND(NOT(PalProcess[@marks]="?"),
      NOT(ISNA(MATCH(PalProcess[@marks],Case[upper],0))))
Lower =AND(NOT(PalProcess[@marks]="?"),
      NOT(ISNA(MATCH(PalProcess[@marks],Case[lower],0))))
Marks =IF(ISBLANK(INDEX(Adjust2,[@index])),"",INDEX(Adjust2,[@index]))
Final =IF(Upper,UPPER([@initial]),IF(Lower,LOWER([@initial]),IF(AND(
      LEN([@marks]),OR([@initial]="",[@initial]="")),[@marks],[@initial])))
```

Output

Below the adjustment rows is the result, still in columns, =TRANSPOSE(PalProcess[final]). Below the input cell is the final palindrome output cell, =CONCAT(TRANSPOSE(PalProcess[final])).

A table is provided to save palindromes, with two buttons to record and review. The record button checks if the palindrome is already in the table, to avoid duplication.

Help

Two demos are provided that perform the inputs and adjustments, with helpful messages. Time between demo actions can be entered in seconds. The demo macros use the Application.Wait method to time the actions.

A collapsible row group gives a transposed view of the processing table, with formula text and data, as well as a button to go to the table itself.

Chapter 11: Conclusion

We began this journey not knowing where it would lead us, with a general unease about the state of our communications and the risks hidden particularly in the Excel files we send and receive every day. This brought us to a candid acknowledgement: principles do matter, and are worthy of an intervention to reestablish them as the foundation of our work.

I've articulated four principles in particular.

Purpose: every work must have an object – a customer, a consumer, a reader, a patron, a fan. Product specifications are just the surface. The real fulfillment is in the discovery and realization of implicit needs and desires, high among them the need to understand and to be understood.

Integrity: the taking of pride in one's work is one of the rare virtuous "takes", like taking responsibility. Integrity is like the unseen welds on the beams that hold up the bridge. It is what you do right without being asked or asking for return, because it is right.

Transparency: openness and honesty in communications is more than not misleading nor omitting truth. It is anticipating and preempting doubt, confusion and mistrust. It's presenting options and revealing details with clean and concise language and format.

Elegance: the union of science and art is one of life's greatest goals. Elegance as a principle holds strength and beauty equally necessary. It connects process and product, giving them both value. It connects producer and consumer, giving them mutual appreciation.

These principles are not new or narrow, they are as old and universal as nature itself. They are easy to understand, and agreeable to everyone. Yet based on the spreadsheet evidence, they are easily overlooked and ignored.

The more things we own and the more space we have to hold them, the more they demand organization. Without organization we can't find what we need, and we lose both function and form.

Excel is a big space to hold our stuff. It demands a strategy to keep what's important secure and accessible, to save us from hoarding, and to make a place where our guests feel welcome and appreciated.

Excel itself is but a convenient, fertile ground where principles can germinate and be nurtured. With practice their value will become increasingly explicit and evident in other aspects of work and life.

About the Author

Doug Bates is a Supply Chain Management professional with CPIM, CIRM certification. He has made a career in both small and large companies of being the go-to expert and trainer in MS Office® and SAP®. He has developed complex solutions, written global standards and training manuals, led change management, and delivered hundreds of hours of training and consultation in several countries.

Doug is now retired from full-time employment, semi-self-employed writing and developing. He also enjoys puttering in his wood shop, occasionally with useful result, arranging and composing piano music, and genealogy. He and his wife Takako have two sons, Jonathan and Joseph.

Resources

Elegant Excel Spreadsheets | Xlegant
https://www.xlegant.com/
Our home, with Blog, Videos, Support
Visit the Store for free VBA and use one-time $50 coupon BOOK50

Excel help & learning - Microsoft Support
https://support.microsoft.com/en-us/excel
From the source...

Excel Visual Basic for Applications (VBA) reference | Microsoft Docs
https://docs.microsoft.com/en-us/office/vba/api/overview/excel
Essential reference for VBA

Xelplus, Excel Courses and Tutorials, Online Excel Videos
https://www.xelplus.com/
Best free video library, professional training for purchase
YouTube channel: Leila Gharani
https://www.youtube.com/channel/UCJtUOos_MwJa_Ewii-R3cJA

Exceljet | Work faster in Excel
https://exceljet.net/
Best free help website, professional training for purchase
YouTube channel Exceljet - YouTube
https://www.youtube.com/channel/UCYJRiP_1kPEPJfstlB4wAbA

ExtendOffice - Best Office Productivity Tools
https://www.extendoffice.com/#
Good free resources. Kutools licensed product for purchase.

Index

Made in the USA
Monee, IL
03 November 2026

67387545R00144